CENSORSHIP IN RUSSIA, 1865-1905

Daniel Balmuth

University Press
of America

Copyright © 1979 by

University Press of America, Inc.™

4710 Auth Place, S.E., Washington D.C. 20023

All rights reserved

Printed in the United States of America

ISBN: 0-8191-0773-5

Library of Congress Catalog Card Number: 79-52510

CONTENTS

    Abbreviations   vi
    Acknowledgements   vii
    Introduction   viii

I. Censorship 1855-1863   1
Alexander II and the censorship 1; Reforms in the censorship office 2; Public opinion and Alexander's reforms 3; Golovnin appointed minister of education 4; Golovnin proposes a more lenient censorship 5; minister of interior Valuev and the periodical press 5; the censorship and political works 6; censorship and the peasantry 7; censorship and public mores 9; Golovnin proposes to transfer censorship to ministry of interior 10.

II. Censorship 1863-1865   13
Valuev's suspicion of writers 13; Polish rebellion and the censorship 14; Nationalism and censorship 15; Provincial press and censorship 15; Expose articles and censorship 17; Mores and censorship 18; Religion and censorship 18; History and censorship 19; Reform proposals in censorship 19; Proposal of a mixture of preliminary and repressive censorship 20; Obolenskii Commission established 20; Proposes to end preliminary censorship for some works 21; Golovnin opposes project 22; New Commission project 23; Amended project becomes law in 1865 24.

III. Censorship 1865-1868   27
Valuev's instructions to censors 27; "Harmful tendency" 28; Attempted assassination of Alexander II in 1866 29; Censorship and the new reaction 30; The courts and the censorship 31; Growth in the number of periodicals 32; Administrative warnings to periodicals 32; The <u>Russian Word</u> and censorship 32; <u>The Contemporary</u> and censorship 33; <u>The Voice</u> 34; I. Aksakov's periodicals 35; M. Katkov and censorship 37; Political works 38; Nationalism 38; Radical ideas and censorship 39; D. Pisarev and censorship 39; Foreign works 40; Burdens of the censors 41; Impact of censorship 42.

IV. Censorship Legislation and The Courts 1865-1872   45
Timashev appointed minister of interior 45; Valuev's failure to revise press law 46; Urusov Commission established to revise press laws 48; Commission's project rejected 50; Timashev prefers administrative measures 51; Committee of Ministers given power to ban books 51; The courts and the case of Pisarev's works 52; Courts reluctant to penalize "tendencies" 54; Censorship dissatisfied with the courts 57.

V. Censorship 1868-1881   59
Amendments to press law 59; Power to ban retail sale of periodicals 59; Power to confiscate works 60; Confiscated works 61; New circulars banning sensitive topics 61; Growth of periodical press 62; Penalties imposed on periodicals 63; Attitude of censorship towards periodicals 63; The Voice 64; The Deed 64; Notes of the Fatherland 65; Reasons for the tolerance of the censorship 66; The Week 69; Messenger of Europe 69; Russian Reports 70; The satirical journals 70; Expose articles 71; Nationalism 71; Jews 72; Growing interest in politics 73; Reaction of censorship to this interest 74; Literature for common people 75; Public mores and religion 75; History 76; Foreign works 76; Censorship administration 77; Burdens of censors 78.

VI. The Crisis of Alexander II's Reign 1878-1881   81
Censorship and the government's reaction to terrorism 81; The subsidized press 82; Liberals ask for censorship reform 83; Loris Melikov proposes to direct the periodical press 84; Loris' concessions to periodicals 84; Special committee to revise the press law 85; Proposal to establish repressive censorship using the courts 86; Penalties contained in the project 86; Alexander's assassination ends chances of the project 87.

VII. Censorship in the Reign of Alexander III 1881-1894   89
Alexander III and the periodical press 89; The liberal B. Chicherin and the press 89; Caution of Loris Melikov in March, 1881 90; Alexander III supports Pobedonostsev and Loris resigns 91; New guardians of the censorship 92; New Temporary Press Rules of 1882 93; New prohibitory circulars 94; Growth of periodical press 95; Growth in number of published titles 96; Censorship restricts growth 96; Weapons of censorship against printed works 97; The Citizen 98; The Voice 98; Notes of the Fatherland 98; Liberal periodicals 100; Russian Thought 100;

Political works 101; Nationalism 101; Jews 102; Critical social thought 102; Public mores 103; History 104; Foreign works 104; Burdens of censors 105; Rejection rate 105; New audience for printed works 106; Impact of censorship 107.

VIII. Censorship in the Reign of Nicholas II 1894-1905   109

Personnel changes in censorship 109; Elenev's memorandum 109; Petitions for reform of censorship 111; Growth in number and circulation of printed works 113; Growing audience for periodicals 113; Provincial press becomes bolder 115; Legal changes in censorship 116; Administrative penalties on periodicals 117; New prohibitory circulars 117; Anti-semitism in censorship 118; <u>Russian Reports</u> 119; <u>Russian Word</u> 120; Political works 121; Socialism 122; Social thought 123; Literature for the common people 123; Nationalism 124; Decadent literature 125; Foreign works 125; Rejection rate of censorship 126; Burdens of censors 127; New boldness of writers 128.

IX. Censorship in 1905 and After   129

Committee of Ministers abolishes some restrictive provisions of the censorship laws 130; New Commission established to revise press laws 131; Commission proposes abolition of administrative penalties and prior censorship 131; Temporary Press Law of November, 1905 ends prior censorship for periodicals in cities 132; New recommendations of Commission 133; Revolution ends Imperial censorship 134; Press Rules of March and April, 1906 abolish prior censorship for most books 135; Emergency press rules cancel new laws 135; Penalties imposed on printed works after 1905 136; Effort to re-establish censorship fails 137; Abdication of Nicholas II 138.

X. Conclusion   139

Statistics on Foreign Censorship   145

Footnotes   199

Bibliography   225

Index   241

Abbreviations

Materialy....1869 .... Materialy sobrannye osoboiu kommissieiu vysoch. uchrezhd. 2 noiabria 1869 g. dlia peresmotra deistvuiushchikh postanovlenii o tsenzure i pechati

Materialy....1905 .... Materialy vysochaishe uchrezhd. osobago soveshchaniia dlia sostavleniia novogo ustava o pechati

SPR 1865-1868 .... Sbornik postanovlenii i rasporiazhenii po delam pechati s 5 Aprelia 1865 g. po 1 Avgusta 1868 g.

SPB .... St. Petersburg

* For English translations of Russian titles of periodicals, see Index

Acknowledgements

I would like to thank those who made this work possible: the Fulbright Commission for a grant to Finland, the Inter-University Committee on Travel Grants, now known as IREX for a stay in the Soviet Union, and the Harvard University Russian Research Center for its ideal environment for research. I also want to thank the many libraries and librarians who have helped me: Helsinki University Library, the Saltykov-Shchedrin and the Lenin Library, The Widener and the Harvard Law School Library, the New York Public Library, Columbia University Library, and the Library of Congress. In particular, I thank the librarians of the reference section of the Skidmore Library for the gracious handling of my requests for books. I also thank the archivists who kindly helped me at the Central State Historical Archive in Leningrad and at the Central State Archive of the October Revolution in Moscow. Even though I may not have acted on their comments, I am grateful for the time and criticisms of Professors Marc Szeftel, Frank Randall, and Daniel Field. Skidmore College was very helpful in supplying money for research and for the typing of this work. I would like to express my thanks to Josephine Lucas for her assistance. Finally, I thank my wife and family to whom this work is dedicated.

Introduction

The history of the Imperial censorship in Russia from 1865 to the 1905 Revolution constitutes an important but little studied aspect of the history of the Empire. The censorship, as in authoritarian monarchies in western Europe in earlier centuries, and indeed in the 19th century, was an important element of social control in Russia. By means of the censorship, the government tried to direct and regulate the material read by its citizens. Its goal at first was to ensure the loyal and unquestioning support of governmental and social institutions in the Empire. On one occasion, in 1848, it even threatened dire measures against those writers who avoided open praise of governmental policies. It never carried through on this threat since the warning alone was sufficient to bring writers to heel and since the emergency which had inspired the threat soon disappeared. After the death of Nicholas I in 1855, the new ruler, Alexander II accepted the appearance of a periodical press and literature concerned with public affairs. The eagerly waiting writers responded with enthusiasm to the opportunity. But soon the appearance of diversity and variety of opinion, the manifestations of a critical spirit, frightened the government. The monster encouraged by the government needed curbing; published criticism of governmental actions or social institutions was seen by the autocracy as inimical to public order. A new Press Law of 1865 was drawn up to help the government regulate published works, especially periodicals. The censorship system that was constituted then persisted with changes down to the 1905 Revolution. All printed works published in the Empire and most foreign works passed the examination of governmental censors either before they circulated or before they were printed.

But the government's control, although thorough, was not perfect. It did not prevent the publication of critical comments on government policies and actions. It did not prevent the appearance of radical and liberal critiques of society and government. Indeed, the Russian revolutionary movement which is often said to have originated during the so-called "revolutionary crisis" of 1861-1862 was nurtured in great part on works published legally within the Empire. Moreover, the government kept tampering with the machinery of the censorship. Already repressive censorship regulations were supplemented by additional regulations that were even more repressive. One minister's repressive regime was followed by another minister's more repressive regime. Penalties increased in number when writers were most free, and decreased when writers kept silent out of fear. Often the "failure" of the censorship to keep this subversive criticism out of printed works is attributed to the inherent stupidity or blindness of censors. It seems incomprehensible to us in the 20th century that government officials could have so inadequately defended the autocracy against attacks by the critical and questioning mind. But so it was. This study is an effort to understand the "failure" of the Imperial censorship. In the course of the study, the policies and actions of censorship officials will be analyzed and described. The goal is to understand the aims of officials as well as to describe their actions.

Censorship during this period has been described and analyzed in a number of excellent works by pre-revolutionary journalists, scholars, and lawyers, particularly by K. K. Arsen'ev, M. K. Lemke, and V. Rozenberg and V. Iakushkin. Soviet authors, especially V. Evgen'ev-Maksimov, I. Aizenshtok, M. Teplinskii, B. Papkovskii and S. Makashin have added much data from the archives to these pre-revolutionary studies.* But the pre-revolutionary studies, aside from limited access to archival material, concerned themselves with the successful effort of the censorship to regulate the printed word, and not its "failure." Soviet authors have often limited their studies to the impact of the censorship on a few radical journals and authors. Their information and their perceptions are invaluable. But what I have done here is study archival material from 1865 down to 1905 with the aim of deriving a more complete picture of the activities of the censorship. I have tried to generalize about the decisions of censors on works involving politics, mores, religion and history on the basis of this archival material. I have studied the material concerning particular journals in an effort to understand the motives for censors' decisions. I have concentrated on the actions of the censors and censorship legislation, giving only slight attention to the administrative structure of the censorship and none to the clerical censorship. The study can only be an overview since I have seen only a few of the more than 13,000 folios in the archive of the Chief Board of Press Affairs in the Leningrad archives. But I have presented here in English, the first general study of the Imperial censorship from 1865 to the 1905 Revolution.

* See bibliography

Undoubtedly readers will be struck by the continuity between the Tsarist censorship and the Soviet censorship today. The demand for a complaisant periodical press, for writers who would cooperate with government aims, has certainly been implemented in the Soviet Union. But it seems to me that the experience of censorship is so widespread in the 20th century that it would be wrong to see only this continuity. What is perhaps most striking to me is the voluntary, self-imposed limitations that the Tsarist censorship accepted, a moderation that unfortunately has disappeared in 20th century politics. The change is perhaps epitomized by an episode involving Alexander II in the years just before his assassination. When a few terrorists had been captured by the police, a meeting at which Alexander was present considered how the government could learn more about the conspirators. The Minister of Court insisted that the captured terrorists should be forced to divulge these names and information. Alexander II answered with dissatisfaction: "How, by torture?"**

** D. A. Miliutin, Dnevnik D. A. Miliutina 1873-1882 Ed. by P. A. Zaionchkovskii 4 vols. (Moscow: 1947-50), III, p. 215 (Meeting of Feb. 8, 1880).

Chapter I   Censorship 1855-1863

Soon after his accession to the throne in February, 1855, the Emperor Alexander II initiated a series of reforms which transformed Russia. Most important were the emancipation of the serfs, judicial reform, and the establishment of representative bodies, the zemstvos. An important but little studied reform changed the press and censorship regulations. This act was immediately connected with the major reforms in that some easing of the pre-publication censorship and some encouragement of the press was initiated by the government to rouse support for the reforms. Greater freedom for the press and literature was contingent on a changed official attitude towards public interest and influence in government affairs. The change was slow and difficult; suspicion of public interference in bureaucratic affairs had a long tradition in Russia. The ideal arrangement for officials was one in which the public, through the press, would support and aid bureaucratic initiatives in reform. The ideal was possible. The Russian educated class was accustomed to following the lead of reforming bureaucrats. But the appearance among journalists and writers of critics of government policy as well as the suspicions of officials thwarted this expectation. Despite these difficulties, reform of the press regulations was pushed by officials. The existing preliminary censorship was modified in 1862 when examination of already printed works was entrusted to the ministry of interior. At the same time an extensive examination of the censorship regulations began, directed to the preparation of new rules. Early in 1863, the censors themselves were transferred to the ministry of interior as well as the committee which was preparing a new law. Finally in 1865, new regulations freeing some periodicals and books from pre-publication censorship were adopted. This chapter is devoted to the period to 1863.

Alexander was a hesitant reformer. His vacillation towards the press can be noted in his remarks and his actions. The Grand Duke Constantine, his brother, was a more convinced advocate of the virtues of publicity. It was he who first proposed to allow discussion of the impending naval reforms in journals, using the naval ministry's journal as a vehicle for this discussion.[1] And it was he who helped persuade Alexander of the usefulness of permitting discussion of the peasant reform, a decision that signalled a new era for journalists.[2] Alexander's announcement in January, 1858 that he intended to permit wide discussion of reform proposals and to prepare a new press law,[3] seemed to mark his conversion to the principle of a liberalized regime in the censorship. But just as he vacillated about emancipation, Alexander was only half-hearted in his dedication to publicity. In November, 1857, he ordered the

Minister of Education to report to him all articles expressing a desire for change so that he might stop those he considered harmful. In passing he noted that "very frequently" judgments about state and public affairs appeared that "are not in agreement with my thoughts, stimulating minds vainly."[4] In May, 1858, he admitted that he had never been an admirer of writers and added that "these are people with very dangerous tendencies and thoughts."[5] Alexander again in December criticized the periodical press for its loose behavior which he blamed on the laxity of the past Minister of Education.[6] A year later he expressed regret that "our century is inclined to malevolent criticism of all government measures." He added, that "journals and newspapers have begun to exceed all measure and print such things which it is impossible to permit in the press in any well ordered state and all the less among us with public education still at a young and undeveloped stage."[7] Clearly Alexander's conception of the role of the periodical press was paternalistic; it was to be encouraged in its useful work and restrained from foolish behavior. It should be mature, and maturity connoted support of its patron instead of thoughtless recriminations. Alexander believed that the task of reform was formidable enough without a periodical press that irritated officials and provoked unnecessary divisiveness.

Alexander's refusal to accept an independent periodical press and his conclusion that it must be guided led him to a number of expedients during the turbulent period of reforms. In December, 1858, he decided to create a Committee of Press Affairs, modeled on similar establishments in western European countries. He wanted this committee to subsidize some writers, direct their activities in an approved direction, and print suitable comminiques periodically. The experiment failed.[8] A year later Alexander proposed an independent body for press affairs which would "leave the press reasonable freedom but stop... this license of the press which must never be tolerated." He gave control of this body to Baron Modest Korf who, with apparent reluctance, prepared a manifesto announcing the new institution, and began discussions about a suitable building for it. But this enterprise also failed. Instead, in 1860 an independent Chief Board of Censorship was established; its functions would be very similar to the old board that had been in the ministry of education.[9] Even this independent body failed to control literature satisfactorily and failed to end the "excesses" of writers. By late 1861, a committee made up of representatives of the ministries of education and interior began work on changes in censorship.[10] Officials had by this time become convinced that only a move from a preliminary to a post-publication, punitive, censorship, not purely administrative changes, could resolve the government's dilemma.

All these expedients were forced on the government by the

public's eager and quick response to the government's invitation to discuss public affairs. The number of periodicals published in the Empire increased rapidly after 1855 reflecting the interest of the public in political and economic affairs. Trade and economic journals were founded to defend the principle of free trade and propagate the businessman's point of view.[11] Popular newspapers catering to literate city people, village teachers, and lower clergy began to appear; three were founded in 1863. The appearance of these new periodicals was encouraged by the government's permission to discuss public affairs, and its decision, in May, 1862, to permit the publication of private advertisements in private newspapers. Soon newspapers were being sold by the issue instead of by subscription although official permission did not come until 1865. By 1866 a Russian Telegraph Agency had come into being, at first to gather foreign and commercial reports, but eventually for domestic news.[12] Political attitudes within Russia's small educated class evolved as interest in public affairs grew. A contemporary witness, E. Feoktistov, in September, 1861, described the majority of enlightened society as liberal, aiming at freedom of the press, public court procedure, a public budget and the end of corporal punishment. Feoktistov however noted that the government's efforts to hold back liberalization contributed to growing dissatisfaction in Russian society. Ironically, the fate of Feoktistov's letter attests to these official restraints; his letter was opened by the Third Section.[13] But if the majority was liberal, a vocal minority led by the writers, N. Chernyshevsky and N. Dobroliubov was radical and another minority was reluctant to accept reforms. All these divisions produced what the government called a "ferment of minds." In turn, the government was quick to see a threat in this "ferment" particularly after student disorders in St. Petersburg University in September, 1861 and mysterious fires in the city in April and May, 1862.

A more precise indication of the government's views and a description of the divisions within the educated public can be found in a memorandum dated April 25, probably 1862, in the Third Section Archive. The report accused writers and professors of propagating atheism or deism, communism, and either republicanism or constitutionalism. The writer actually distinguished between extremists who wanted to change society completely, more moderate advocates of republican government like that of the United States, even more moderate advocates of monarchy limited by a representative body, and finally the most moderate group who simply wanted reforms of the courts and the police as well as a free press. While noting that this last group deserved "esteem,", the writer added that a free press required the establishment of trustworthy courts as a precondition. He also suggested that all these political and religious ideas "dispose minds" towards political movements directed against the government. To oppose this threat, he proposed a whole series of measures by the police, the church and the ministry of education.[14] The writer's suggestion was apparently acted on after the fires in St. Petersburg in May, 1862. That same file contains copies of orders banning public lectures in St. Petersburg in June, 1862 and closing public reading rooms and Sunday schools that same month.

This agitation within the government at the new independence of writers and professors and their reluctance to serve as complaisant assistants of the government in the task of reform provided the setting for the activity of A.V. Golovnin, the acting Minister of Education appointed in December, 1861. Contemporary judgments of Golovnin were mixed. Feoktistov, a subordinate of Golovnin, called him a limited and confused person who never learned the errors of liberalism. The reformer Nicholas Miliutin thought he was a mediocrity with high pretensions. On the other hand D. Miliutin called Golovnin a conscientious advocate of progress.[15] He had served under Grand Duke Constantine in the Naval Ministry and his reputation was that of a liberal. His program was also liberal in that he hoped that a mixture of concessions and generosity towards favorably disposed writers and stern repression of the malevolent could create the malleable journalism and literature that Alexander desired. In his memoirs, Golovnin notes that in order to protect the government, he tried to move cautiously in the direction of freeing the press. He prepared favorable reports on articles to dispose Alexander towards the press; he distributed favors, sometimes monetary but more often privileges such as the receipt of foreign books without censorship and permission to publish private advertisements; and at the same time, he tried to maintain a vigilant censorship.[16] He was assisted in his efforts by his friend, V. A. Tsey, who became chairman of the St. Petersburg censorship committee in March, 1862.

Golovnin's liberal attitude was not unique among officials. In January 1862, the head of the police, Prince V. A. Dolgorukov advised the Minister that discussions of reforms prior to confirmation might be permitted. He thought private warnings would suffice to keep journalists in line.[17] At the same time, he was advising the fifth expedition within the Third Section, the censorship division, to report useful proposals by journalists as well as anti-government articles.[18] But Dolgorukov's leniency was as mixed with caution as Golovnin's. Early in 1862, Tsey warned Golovnin of the bitter lessons to be drawn from the French experience in the 1770s and 1780s. Then, for lack of effective control by the government, literature had helped to undermine the government. Tsey feared that the extravagencies of journalists might have unfortunate consequences on an impressionable public. For this reason, he urged the publication of a new code that would warn censors and writers about impermissible subjects. Although opposed to a punitive censorship, that is the punishment of culpable articles after their appearance, he was willing to graft onto the existing preliminary censorship punitive measures against authors of socialistic or communistic articles. He concluded his recommendations with the advice that these punitive measures should be combined with measures to eliminate sources of irritation in society.[19]

Tsey's willingness to mix leniency with harshness in order to restrain writers was in fact Golovnin's program. Neither was as yet a complete supporter of an unrestricted periodical press. Tsey's influence on his friend explains Golovnin's proposal, in March, 1862, to divest himself of the supervisory aspect of the censorship.[20] The proposal, approved by Alexander, retained the censors in the ministry of education but transferred the Chief Board and its examiners of printed works to the ministry of interior.[21] Golovnin's decision to rid himself of policing responsibilities eased his task. He could now pose as the defender of the press and join with writers to condemn the harshness of edicts that emanated from the ministry of interior. At the same time he did not expose the government to the threat presented by an unrestrained press. Governmental security remained important to him. For this reason he prepared the new Temporary Censorship Rules of May, 1862 and in June, 1862 proposed the closing of the radical journals The Contemporary and Russian Word, a recommendation that was changed by the Council of Ministers to temporary stoppage to avoid the need for a special Imperial order.[22] Throughout 1862, Golovnin played his difficult role of vigilant sentinel and generous patron of literature. In this ambiguous role, he made use of the services of the supervisory censorship directed by P. Valuev, the Minister of Interior from April, 1861.

Golovnin describes Valuev critically in his memoirs, saying that Valuev tried to stir Alexander against the press in order to further his repressive policies.[23] Valuev was indeed suspicious of the press. An episode in May, 1862, is indicative. Here Valuev complained to Golovnin that a poor translation of a Polish language communique that had appeared in Russian Invalid was "hardly accidental" considering the previous editorial policies of the newspaper. He asked Golovnin to have editors certify the accuracy of their translations henceforth, a request Golovnin refused on the grounds that censors were limited to examination of the text alone. Valuev responded with a citation of another article of the Censorship Code which enjoined censors to be guided by the spirit as well as the letter of the law. The spirit of the Code, said Valuev, required the prevention of "any kind of harmful consequences from the printed word." Despite this rejoinder, Valuev now requested only that the matter be brought to the attention of editors and censors informally. Golovnin acceded.[24] Valuev saw journals as exponents of points of view or policies which could be ascertained over a period of time by considering their selection of articles and, only occasionally, by overt statements. Particular violations were important to him as much because they exposed the editorial point of view as because they were illegal. Another indication of his attitude towards the press is a remark, in an 1865 report on the press, that hardly any issue of a periodical appeared without some changes made by censors. Thus, he argued, a "true idea of the spirit and general state of mind of our press" could not be acquired only from reading what was printed. In the context, Valuev's remark was critical. Still, like Golovnin, Valuev thought it was possible to manipulate the press and so guide public opinion.[25] To that extent his differences from Golovnin were differences in attitude rather than goals. Both sought to control the press and literature.

Valuev's suspicions about literature and the press were combined with sympathies towards political reform in Russia. Like Golovnin, his policy was "two faced" in that in 1863 he proposed, without success, a reform that would have changed the State Council into a legislative body with some popular representation. His desire for reform was however subordinate to his deference to the will of Alexander.[26] Accordingly he was often obliged to criticize periodicals that proposed the exact reform he himself desired. His "duplicity" probably explains why contemporaries judged him harshly even while they acknowledged his intelligence and ability.

The political sensitivity of Valuev and the supervisory censorship after March, 1862 and the difference in attitude and responsibility between Golovnin and Valuev is apparent from their correspondence in 1862, especially in cases involving politics. In June, 1862, Valuev wrote to Golovnin about a series of statements in an article in Russian World: that the press laws of a nation parallel its political structure; that the egalitarian commune is a fundamental form on which Russian development should be based; that the political life of a people is a sign of its vitality; that absolute monarchy has become antiquated in Europe; that government should devote itself to awakening the moral forces in society and give these some scope; and that the people should have some voice in the declaration of their needs. Valuev found all these remarks impermissible.[27] Golovnin did not quarrel with this report or two others in which Valuev cited impermissible discussions of the disparate interests of southern and northern Russia and impending reforms in the bar and finance ministry such as the elimination of bribery.[28] But he did take issue with Valuev in connection with an article that Valuev accused of juxtaposing, unfavorably, extremists of the left in society and extremists of the right in the government. According to Valuev, the author had argued that the two extremes nurtured each other.

Thus, the fires in St. Petersburg had led to severe measures such as the closing of the Sunday schools, the chess club and reading rooms. Golovnin countered on August 7, 1862 with an extract from the censor's explanation. The censors said the article appeared in two parts, in the first of which, after juxtaposing the two extremes, the author described the extremes as representing different groups among journalists and society. The second part of the article listed a series of news items without comment and included the measures noted by Valuev. To support his judgment, the censor noted the journal's praise of the government's past reforms and its intentions to continue these policies.[29] This disagreement between Golovnin and Valuev was partially based on a matter of fact. But to a great extent, their disagreement reflected their different attitudes and responsibilities towards the press. Valuev, fearing Alexander's reaction, preferred silence or almost unquestioning support from the press. Golovnin would accept support of the government's reforming policies.

Valuev's reluctance to give the press the opportunity to criticize government measures appeared also in his treatment of articles on the peasantry. He protested against a criticism of a provincial office's decision[30] as well as criticism of the Emancipation Statute[31] and a tale detailing the abuse of house-serf.[32] A proposal to endow houseserfs with land was condemned by Valuev[33] and he accused another article, critical of a court's rejection of a peasant suit against a landlord, of possibly stimulating hostility between classes.[34] Another article that caught Valuev's attention described a dispute between a lowly restaurant attendant or "bufetchik" and four landowners. The dispute ended with the closing of the counter, thus depriving the owner of his income. Golovnin objected to Valuev's judgments and answered that abuse of power rather than publicity about such abuses was more likely to stimulate hostility between classes.[35] Golovnin's argument was sound but so was Valuev's. Unfortunately for Golovnin, Valuev's policy of hounding criticism from periodicals was easier to implement than Golovnin's policy of tolerating moderate criticism. Golovnin must have recognized the problems inherent in his combination of concessions and rigor. The archives contain an original of a letter by Golovnin asking for guidance from the minister of justice as to whether decisions of government courts on peasant affairs might be criticized. But the request was crossed out and replaced by words indicating Golovnin's agreement with Valuev's comment.[36]

Golovnin did not always defer to Valuev. On one occasion Valuev condemned an article which referred to ineptitude by lower officials in the State Bank administration. Golovnin informed the Minister of Finance who answered that since the Council of Ministers had permitted publicity concerning abuses within the administration he would agree with Golovnin that the article was permissible.[37] Golovnin could not however gainsay Valuev's sensitivity to "expose" literature that in a transparent way referred to abuses by specific individuals. These "exposes" were called slanderous by Valuev.[38] A particular offender was the section "They Write to Us" in the satirical periodical The Spark. Because the section was continuous and because the names used to conceal person and place were consistent, the government decided that attentive readers might be able to decipher the "exposes." For this reason, in July, 1862, the censorship banned further printing of the section.[39] Golovnin's policy remained vulnerable to the charge that it might undermine trust in governmental institutions. This was Valuev's contention in a case in which a local office of the Chief Board of Routes of Communication was pictured as ignoring a petition of local shipowners.[40] Golovnin was also vulnerable to the charge that a whole class of officials was being condemned indiscriminately. Such was Valuev's criticism of an article in which the author referred to the peasants' need to purchase immunity from captious officials.[41] Valuev was right; the disclosure of abuses would undermine trust in governmental institutions. Golovnin did retort that abuses and the concealment of them did more to undermine trust. Colovnin was also right. But his liberal position was more difficult to implement than the more traditional distrust of literature exhibited by Valuev.

Another significant indication of the differences between Valuev and Golovnin appeared in their attitudes towards the use of Yiddish in printed works. Valuev wanted to ban the printing of such works except when they were religious or moral in content. He argued that a commission of rabbis had approved this proposal and its result would be to encourage the spread of German and Russian. Besides, he argued literate Jews looked on Yiddish with contempt. Golovnin retorted that the prohibition would encourage a feeling of martyrdom among Jews and reinforce a preference for Yiddish. He thought that in fact Yiddish was becoming less important but that a governmental prohibition was not justified either politically or pedagogically.[42] In this case, Valuev's penchant for administrative decrees is clearly set off from Golovnin's willingness to tolerate and even encourage a gradual social process without overt interference by the government. Valuev was very much the bureaucratic reformer while Golovnin was hesitantly putting forth a liberal, laissez-faire, program for the government. Since Valuev's policy was more traditional, Golovnin went to some pains to allay bureaucratic suspicion of literature by flattering appraisals of writers and journalism.[43]

The gap between the policies of Golovnin and Valuev is displayed also in an episode involving Leo Tolstoy's periodical Iasnaia Poliana which Valuev accused of undermining religion and morality. Valuev believed that the evil of the journal appeared in the extremism and the falseness of its "tendency" and spirit.

But he also noted, paradoxically, that the danger from Tolstoy was that he could not be accused of malice or conspiracy. The paradox can be resolved. In a manner customary among higher officials dealing with printed works, Valuev implied that educated folk would suffer little harm from Tolstoy's work but that malicious and ill-informed teachers would develop harmful ideas on the basis of Tolstoy's position. Valuev was also, in a manner customary among censors and other governmental officials, using the word "tendency" in two senses: to apply both to the author's intention, conscious or not, and to the impression produced by a work, intended or not. Golovnin did not share Valuev's fears. He absolved Tolstoy of the charge that his thinking was anti-religious and although he called the author's pedagogical views incorrect, he did not think this was cause for suspicion. Unlike Valuev, Golovnin did not believe that because Tolstoy's views were open to criticism, they should be regarded with suspicion.[44]

Valuev and Golovnin quarreled in May, 1862 about an article that had appeared anout a newly proposed society to aid needy youths in Moscow. Valuev thought the appearance of the article unsuitable because the society had not yet been approved by the government. Golovnin answered at length:[45]

. . . many sided consideration of such undertakings by private persons in journals and newspapers (may) have a good influence on the proposed institution...(and) may preserve the inexperienced and thoughtless from participation in an undertaking which has no foundation. It is very probably that if at an earlier time free consideration of such proposals of private persons had been permitted, then a few share companies in which many families lost their capital might not have come into existence.

Golovnin's appreciation of the value of publicity and his acceptance of the idea that the government should not interfere in the discussion of ideas had its limits. When Valuev reported, in May, 1862, that an article in The Contemporary (Sovremennik) the previous February had propounded the socialist idea that equality of taxation required equality of income, Golovnin made no rejoinder.[46] Golovnin was moving towards a liberal position but by no means was he prepared to imperil the security of the state and society by giving free rein to outspoken radical views. There is little truth to the critical comment of E. Feoktistov, an aide to Golovnin in 1862 who later became an outspoken conservative. Feoktistov, after crediting Golovnin with the belief that every opinion, however wrong, should be expressed without hindrance while the ministry watched the struggle, adds that it is difficult to think of anything more liberal or more stupid.[47]

On the other hand, Valuev's suspicions seem to have had few

limits. He objected to the appearance in a non-scholarly periodical of a reference to the moral depravity of Emperor Peter III, fearing harm from this information.[48] When an excerpt from Hugo's Les Miserables appeared in a periodical, Valuev argued that its anti-religious and democratic views could only undermine religion and the monarchy.[49] Golovnin gave no counter-argument. But when Valuev attacked an article by D. Shcheglov that had been published with Golovnin's express permission in Library for Reading, Golovnin did respond. The article defended a punitive, post-publication, censorship on the grounds that it would allow to all the possibility of presenting as well as refuting arguments in print. Golovnin parried Valuev's indignation by insisting that prohibition of the article might have led to its circulation in manuscript. In turn, the excellent refutation which was published elsewhere would have been impossible. The Minister argued that refutations were more useful than simple prohibitions and added that the Temporary Censorship Rules of May, 1862 which Shcheglov criticized, undoubtedly had inadequacies.[50] Golovnin had his own criticisms of the article, based on his belief that the impressionability of the great bulk of the population had to be taken into account. Further, he disagreed with Shcheglov that censors, in their ignorance, would incorrectly attribute socialist ideas to authors. For Colovnin the choice he faced was simple: either harshness for all or harshness for selected journals and writers. He much preferred the latter policy.

Valuev's position was indeed less devious. Ironically Valuev would have been forced to agree with an argument present by The Contemporary in its March, 1862 issue. The journal noted, tongue in cheek, after an investigation of French censorship legislation, that a "conscientious investigation" could lead to the conclusion that continuation of the preliminary censorship was necessary in Russia. The implication of the article was that otherwise the periodical press could not be restrained from expressing its hostile attitude towards the government. Valuev condemned the article but his many letters to Golovnin indicate his very clear suspicions about the antipathy of journalists.[51]

Since Valuev's attitude was more traditional in the bureaucracy, Golovnin had to struggle hard for his more discriminating policy. He tried to allay the Emperor's suspicions about the press by forwarding "well intentioned" articles to him and proposing some support of useful journals. But he did not conceal from Alexander the sins of the press, and sent forbidden articles to him. A collection of unpermitted articles was prepared by the ministry and published.[52] But in December, 1862, after the Obolenskii Commission, established to prepare a new censorship code, presented its report to him, he had to end his ambivalent policy. In December, 1862, on the basis of a critical evaluation of the work of the Obolenskii Commission by his Vice Minister, Golovnin attacked the project and proposed the establishment of transitional censorship rules pending reform of the courts. More importantly, he raised the question whether the censorship should remain in his ministry. Alexander ordered Golovnin to present his views to the Council of Ministers.[53] The final product of Golovnin's thought was an extended report to the Council on January 10, 1863. Aside from recommending transfer of the entire censorship to the ministry of interior, Golovnin here presented his liberal credo.

Citing general complaints about the effectiveness of the censorship, Golovnin attributed its faults to the inability of the law to set down precisely what can and what cannot be printed. Only a punitive censorship in which printed works would be subject to the courts could satisfy writers and the government. He admitted that Russian society was "morbidly sensitive" to the printed word. Until the courts were reformed, a punitive censorship was impossible; indeed, freedom would soon lead to reestablishment of the preliminary censorship. Golovnin indicated that he now agreed with the Obolenskii Commission on the need for transitional measures. The question for him was whether the ministry of education or the ministry of interior should conduct the censorship in this transitional period. He argued that his own ministry was a protector of enlightenment which was a product of the "free dispute" of various opinions from which truth emerged triumphant. The censors, said Golvnin, protect the momentary truth and so limit deliberation. His ministry had tried to extend the borders of permissible discussion recently. But in a time of awakening intellectual life, the task of censors became very difficult as they sometimes erred while holding back the powerful enthusiasms of literature. Concluding his credo, Golovnin offered to turn over the censorship and the project to the ministry of interior.[54] There was some debate on Colovnin's proposal, enough to require two separate meetings. Golovnin was apparently criticized and, according to Valuev, was accused to perpetrating some trick on Valuev by his proposal. But approval finally came and on January 14, 1863 control of the preliminary censorship and the Obolenskii project passed into Valuev's hands.[55]

Golovnin's acceptance of the liberal notion of the "free exchange" is clear from his statements. But what is also clear is that he tempered his commitment to liberal ideas by a thorough acceptance of the need for security. His decision to hand over the censorship and the project to Valuev indicated his reluctance to sully his reputation for liberalism by implementing illiberal decrees. This was the verdict of contemporaries. Golovnin's action may also have been determined by a judgment that a truly liberal censorship would not be tolerated by Alexander. Colovnin implies as much in his recollections. There he recalls that his goal was to "give greater scope to the printed word", eliminate arbitrariness from the censorship and punish crimes through the courts. But "events...which did not permit extension of the rights of the press--proclamations, actions of foreign agitators, intrigues of revolutionary propaganda, in particular Polish" nullified the good results of his efforts. Because these conspirators counted heavily on the use of periodicals, the government increased the severity of the censorship and forced postponement of concessions to the periodical press. Golovnin's account is essentially true except for his effort to make his actions in 1862 appear to be dictated by circumstances rather than his own choice; for example, his remark that extraordinary measures made the job of minister more and more impossible and placed him in a position "opposed to the entire direction of the government."[56] What Golovnin does not say is that he found the censorship to be a political embarrassment and decided in January, 1863, to rid himself of it. His hope may have been for greater freedom for the press but his decision indicated that he was unwilling to risk his position by taking a responsible and active role in achieving this goal.

Golovnin's abdication meant that Valuev would have his opportunity to control the censorship and guide the press in the next few years. Liberalism, even when tempered by harshness towards a few malcontents now gave way to a stern paternalism under which literature and the press would be under pressure to become compliant assistants of the government in the work of reform. Dissent, whether systematic or not, would be suspect and criticism would have to be well meaning to be acceptable. Moreover Valuev's paternalism, like that of Alexander, was seasoned by a great distrust of journalists and literature. The desire of writers for independence and their refusal to become unofficial agents of the government, even more than any overt expression of harmful tendencies fed this suspicion. Such were the conditions under which literature lived from 1863 to 1865 and under which a new censorship code was prepared.

Chapter II   Censorship 1863-1865

With the transfer of the censorship and the Obolenskii Commission to the ministry of interior, the spirit of accommodation that Golovnin had fostered ended. Valuev did not believe that truth would emerge triumphant in the free competition of ideas nor did he believe that subversion of the government was the work of only a few writers. For him the very independence of writers, whether sympathetic or hostile to the government, was a threat to the government. Prince Obolenskii, in the first meeting of the reorganized Obolenskii Commission, expressed Valuev's attitude when he pointedly lectured members that truth did not always triumph in literature. He insisted that the censorship by nature was arbitrary even when cloaked in the forms of law, and he argued that this arbitrariness was justified.[1] Valuev remained suspicious of writers during the period from 1863 to 1865. In addition to persuading writers to support the government, Valuev used threats and force to ensure a compliant literature. He also made use of an official newspaper of the ministry, Northern Post, as well as subsidies to writers and publishers. But the threat of sanctions rather than a benign optimism was the dominant note in Valuev's policies.

Valuev's circular to censors on January 29, 1863 is indicative. He there ordered censors to give special attention not only to particular thoughts but the "general direction" or tendency of each separate article and the publication it was to appear in. He advised censors to inform editors and authors privately that because of the disorders in Poland and the impending reform of the press laws, censors were not to permit that which "contradicts the fundamental ideas of our state structure and root conditions of public order." Valuev, in clarification of his statement, explained that a few journalists aimed at the "systematic condemnation (okhuzhdenie) of government decrees" and the publication of information that might be irritating. He further advised censors to warn journalists of his power to stop a publication temporarily; finally, he ordered censors to forward requests for new periodicals directly to him.[2] This order deserves some analysis. The concept of a "general direction" or tendency was an old one in the censorship. It referred to the attitude or editorial policy of a censored journal which conveyed by the selection of articles, allusions, and sometimes by silence the assumptions which the author did not dare express because of the censorship. "Direction" also connoted an attitude expressed over a period of time. The direction might however, as interpreted by the government, be an attitude of which the author or publisher himself was not conscious. Used in this sense, the journal might be condemned because the government was displeased by the impression an article or series of issues might create. If a particular author consistently wrote articles that produced

13

an unfavorable or displeasing impression, the government might accuse him of having, or exhibiting, a harmful direction. This constituted the "systematic condemnation" that Valuev was referring to. Considering the fact that the government did not concern itself with the actual attitude of writers nor with the actual observed impact of an article, the scope given to arbitrariness was great. Valuev's advisory in effect allowed censors to interpret an article on the basis of the author's attitude in the past, or the attitude of the journal, or even the particular conditions in Russia at the time the article appeared. Valuev's use of the concept of "direction" gave clear sanction to arbitrariness.[3]

During the period from 1863 to 1865, important reforms were instituted such as the zemstvo reform, the university and school reforms and the judicial reform. Although Valuev was suggesting in 1863 an audacious reform, the admission of public representatives to the State Council, he tried to prevent periodicals from setting forward similar proposals. Thus, he ordered censors to stop articles recounting the virtues of representative government either specifically as in the case of a Dorpat newspaper or generally as in references to historical precedents for representative government in Russia.[4] After the zemstvo law had become public knowledge, he ordered censors to prevent speculation about the possible widening of their competence.[5] When the Moscow Reports considered the question of the state peasants, Valuev ordered the censorship to forbid articles on the subject because the measure was then being considered by the government.[6] Valuev's concept of the role of the periodical press required limitation of its privileges. He treated it as if it were another branch of the government bureaucracy whose function was to act as a supporter of government policies. Since the press, whether or not it was sympathetic to the government, wished to be either independent or to set its own terms for its support of the government, conflict between it and Valuev was inevitable.

The Polish rebellion which began in January, 1863 was a particularly sensitive issue in this period. Extreme nationalists like Ivan Aksakov argued that Russian officials were not taking a sufficiently patriotic attitude. He suggested, in The Day, that Russians might well learn patriotism from the Poles. Although Valuev forbid repetition of such remarks, Aksakov, a few months later, returned to the subject and alluded, indirectly, to the lack of a Russian spirit among officials.[7] Valuev condemned an article that proposed harsh policies towards Catholic monks on the grounds of their collusion with Polish rebels.[8] But Valuev was also alert to criticism of Russian patriotism.[9] Caught between an ardent patriotism which questioned the effectiveness of official policy towards Polish rebels and a minority opinion that opposed this patriotism, Valuev ordered in February, 1863 that all news from Poland be taken from official newspapers and news about Poland be censored by one specially chosen censor.[10] When periodicals evaded this order, he reiterated his earlier instruction,[11] now permitting citation of semi-official newspapers. A specific example of these evasions was an article in *Northern Bee* early in 1863 which noted that the Russian army had been ousted from a few cities by the rebels. Valuev criticized such articles because they might lead to distrust of official bulletins.[12] But the curiosity of the Russian public and the ingenuity of journalists were so great that over a year later, in 1864, Valuev had to demand again that news of the actions of the military command be taken only from the semi-official *Russian Invalid*. The ostensible reason was to prevent foreigners from drawing incorrect conclusions about the persistence of the rebellion.[13] But the real reason was Valuev's sensitivity about the Polish question. His decision to abruptly end the polemic about Poland between the patriotic *Moscow Reports* of M. Katkov and the semi-official *Journal de Ste. Peterbourg* confirms this conclusion.[14] Despite failures, Valuev consistently tried to control periodicals.

Polish nationalism was not the sole irritant in 1863. Ukrainian or officially, "Little Russian" nationalism was the topic of a special and secret letter from Valuev to Golovnin in July, 1863. Referring to the argument in the press about whether a "Little Russian" literature existed, Valuev accused some writers of harboring political aims that were masked by the ostensible goal of spreading literacy among Ukrainians. He noted that educated "Little Russians" saw little value in propagating "Little Russian" works since they could not be used as school texts. He also accused Poles of spreading the fallacious idea that a unique "Little Russian" language existed. On these grounds, Valuev forbid publication of a New Testament in "Little Russian" and forbid the publication of all except belles-lettres in the language pending a final decision of the question of teaching "Little Russian."[15] A few years later the ban on the publication of Ukrainian works was extended. Even Baltic nationalism became a problem when Russian patriotism became particularly strident. Valuev found it necessary to condemn an article in a Dorpat newspaper which claimed that Lutheranism was being persecuted by the Russian state.[16] A fictitious tale from the 17th century in a provincial newspaper which suggested that Smolensk was a Lithuanian, not a Muscovite city, was criticized by the censorship late in 1863.[17]

The provincial newspaper press was affected by the new surge of interest in public affairs. These newspapers except for a few that were privately published, were usually issued in two parts, an official and an unofficial part. Although the government made some effort to encourage these newspapers, it kept close watch on them through the local vice-governors who acted as censors. For example, in permitting a few provincial newspapers to print political news in 1863, Valuev ordered that all such news be reprinted from official publications.[18] In July, 1863, Valuev advised governors that local provincial newspapers were publishing critical comments about local institutions that exceeded the limits of propriety. For the future, he ordered that disclosures of defects be permitted only when the government's remedy for the problem was also published.[19] Valuev's solution to the dilemma posed by local newspapers was ideal but he could not enforce it, despite his many attempts to do so. Early in 1864 he ordered some provincial newspapers to take their national news directly from Russian Invalid, the Market Reports, the Journal de Ste. Peterbourg, and Northern Post all official or semi-official newspapers.[20] On another occasion he condemned polemical articles that he thought verged on libel.[21] In March, 1865, Valuev accused official provincial newspapers of printing "expose" articles about private individuals or officials and other articles critical of government actions in peasant affairs, the schools or local government. He demanded that the newspapers coordinate their activities with the government since unlike private publications, these provincial newspapers must reflect the government's views. Valuev asked the governors themselves to enforce this decision especially in view of the imminent opening of zemstvo assemblies. In particular, Valuev wanted to prevent the appearance in provincial newspapers of reports of zemstvo discussions except in excerpts, as approved by the governor.[22] This clear edict was violated. In July, 1865 Valuev had to reaffirm the order and used the occasion to empower governors to replace editors and censors in case of violations.[23] Valuev's difficulties with these semi-official provincial newspapers indicates that his goal of making the private press a handmaiden of the government was a formidable task.

The history of the Voronezh Sheet (Listok), a private provincial newspaper, illustrates the caution of the government. In 1862 the local gendarme official informed the Third Section of the "bad" tendency of the newspaper as shown by its penchant for libelous statements. Two years later, Valuev complained about the tendency of the newspaper in connection with its printing of judicial circulars.[24] A few months later he banned the newspaper for eight months. When the publisher was about to renew publication, he asked permission to appoint a new editor. The local gendarme officer noted that the new editor had been discharged from a newspaper in the past because of its bad tendency. For this reason he thought it unlikely that the Voronezh newspaper would be run suitably. The publisher was forced to appoint another person as editor. Despite this careful scrutiny, the new editor did not make the newspaper irreproachable. In 1866 the gendarme officer complained of the scurrilous character of its articles. A few weeks after this complaint, the publisher proposed a new editor whose qualifications were examined by the gendarmes. The officer noted his "free form of thought" but added that up to now no accusation of unreliability had been made against him. On this basis the Third Section advised the Chief Board of Press Affairs that the new editor was acceptable.[25] The archive folio on the newspaper ends here; apparently the new editor ran the newspaper to the satisfaction of the Third Section.

Despite the obstacles imposed by Valuev, the periodical press would not be silenced completely. An especially popular form in the press was the "expose" article which disclosed administrative abuses without directly naming the officials involved. The official stance was to allow such disclosures because they provided assistance to the government. Such at least was Valuev's statement in a secret advisory to the censorship in July, 1863 which added, however, that the abuse was not to be treated as a typical action. Valuev also appended a note whose purpose was clearly to mitigate the harm he expected from "expose" articles. He suggested that censors should exercise care that "expose" articles be accompanied by articles favorable to the administration because "systematic declaration of inadequacies alone, in the light of improvements now being made by the government....shows not an aim to uncover the truth but a systematic attempt to irritate minds and plant distrust in them."[26] Valuev's fine distinction was difficult to implement; but to that end he advised official and semi-official publications to counter "unfounded" reproaches of the government by printing, frequently, articles which detailed the government's efforts to improve its practices.[27] About a year later, in 1864, Valuev again complained about baseless "expose" articles and ordered Moscow censors to demand from publishers the names of the sources for the information. He told the censors to explain to publishers that the ministry had no intention of concealing abuses. It wanted however to prevent the printing of "exposes" which originated simply from personal malice or an animus against the government.[28] In all probability Valuev was not being disingenuous. He very likely was sincere in his desire to uncover abuses and he was aware that here the periodical press might be useful. But he was also conscious that "exposes" threatened the prestige of the government. His solution to the problem was to insist on "exposes" that carefully noted official efforts to eliminate abuses or described the abuse as unique. But the evidence seems clear that he had great difficulty enforcing his program.

Journalists persisted in their independence. One periodical accused a doctor in Tiflis of abuses and the censor was reprimanded.[29] Another charged a provincial secretary with abuses and the censors were ordered to stop the article because the case was being investigated.[30] One journalist even defended an official against an accusation, an action that Valuev considered inappropriate.[31] When The Day printed an accusation of bribery in connection with a woman's school, all of which were under the

17

patronage of the Empress, the Committee of Ministers objected on the pretext that the article was unsigned.[32] One case indicates that the Russian public was learning to make use of publicity: Moscow Reports was implicated in a suit by members of the Moscow Board of Public Order (blagochiniia) against the Moscow Duma because a letter of a member of the Duma reproaching the Board had appeared in the newspaper.[33] This stubbornly independent attitude of the press made Valuev's task difficult. He wanted to use the press and he appreciated the value of publicity. But he was also aware of the dangers it posed, especially when it became insubordinate.[34] And the press instead of reflecting the views of officials became a mirror reflecting the disorders and disquiet of society.

How could the press aid the government in the task of preserving morality in society? In November, 1863, Valuev thought he had devised an answer. He advised censors that ridicule of moral inadequacies was permissible so long as names were not mentioned and immorality was not presented to readers in an attractive or enticing form.[35] On the surface the admonition was clear. When implemented however, the order led the Council on Press Affairs to condemn a description in V. Krestovskii's novel, Petersburg Slums (trushchoby) of the drunkenness of a young woman for its shocking details.[36] Valuev thought that a novel by Boborykin, The Power of the Land (Zemskiia sily) appealed to prurient minds and ordered a reprimand to the censor who permitted it. Only a month before he had advised censors to be cautious in examining the novel.[37] If censors could misunderstand an explicit order of Valuev, writers could with justice plead that they found it difficult to distinguish proper from improper references to morality.

One of the duties of the censors was to aid the clerical censors, who censored religious and dogmatic works, by defending religion in secular works. The growing importance of Biblical and religious criticism made the task of the censors difficult. For example, the censors passed a five volume encyclopedia without consulting the clerical censors beforehand about a few culpable places. The places included a statement that, with the advent of Christianity, Christian saints supplanted pagan priests; another referred to the "sober" teachers, the Gnostics, whose preachings were ignored in favor of those of Christian ministers.[38] A reference to the greed of parish priests who refused to bury an old woman without payment troubled the censors.[39] A review of an exhibition of paintings by Gey (Ge) was vigorously condemned by the censorship because the reviewer suggested that the painter was the artistic counterpart of an unnamed European author whom the censors decided was the Biblical critic, E. Renan.[40] Works of the Schismatics, who had broken with the Orthodox Church in the 17th century, were permitted but only when their "absurdities" were refuted.[41] The secular censors working in combination with the clerical censors, whose reputation for vigilance was proverbial assured tight control over works involving religion. Even praise of an official Committee for the Improvement of the Way of Life of the Clergy was restricted.[42]

The sources contain less material on the censorship of historical works than on works relating to religion. The St. Petersburg committee rejected two pictures in an illustrated history of Russia, one of a banquet in the palace of Ivan IV and the other of the death of Ivan on the grounds that the work, intended for the common people, depicted popular entertainers (skomorokhy) and sudden death by the sword. The publisher complained and the Council on Press Affairs acknowledged that a publication costing eight rubles could not indeed be intended for the common reader. Still the Council decided that the unpleasant subjects depicted in the work were not suitable for the audience of children at which the publication aimed. The Council ruled, while permitting the work with some changes, that henceforth publications designated for pupils should not sketch primarily the dark side of Russian history.[43] The Council was disingenuous since it would take exception even to the incidental description of "dark" events. Still, thoroughly scholarly works because of their limited audience might escape these restrictions.

During these years, 1863 to 1865, while a new press code was being considered by the government, Valuev tried to keep literature and the periodical press on a tight rein. He would have preferred a press that acted as a handmaiden to the government. Instead, as the cases indicate, writers and publishers behaved in an unruly manner. They chafed and struggled and succeeded in printing information that displeased the government. In no sense could the activities mentioned above be called anti-government or subversive. Writers and publishers were trying to publish what they thought would educate the public and excite their curiosity. But Valuev insisted on seeing some of these efforts as subversive. His attitude is epitomized in his judgment, in August, 1863 that the "most significant part of our literature" exhibited a "not well intentioned tendency."[44] Armed with control of the censors and the power to deny a periodical the right to print private advertisements,[45] Valuev fought to direct the press and literature. Perhaps, as a bureaucrat, he found it difficult to replace the old custom of paternalism with a more tolerant attitude towards the activities of independent citizens. Under his aegis, the new press law of 1865 was prepared.

II

The preparation of the new press law was the work of the Obolenskii Commission, so named for its chairman, Prince D. A.

Obolenskii. Prior to the Commission's establishment, in March, 1862, an ad hoc committee composed of two representatives of the ministry of interior and two from the ministry of education had considered an earlier proposal for reform by the then Minister of Education, Admiral E. V. Putiatin. Putiatin, alarmed by the radicalism of The Contemporary and The Russian Word, had recommended in November, 1861 that all journals be required to post a bond that would be forfeited if regulations were violated. Such a measure was in principle incompatible with a preliminary or preventive censorship since it would hold writers and publishers responsible for printing material that censors had read and approved. Alexander avoided a decision at the time by turning the question over to the ad hoc committee.[46] The committee considered Putiatin's recommendation as well as a petition of editors and publishers asking for the privilege of printing articles on their own legal responsibility without preliminary approval by the censors. What they were demanding was a "punitive" system, that is the abolition of the preliminary censorship, the author's or editor's responsibility for published works, and allowing the government the opportunity to prosecute the authors or publishers of "illegal" works. On the surface, it would appear that Putiatin and the petitioners agreed on the nature of the reform they desired. But in fact, both sides agreed only on the intolerableness of the existing system and even then, the reasons for their dissatisfaction were different.[47]

The disparity in motives was clear from the recommendation of the ad hoc committee in February, 1862. The two representatives of the ministry of education, in a joint report, opposed a punitive system on the grounds that it was appropriate only to countries with public legislative bodies and that freedom for authors would be extremely dangerous in Russia. They proposed a mixed system combining repressive features of both the punitive and preventive censorship.[48] The two representatives of the ministry of interior filed separate reports. They too recommended a mixed system but saw it as transitional to the eventual abolition of the preliminary censorship. But their notion of a punitive censorship was clearly distorted to prevent the spread of dangerous works; they proposed to have printed works examined before distribution although after printing and to hold authors responsible for printed but undistributed works.[49] Golovnin, when he proposed, in February, 1862, a revision of the censorship regulations with a view to replacing the preliminary censorship by a punitive system that would rely on the courts, clearly split with the ad hoc committee. But by mid-March, 1862, when he issued instructions to the Obolenskii Commission, he had changed his position. Now he contemplated a mixed system which would include repressive elements from both kinds of censorship.[50]

The Commission took about eight months to prepare its conclusions, soliciting the opinions of writers as well as investigating thoroughly the press laws of Germany, and other European countries. The Commission's conclusions were submitted in October, 1862.[51] Like Golovnin after March, and the ad hoc committee, the Commission decided that a punitive system was impossible because of the lack of courts, the public's unfamiliarity with "insolent" speech and the possibility of abuse. But on the other hand, the Commission condemned the existing preliminary censorship chiefly because of its ineffective control of literature but partly because of the negative effect it had on writers. On these grounds, it proposed a mixed system as a transitional measure.

Despite the suspicion of writers indicated by the Commission's fears of "insolent" speech, the Commission was concerned that harsh regulations might stifle literature. In connection with a suggestion that freed periodicals post a high monetary bond, the Commission noted that such a measure had been used in France to assure the government that only wealthy individuals would become publishers. But the measure, noted the Commission, had not prevented the appearance of journals hostile to the government, nor could the Russian government expect a more "correct" direction from "capitalist profiteers." The Commission argued further that a high bond might suppress periodicals which serve as a means of education and a medium for the expression of public interest in public affairs. Moreover, said The Commission:

> For the government itself, journalism serves as the best and irreplaceable means of following the state of minds at a given time and knowing the true needs of the various classes and locales. Wherever journalism is not developed or is suppressed, there the government is deprived of one of the most important aids for consideration of the state of society. Without it it must act gropingly, at random, without any guarantee of success of its most well intentioned enterprises. Let the law prosecute and punish abuses of the press but general repressive measures against journalism in general...falling with all its force not only on a journal with a harmful direction but on well intentioned journals may only yield the most deplorable consequences for both society and the government.[52]

As is clear from this statement, the Commission sought to accommodate the needs of literature and the government without endangering the state's security. Its motives were mixed as was the system it proposed.

The Commission's project freed works of twenty or more printed sheets (320 pages in octavo), all official publications, publications of scholarly institutions, and all works in Greek or Latin from preliminary censorship. Freed publications would be subject to a punitive system closely resembling that in

Napoleon III's press law of February, 1852. The government could prosecute authors for violating the law. Until new courts were established everywhere in Russia, freedom would be restricted to works published in St. Petersburg and Moscow. Periodicals could be freed from censorship only with the consent of the minister of interior. These would be liable to judicial and administrative penalties. The latter might be imposed when a "harmful tendency" was noted, an offense which the Commission frankly admitted would not be acceptable in the courts because of vagueness.

The Commission, considering independence of the censorship authorities a necessity, gave control of the censorship and the punitive system to a Chief Board of Press Affairs, composed of a five man council and chairman, all part of the ministry of interior and subject to the minister. The council would read printed works and decide either on prosecution or, in the special case of periodicals, administrative penalties. Council decisions could be rejected by the minister. Moreover, the minister would have the authority to permit new periodicals, to free them from censorship and to prepare instructions for censors.[53]

With respect to the preliminary censorship, the Commission used as a model the code prepared by the minister of education in 1859 that was rejected by the State Council. It preferred to avoid precise instructions to censors, acknowledging that the task of censoring involved arbitrariness and coercion. Besides, the Commission believed that a profusion of instructions were testimony to a distrust of the censor when in fact the government must place its trust in the censor. The Commission agreed, without any explanation, to retain the censorship of foreign works, and it made no proposal concerning the clerical censorship and the censorship of theatrical works.[54] In all, the Commission had produced a project that mixed a few concessions, carefully hedged and elaborately justified, with a strengthened censorship administration.

Baron A. P. Nicolai, Golovnin's Vice Minister, examined the project and criticized it for its mixture of punitive and preventive measures. He preferred an exclusively punitive system but nevertheless hesitated to propose such a radical change until the press became accustomed to "cool" speech and the government less dependent on administrative penalties.[55] Obolenskii rejected this argument and praised the virtues of gradualism and argued the dangers of inaction.[56] Finally Golovnin himself attacked the project as hostile to literature and the press and suggested preparation of new rules for a transitional period until the judicial reform took effect. Most important however was Golovnin's recommendation that the government decide which ministry should control the censorship before it considered the project. The emperor ordered Golovnin to present these remarks to the Council of Ministers which Golovnin did in January, 1863.[57] At that time Golovnin presented a long report which, with resounding phrases, defended the doctrine of the free market place of ideas, argued for a punitive censorship, and recommended transfer of the entire censorship and the project to the ministry of interior. After some debate in the Council, at two separate meetings, the Council approved the transfer which took place on January 14, 1863. Now the project was in Valuev's hands.[58]

Despite Obolenskii's bitter rejoinder in which he insisted that the project conformed to Golovnin's instructions and that Golovnin had read and approved most of the project before its official presentation, it would appear that Golovnin was justified in criticizing the project. His instructions had not suggested transfer of the censorship to the ministry of interior, as the project intended, and even these instructions which advised a mixed system represented a compromising of Golovnin's original views.[59] Obolenskii expressed his bitterness in the first meeting of the new Obolenskii Commission which met on February 19, 1863. Here he directly countered Golovnin's defense of the free market place of ideas by arguing that truth does not always triumph in the free competition of ideas.[60] The new Commission, chosen by Valuev, retained Obolenskii as chairman, the same secretary and I. Andreevskii, a professor of police law at St. Petersburg University. Seven new members, three of whom ostensibly represented the ministry of interior replaced four members of the old commission. After three months in which the Commission met as a group fourteen times, a new project was prepared and presented to Valuev in June, 1863. In most respects the new project was similar to the old. However, a majority of the Commission did recommend a few more liberal provisions. For example, all periodicals in the capitals might choose freedom; the original project had allowed the Minister of Interior the power to confer this privilege. The new project required only half the monetary bond of the original. A minority of the Commission favored expanding the authority of the Council of the Chief Board at the expense of the minister's power but failed to introduce this change into the project. Ultimately the conservative minority position triumphed because Valuev revised the project before submitting it for review; he systematically eliminated the liberal provisions that the conservative minority had opposed.[61]

Golovnin and other high officials examined the project after June, 1863. Golovnin's comment was in conformity with his previous statements: he opposed administrative penalties and suggested alternatives that would do less violence to the property rights of publishers. Valuev's rejoinder was ad hominum; he reminded Golovnin that his own Temporary Censorship Rules of May, 1862 included administrative penalties.[62] Baron Korf, head of the Second Section of the Emperor's Chancery, made some lengthy comments which in theoretical terms favored a punitive censorship but in the end accepted the mixture offered by Valuev. He proposed that the power of imposing administrative penalties be taken from the minister and given to the Council and he wanted to free books of ten or more sheets from preliminary censorship. Valuev rejected these liberalizing amendments.[63] He also rejected similar proposals by the Minister of Justice, D. N. Zamiatnin and Count V. N. Panin, who had replaced Korf as head of the Second Section by September 1864.[64] Valuev thus rejected all amendments and presented the project to the State Council in November, 1864.

The Department of Laws of the State Council devoted a number of meetings to the project and proposed a few amendments, the most important of which would have required approval by the Senate, the highest court of the Empire, of decisions to suspend a periodical.[65] Opposition to the project was even stronger in the State Council. Here the attack was led by the War Minister, D. A. Miliutin. Valuev had earlier stubbornly refused to make concessions even when warned by the Grand Duke Constantine Nikolaevich. Now, however, Miliutin demanded that the new legislation should take the form of separate edicts as befitted transitional measures. Further, he wanted to free works of ten or more sheets from the censorship, increase the Council's power vis-a-vis the minister, give the Senate a voice in suspending a periodical, and allow periodicals to decide whether to be uncensored. (Here Miliutin wanted to restore the provision of the project that Valuev had changed to allow the Minister to decide the question). E. P. Kovalevskii, a former Minister of Education, supported Miliutin in the State Council arguing that administrative penalties were unnecessary since freed works would be examined before their distribution. The debate ended when the State Council accepted Baron Korf's suggestion to return the project to the Department of Laws for revision.[66]

In the face of this setback, Valuev revised the project before submitting it again to the Department.[67] Despite these changes the Department forced additional changes in the project in meetings of March 10 and 13, 1865. Now, ten sheets would be the required minimum for liberation from censorship, and the new law would take the form of separate edicts rather than a code. Moreover, a majority of the Department favored increasing the power of the Council and the involvement of the Senate in decisions to suspend a periodical. These two issues were taken up again in the full State Council on March 24, 1865.[68] But in the Council, Valuev had the support of the Emperor and so was able to win a compromise. Valuev was given the authority to suspend a periodical temporarily by his own decision; permanent suspension became the prerogative of the Senate. On the second issue, the powers of the Council, Valuev won and received complete authority over the Council on Press Affairs. Thus, with Alexander's support, Valuev reversed the judgment of the majority in the Department of Laws. The Emperor signed the new press law on April 6, 1865 and it went into effect in September, 1865.[69]

The new law was published as two separate enactments. An imperial ukase delineated the various concessions to the press while an opinion of the State Council, confirmed by Alexander, contained details, especially the new controls over the press. Despite the fears of some journalists, some of whom even contemplated remaining under the preliminary censorship, the new law represented a substantial liberalization of censorship laws.[70] Periodicals in St. Petersburg and Moscow could be freed of preliminary censorship on request. In return they would be subject to administrative penalties, which could be imposed by the minister and the Council, as well as court imposed penalties for violating the law. Moreover, the new law required examination of periodicals after printing but prior to distribution, during which period the government might ban a work pending the initiation of prosecution. This vestige of the preliminary censorship also applied to uncensored books. But authors of books were more fortunate than publishers of periodicals since books, unlike periodicals, were not subject to administrative penalties. The confiscation of books could only occur when the government began prosecution and only the courts could punish an author. The main defect of the law was not, as Valuev wrote in 1868, that the liberal features had encouraged the false notion that the reform was intended as a concession to the press.[71] It was that as a result of Miliutin's efforts, the section of the project that included a list of press crimes was excluded from the project. Thus, the effort to base the censorship on law and the court system was weakened from the start. It must be admitted, however, that these provisions, drawn from the Penal Code, were inadequate in defining press crimes. This inadequacy encouraged the bureaucracy to avoid reliance on law and return to the tested system of administrative action. Valuev quickly turned to such measures in his effort to produce a compliant literature and press.

Chapter III   Censorship 1865-1868

In September, 1865, the new press laws went into effect, greeted by many as the beginning of a new era. The new grant of freedom was limited however and during the first few years, Valuev tried to establish even more limitations. In part, Valuev's moves to restrict the press were dictated by unusual events such as the attempted assassination of Alexander II in April, 1866. In part, the change in policy was a product of his experience with the new law. This experience led him to show an increasing preference for administrative measures over court procedures that set a precedent for censorship officials after him. Even his goals changed in the course of his administration. In 1865 he thought that the law in combination with efforts to influence the press would give him the control he desired. A few years of experience with the press persuaded him of the vanity of this hope. By 1867 he was less optimistic that he could direct the press; now he advised the Chief Board to concentrate its efforts on the prevention of evil. Throughout the changes in policies and goals, Valuev made use of a careful mixture of conciliatory and repressive measures.

Valuev's cautiousness appeared in his instructions to censors on August 29, 1865 on the eve of the introduction of the new press law. He listed a number of possible criminal violations of the new law: the questioning of the truths of Christianity, attacks on autocracy and "rooted" ideas of social and civic morality, or on property rights, and the stimulation of hostility between classes. Then Valuev stated some guiding precepts for censors. He proposed that the "leniency" enjoyed by censored publications up to now must end. Henceforth censored publications would be considered to be specially approved and licensed publications which consequently would not be permitted to express views different from those of the government. He advised censors to devote special attention to periodicals which could convey their views over a period of time by hints, repetitions, and innuendo. All of these, said Valuev, could be understood as characterizing a periodical's "ruling view." Individual articles should be judged by censors, said Valuev, in the light of this "ruling view" and all willful violations were to be noted by the censors. Harmful violations would be prosecuted under the law. But even improprieties that were legal should be recorded, according to Valuev, because in the course of time these might become the basis for judicial prosecution. Valuev carefully added that such legal improprieties were significant only for periodicals with a harmful tendency; the errors of well intentioned periodicals could be treated leniently. Valuev's intention, to use the law as a means of applying pressure on selected periodicals, was also apparent in his advice to censors to consider, when examining an article, the personnel of the periodical, its attitude towards the administration in general and towards abuses within it, and the presence of commoners among its readers. "Expose" literature for those censored periodicals in the capitals which were bold was to be signed and very explicit in its target; provincial periodicals, because they had no option but to be censored, might be given more freedom in this area. The minister concluded his injunctions to censors by instructing them to weigh the motives behind violations, the contemporary situation, and finally whether the courts would uphold prosecution. He feared that unsuccessful prosecutions would discredit the government and publicize the accused article.[1]

Valuev's lengthy instruction is worth analysis. It shows that he saw the new law as a possible impediment, but also an aid to him in his task of securing the government against the press and literature. A parallel to his resigned agreement to be restricted by the law in pursuing the guilty was his conviction, traditional in Russian police agencies, that motives and intentions, conscious or unconscious, and consequences, intended or unforseen, were of greater concern to the censorship than the actions themselves. The implication of Valuev's instructions was to assume that the worst possible motive and consequence of any article had been in fact intended by the author. This was a recipe for suspicion. In this vein, Valuev argued, in January, 1867, that while some people assumed good intentions lay behind most actions of the periodical press, whether good or bad, he preferred to treat the press as fully aware of and responsible for its actions.[2] Here Valuev would seem to have argued that the motives of journalists were always conscious and by implication, often malicious. But actually, all that Valuev was saying here was whatever the possible consequences of an article, he would act as if the author had intended these results. Again, the practical import of Valuev's instruction was to suspect the writer. Such an attitude in the censorship produced arbitrariness. An author's motives or the possible consequences of his article would be considered more important than his action and might become the basis for an accusation. And while the government could use either a presumed motive or a possible consequence to argue its case, the author could not easily prove the purity of his motive and the harmlessness of his action.

The arbitrariness of the notion of a "harmful tendency" was acknowledged by the Obolenskii Commission and later by the official newspaper of the ministry of interior, the Northern Post. According to the newspaper, which spoke for Valuev, the evil represented by administrative penalties for a "harmful tendency" was balanced by the evil of bad intentions on the part of journalists; in any case, concern for society's reaction would make the government cautious in applying this measure.[3] Still, as interpreted by the Senate in 1869, the concept of "harmful tendency" became almost inscrutable. The Senators started from

the position that the tendency of a periodical was equivalent to
its character, tone, or attitude, and reasoned that even a well
intentioned tendency could coincide with dangerous actions. But
then the Senators argued that doctrines were only one factor in
distinguishing a periodical's tendency. The audience, the
attractiveness of the form, and the circumstances of the time
were also to be considered in determining a tendency. Thus, the
Senators freed   the term "tendency" from its original
connection with intention, motive, and aim. In effect, the
Senators concluded that a "tendency" was equivalent to an
"impression" or "influence". The General Assembly of the Senate
accepted this specious reasoning and commented: "With the un-
ending variety of thoughts expressed in literary works, positive
law cannot foresee and severly define all these cases when disclosure of a thought may produce harm and consequently be subject
to punishment." In conclusion, the Senate decided that intention
and the appearance of an evil, two components of ordinary crimes
according to law, could not always be proven since the evil might
appear in the course of time and might be independent of the
author's intention.[4] Thus, "tendency" as interpreted by Valuev
and the government might include any or all of the following:
the ideas, attitude, or tone of a periodical, the motive of the
author; the audience or attractive form of a work, the impression
produced by the work, the immediate or potential danger that
might be stimulated by a work, and the circumstances at the time
the article or work was printed or even some situation conceiv-
able in the future. What all these locutions reduced to was a
definition of a "bad tendency" as one which displeased the
government. And in deciding what it did not like, the government was free to use motives, actions, or possible consequences
as the basis for its judgment. Only the reaction of society
would restrain the government. Considering that this formula
for arbitrariness was built into the new Press Law, it is
surprising that by January, 1866, 16 periodicals had chosen freedom. A year later the number reached 19 and by January, 1868,
27. Perhaps the alternative posed by Valuev, becoming semi-
official spokesman of the government's views as censored periodicals, dictated the choice.

Despite the enormous power the law gave him, Valuev was
ambivalent in his attitude towards it. In October, 1866, he
referred to the prevalence of materialism and egalitarianism in
literature and the periodical press as well as a pervasive distrust of the government. He thought that precise execution of
the laws as well as greater government influence over the press
might restrain it. But his confidence in the law, never strong,
diminished,[5] especially after the unsuccessful attempt on the
life of Alexander II by Karakozov in April, 1866. As a direct
result of the attempt, Golovnin, the Minister of Education, was
discharged and Prince V. A. Dolgorukov, the head of the Third
Section and Prince Surorov, the St. Petersburg governor, retired.

Alexander also appointed a special inquest commission headed by the victor in Poland, the "hangman", M. N. Murav'ev. The commission decided that the laxity of the ministry of education was responsible for the dangerous ideas abroad in the land and demanded forceful measures to end attacks on the government and its principles in the press. A new special committee under the leadership of Prince Gagarin, chairman of the Committee of Ministers, considered these charges as well as some proposals by the new head of the Third Section, Count Peter Shuvalov and made a series of recommendations. One proposal was the immediate closing of The Contemporary and Russian Word. Moreover, the committee decided that because the government's authority over the press was too restricted, some changes should be made in the press laws. The committee also advised the closing of informal free schools, the investigation of the political reliability of teachers and private tutors, and an increase in the power of provincial governors. The broad character of the committee's attack on "free thought" is indicated by its proposal to ban all student associations, mutual aid societies of typesetters and printers, as well as "nihilistic dress"----long hair, blue eye-glasses for men and short hair and crinolines for women. So sweeping were these proposals that a few committee members objected, seeing in them a complete rejection of the Emperor's reforming policies up until then.[6] But Alexander confirmed the recommendations. At the end of May, 1866, a special Imperial order banned The Contemporary and Russian Word for their "persistence" in maintaining a bad tendency.[7] The committee had been more precise; it had condemned the two journals for purveying socialism and nihilism.

Valuev turned what might have been considered a defeat for him into an opportunity to sharpen the government's weapons against the press. At the end of April, he presented a memo to Alexander criticizing the predominance of materialism and leveling tendencies in literature. He suggested that with the cooperation of the courts this literature might be kept in limits. In early May, he wrote to Murav'ev implying that the staff of Russian Word had created a milieu in which the thought of murdering the Tsar could develop. Then, at the end of May, 1866, the head of the Chief Board, M. Shcherbinin, advised censors to give special attention to the satirical periodicals The Spark (Iskra), The Alarm Clock (Budil'nik) and Diversion (Razvlechenie) and other humorous periodicals dealing with politics and accessible, because cheap, to the common people.[8] Valuev also delivered an extended instruction to censors on the same day in which he warned them to be watchful for ideas opposed to religion, morality, the social order, **loyalty to the throne, and property.** Warning that the periodical press was a "double-edged sword" capable of good and evil, he admonished them to keep it within bounds and prevent the purveying of "destructive theories" and "false teachings" detrimental to the state's unity, harmony between classes, and religion. Finally, he advised them to give special attention to pedagogical works and those directed at the common people. Shcherbinin repeated the warning on July 10, 1866.[9] At the end of May also, Valuev secured Alexander's consent to prepare revisions in the press code.[10] Valuev now had an opportunity to amend the press laws.

One of Valuev's main problems with the press law was the insistence of the courts on adherence to the word and spirit of the law. The luck of Valuev with the courts was mixed. Court cases tended to be appealed and as a result cases lingered. From September, 1865 to the end of 1866, the censorship initiated cases against thirteen publishers and editors and by March, 1868, seven cases were still being considered.[11] But on the other hand, by early 1869, of 13 judicial proceedings begun by the government, the prosecution had won ten.[12] The slowness of the courts irritated the censorship. Another source of irritation was the disagreements between the prosecutor and the censorship about the validity of the charge. Judicial officials insisted that the prosecutor must have some voice in framing the indictment. In the end the State Council conceded to Valuev in December, 1866. The prosecutor would have to accept the indictment of the censorship administration and "officials". In case of doubt, the prosecutor could ask the minister of justice.[13] Another troublesome issue involved the use of jury courts. After two cases had been initiated in a jury court, the State Council ruled in that same December, 1866 law that press cases should be considered by a higher court, without a jury, as a court of first instance.[14] Another major complaint that Valuev had against the courts was the opportunity a court trial gave to clever attorneys to defend their clients and sometimes win their cases. On one occasion, an attorney argued that because the censorship had stopped the sale of his client's publication, the author could only be charged with the intention to violate the press laws, not a violation. The court rejected the argument but nevertheless imposed a lesser punishment on the defendant than the prosecutor had requested.[15] The opportunity the courts gave to the accused to defend himself restricted the censorship in an unaccustomed way.

Valuev did not have to rely exclusively on the courts to maintain pressure on periodicals. The law allowed the censorship not only to bring a periodical before the courts but also to issue administrative warnings. Three warnings brought a ban for up to six months. Complete suspension, according to law, could result only from a direct Imperial order, a decision of the Senate, or a decision of the lower courts which might be appealed ultimately to the Senate. Up to 1869, 46 warnings were issued and ten periodicals suspended temporarily. Moreover, special Imperial orders had closed The Contemporary, Russian Word, and The Muscovite (Moskvich).[16] The warnings affected a small number of private uncensored periodicals of general interest. In 1867, six periodicals received 15 warnings.[17] In fact, of the 289 periodicals published in the Empire in 1866, only 22 were private uncensored periodicals; in 1867, the figures were 313 and 31.[18] Thus the full weight of administrative measures fell on this comparatively small number of periodicals of general interest that had paid the monetary bond.

But the number of periodicals grew after 1865. By the beginning of 1868, the number was 317 as compared to 254 when the new law went into effect.[19] Son of the Fatherland had the largest circulation of any periodical, 15,000, while The Voice, a newspaper published by A. Kraevskii, had about half that number in 1868. The "thick" journal, Notes of the Fatherland, which had just come into the hands of N. Nekrasov, had only a circulation of 5,500 in 1868 while the financial Market Reports, (Birzhevye Vedemosti) which sometimes contained articles of general interest, sold a thousand more copies.[20] In addition to copies sold by subscription, copies might be sold on the streets of St. Petersburg or Moscow or sold from the publisher's office. This public sale was a privilege that the government could grant.[21] Although the effective audience of periodicals was much greater than the circulation figures would indicate, still the government's fear of periodicals seemed disproportionate.

Against this periodical press, the censorship disposed of a number of weapons aside from the courts and administrative penalties. It kept a record of suspicious articles. During the period from September, 1865 to the end of 1866, it recorded nine articles from Moscow Reports (Moskovskie Vedemosti), eight from The Voice, and five from the St. Petersburg Reports (S. Peterburgskie Vedemosti). Five unofficial and private warnings were given to The Voice in that period as well as three to the newspaper The Week (Nedelia).[22] In 1868, censors rejected twenty-six articles for censored periodicals.[23] These threats to the press were supplemented by a public warning to periodicals that previous publication of material separately did not guarantee a periodical immunity from prosecution when it reprinted the material.[24] Another indication of suspicion of periodicals was the withdrawal, in 1866, of the privilege Golovnin had generously conferred on a few editors, to receive foreign publications without censorship. Henceforth the Minister could extend this privilege at his discretion.[25]

The radical periodicals The Russian Word and The Contemporary were considered the most reprehensible by the censorship. With the inauguration of the new press law The Russian Word freed itself of the preliminary censorship. By December, 1865 it had received its first warning for articles preaching communism and socialism and its cynical attitudes towards morality and marriage.[26] Less than a month later came a second warning for

articles by D. Pisarev and N. V. Shelgunov in the November
issue.[27] A report by the famous author of Oblomov and member of
the Chief Board of Press Affairs, I. Goncharov, served as the
basis for this warning. He accused Pisarev of emphasizing the
age-old character of the struggle between reason and religion.
Shelgunov's guilt was to argue that workers' associations aimed
to change the social and economic structure. Goncharov thought
that judicial prosecution would be a more appropriate and more
severe punishment than a warning but the Council decided otherwise.[28] Another report by Goncharov followed soon after citing
articles by P. Tkachev and Shelgunov. Goncharov proposed to
await a more favorable occasion for a third warning but the
Council decided to act. On February 16, 1866 the journal
received a third warning wnd was banned for five months.[29] Before
the journal could renew publication, an Imperial order in May,
1866 banned the journal completely.

Even after the ban the censorship pursued the journal. The
publishers prepared an anthology of selections which Goncharov
reviewed in March, 1866. He noted in it a sympathy towards the
Enlightenment's critique of religion but thought there were no
adequate grounds for prosecution. Since, as a book, the work
could not be punished administratively, the case ended here.[30]
The journal was considered dangerous, so dangerous that it could
be argued that the journal was punished more for its reputation
than for what it printed. Goncharov, a lenient examiner,
suggested in one report, that Pisarev should be refuted, not
punished. But significantly he also commented that the articles
he was reviewing might have passed without notice in another
journal. Because of the reputation of the journal and because
The Contemporary had only recently been warned for a similar
article, he had recommended the first warning to the journal.[31]
Goncharov's leniency was partially a pose. For at the same time
that he condescendingly called Pisarev's article "The New Type"
an "abuse of mind and talent", he expressed fear that "young
dreamers" might be attracted by the article.

The Contemporary received similar treatment. Its first
warning came in November, 1865 for articles critical of marriage,
capitalism, and property.[32] A second came the next month based,
in part, on M. Antonovich's article which was accused of ridiculing
the Imperial regime and expressing improper judgments about Orthodoxy. Goncharov, who reviewed this issue, argued here that the
culpable articles could do no harm to society. But the Council
disagreed and issued a warning.[33] No further warnings were issued
but N. Nekrasov, the publisher, feared the imminent closing of
the journal. Contritely he wrote to Shcherbinin, the head of
the Chief Board, that he was prepared to close the journal but
wanted a year without warnings or temporary suspensions to prepare
for its demise. Informally Nekrasov was reassured and in fact,
the attitude of the censorship seemed to soften. But the journal

found itself in financial difficulties also; subscriptions had fallen from 4000 in 1865 to 2100 in January, 1866.[34] Then, in May, 1866, after the Karakozov episode, the Council, on the urging of Valuev, threatened the weakened journal with prosecution for publishing the article "The Problem of the Young Generation."[35] The article had described the pre-emancipation gentry as a parasitic class which had lived at the expense of the peasantry and predicted that the future belonged to the industrious kulaks and industrialists. Despite the permanent ban of the journal that was a product of the various special commissions in 1866, charges were lodged against the author, Iurii Zhukovskii and the editor, A. Pypin. The accusation, insult to the honor and dignity of the gentry, was challenged by K. K. Arsen'ev, the defense attorney, since the gentry were not a corporate person capable of being insulted. Arsen'ev convinced the lower court, but an appeals court overturned this verdict in October, 1866. Pypin and Zhukovskii were arrested for three weeks and fined 100 rubles each.[36] Arsen'ev based his defense on the premise that the prosecution of remarks critical of any class could be justified only by a compelling state interest. Otherwise, the civic activity of all classes was an object of free judgment. To his surprise, the court found that the state had an interest in curbing abuse or insults because such were crimes against social propriety and good order.[37] The government was vindicated and other journalists would take note.

    The Voice had difficulties with the censorship mainly because it tried to be a vigorous spokesman of liberal nationalist sentiment. Its first warning came in December, 1865 for a "completely and consistently" harmful tendency. This sweeping indictment was based on the newspaper's improper judgments about government measures, insults to officials and the gentry, and its incorrect depiction of history with the "obvious" aim of arousing sympathy for the government's opponents.[38] Not content with this penalty, the censorship took the publisher A. Kraevskii and a young contributor to court. The lower court imposed a fine of 200 rubles on Kraevskii but on appeal, the Senate raised the penalty to two months arrest. On Kraevskii's petition, Valuev asked the minister of justice to reduce the penalty to house arrest.[39] A second warning was precipitated by an article suggesting that some government positions were sinecures. The warning cited "systematic and unfounded reproaches" to the government.[40] A third warning and suspension for two months came in December, 1866 for slander of high police officials.[41] In 1867 came two new warnings for improper consideration of political questions and for casting suspicion on the Baltic Germans.[42] This vendetta against The Voice differed from the campaign against the radical journals. The Voice was not accused of propagating dangerous ideas but of excessive criticism of government policies. Valuev's measures succeeded in changing the attitude of the newspaper to the government's satisfaction. A yearly report by V. Fuks, a member of the Council of the Chief Board, noted at the end of 1867 that the newspaper had become more moderate since its suspension. Where it once had been "cosmopolitan" in attitude, it had now become nationalistic.[43] The reformed newspaper did not receive another warning until 1872.[44]

Like Kraevskii's, the nationalism of Ivan Aksakov was also associated with a claim to criticize the government. His Slavophile newspaper, The Day (Den'), found itself in difficulty almost immediately after it was freed of preliminary censorship. Goncharov, the reader for the Chief Board, proposed to prosecute the newspaper on the basis of material in the first two uncensored issues. The Council agreed with him but Valuev demurred. Later Goncharov reported on the tendency of Aksakov to present his newspaper as a tribune of the people. In the light of Valuev's earlier decision, he did not recommend any action. But in his later surveillance, he noted many improper articles, particularly those dealing with the Baltic Germans. In one of the last issues of the newspaper, Goncharov found a particularly reprehensible article that criticized a proposal to allow state peasants to purchase their land from the state. Goncharov commented that if this proposal had not yet been accepted by the government, then The Day was spreading false rumors; if the government had accepted the measure, then Aksakov was undermining this decision. Having posed the question, Goncharov refrained from a recommendation. Perhaps he realized the absurd predicament he had set for the press, which demanded the right to comment on public affairs, and for the government which claimed to grant this right. But Goncharov's question does show how unaccustomed censors were to the new freedom granted to writers to comment on public affairs. In any case soon after, The Day ended publication for financial reasons.[45]

Aksakov found new financial backers and soon his new publication Moscow (Moskva) received its first warning for "sharp" judgments about church-state relations.[46] A month later the newspaper received a second warning for criticism of passport regulations which the censorship thought might shake public trust in the government.[47] Then, in March, 1867 Valuev personally decided to issue a third warning to suspend the periodical for four months because of Aksakov's editorial which, in criticizing the Lutheran clergy, called for free competition between Lutheranism and Orthodoxy in Livonia. Valuev said such competition was not desired by the government. The warning also cited a tendency in the periodical to arouse hostility between different parts of the population.[48] When Moscow reappeared after the ban, Aksakov criticized the edict that suspended the periodical. For this action, he received a new warning.[49] A peaceful few months followed but Aksakov received two warnings in November, 1867 and his periodical was again suspended for four months. On this occasion, Aksakov's criticism of tariffs on foodstuffs and his subsequent criticism of the warning for this article were interpreted by the censorship as a persistence in his obtuseness.[50] After this ban, Aksakov, supported by what Valuev called a "few honored inhabitants" of Moscow, secured permission to publish The Muscovite (Moskvich) as a business periodical. Valuev was angered by the tone of the new newspaper but especially by Aksakov's stratagem. He asked the Committee of Ministers to ban the newspaper. The Tsar agreed and so allowed the proposal to be put before the Committee without the usual delay. In February 1868, the newspaper was banned.[51]

The irrepressible Aksakov renewed Moscow in 1868 and soon received a new warning for complaining of unfair treatment and suggesting that thorough-going compliance with the press law would allow evasion of the intent of the law.[52] A second warning came that same month, April, 1868, for criticism of government measures.[53] A third warning and suspension for six months soon followed. At the same time the Chief Board decided to ask the Senate, in accordance with the as yet unused provision of the press law, to ban the periodical permanently. The Senate divided on the issue. As a result the Minister of Interior, now A. E. Timashev, took the case to the State Council which supported his request. In 1868 Aksakov was, at least temporarily, silenced.[54]

Why did Aksakov receive this extraordinary treatment, as harsh as the treatment of the radical journals and yet lenient? An official of the Council on Press Affairs called Moscow essentially "patriotic" and "well intentioned". This would explain the government's patience in dealing with him. But the same official accused Aksakov of "sharpness" and "strange one-sidedness.".[55] In other words, Aksakov's attitude was irreproachable but his actions doubtful. Aksakov's case forced the government to do some deep thinking about the meaning of the word "tendency". Ultimately, while some Senators and members of the State Council interpreted the word narrowly to imply attitude and intent, and found Aksakov to be patriotic, the majority of Senators and members of the State Council decided that a "tendency" was equivalent to the impression a work produced. They concluded that Aksakov's criticisms of officials constituted an anti-governmental "tendency" which "could hardly not undermine" esteem towards ideas he supposedly defended.[56] Tendency was no longer a property of an author, journal, or article. It became a disembodied idea or spirit that was attributed to an article but could just as easily be explained by the sensitivity of readers or the political situation at the time. Aksakov's guilt however was compounded by his "sharpness", his caustic pen and forthright conviction. Forthrightness and directness were combined in Aksakov with an assertive independence. This independence was not the kind of attitude that the censorship wished to encourage among journalists, even patriotic journalists.[57]

The same flaw explains the many difficulties experienced by M. Katkov, the conservative entrepreneur in journalism in publishing his <u>Moscow</u> <u>Reports</u> (<u>Moskovskie</u> <u>Vedemosti</u>). Katkov, whose influence explains his nickname, the "Thunderer of Strastnoi Boulevard," came into conflict with Valuev in March, 1866. His newspaper received its first warning for implying that some officials were not partisans of a unified Empire.[58] A second warning followed in early May for an editorial accused of arousing distrust of the government.[59] At the same session of the Council, an editorial which disputed the government's authority to impose warnings was reviewed and the Council decided on a third warning. The newspaper was suspended for two months and deprived of the important right to print government advertisements.[60] Katkov almost decided to abandon the periodical but was encouraged by the Emperor to remain as editor under special protection.[61] Nevertheless the newspaper stopped publication for about ten days and reappeared only because the owner, Moscow University, replaced Katkov as editor temporarily. In June, 1866, Katkov returned to his position and resumed publication on a new basis.[62] His authority and prestige and his influential partisans, Count Murav'ev, A. A. Zelenoi, Minister of State Estates, and D. Tolstoy, Minister of Education, allowed him an exemption from the subordination demanded of other journalists. When Valuev again attacked the newspaper in November, 1866 the Emperor, despite his own irritation at the harsh tone of the newspaper, asked Valuev to bring his complaint to the Committee of Ministers. Valuev however decided not to pursue the issue further and the Committee of Ministers accepted this decision.

The secret of Katkov's comparative immunity lay, in part, in his views. Like Aksakov he was nationalistic; like Aksakov he attacked the bureaucracy; and like Aksakov, he was forthright in his opinions. But unlike Aksakov, his political orthodoxy was impeccable, and more important, the circulation and influence of his newspaper was greater. The government had long sought a spokesman that would influence the public. It created the <u>Northern</u> <u>Post</u> and other official and semi-official newspapers to present this pro-government point of view. But none had the influence of the <u>Moscow</u> <u>Reports</u>, perhaps because of Katkov's appearance of independence, a quality that the government often sought but never sanctioned for its semi-official newspapers. Indeed one might argue that Valuev's attack on the newspaper helped to preserve Katkov's reputation for independence.

Most of the work of the Chief Board was devoted to the small number of private uncensored periodicals. Thus, in 1868, censors were advised of 26 unacceptable articles that censors had permitted but were informed of 83 uncensored articles. What was unacceptable to the censorship is disclosed by the character of the cases it considered. Sexual morality, a traditional concern of censorships, was important in only a few cases.[63] Most often censors were concerned with political cases and works critical of government policies or personnel, or reputed to arouse hostility between classes.[64] Cases involving foreign policy also concerned the censors. But new concerns, such as the zemstvos and invidious comparisons of zemstvo representatives with bureaucrats or analyses of the new judicial system led to incidents in the censorship. The bulk of the cases show that the Imperial censorship regarded the defense of the political system as its main task. The large number of such cases does not prove that the regime was under continual onslaught. They show instead the extreme sensitivity of the government to incursions by writers into its formerly exclusive rule in politics and public affairs.

Political considerations explain the attention given to a polemic between Baltic German and Russian periodicals that developed late in 1865. The background of the polemic was a government decree requiring the study of history in Russian and the use of Russian in official procedures. Baltic German newspapers argued with capital newspapers about the issue until Shcherbinin, in December, 1865, ordered censors to forbid further articles on the subject in the Baltic press. He justified this one-sided measure by the specious argument that since the Baltic press has started the polemic, they should make the first concessions. He also implied that the arguments it had used encouraged the suspicion that it sought the Germanization of the area. The errors of the Russian press Shcherbinin imputed to an "honest and worthy" but regrettable one-sidedness.[65] The issue did not die. In February, 1866, against the advice of the Riga censor, a German professor at Dorpat University, Shcherbinin prohibited the reprinting in the Baltic press of articles from the capital press on the grounds that the censored provincial press required tighter control than the uncensored capital press.[66] Shcherbinin's 1865 instruction was reaffirmed in October, 1867 to prevent the Baltic press from criticizing the government's original decree.[67] Some effort at evenhandedness is apparent in the reaffirmation of the ban on polemic in December, 1867 after an editorial in the Moscow Reports on the subject.[68] Nevertheless, the policy of the censorship clearly gave some advantage to the capital press and its Russian nationalism.

But nationalism could be too fervent. Goncharov reported in May, 1866 on a book, The Future of Russia that he accused of exhibiting the same point of view as Katkov. The author suspected a conspiracy behind the Karakozov attack, condemned the bureaucracy as alien to the Russian people and as distorters of the Imperial will, and opposed Polish and German influences within the Empire. Goncharov wanted to exclude these passages; when the Moscow Reports was soon after suspended, he used the occasion to recommend confiscation of the work, a censored book. In the end he decided that the best policy would be to allow the work to pass unnoticed by the public and the censorship.[69]

Goncharov's actions show that Valuev tried to impose limits on expressions of nationalism. But Katkov's success indicates that Alexander and higher government officials did not share Valuev's moderation. They were prepared to use nationalism to rally popular support even if such support entailed some freedom to criticize the bureaucracy.

Unorthodox views on society and in particular expressions of materialistic ideas were carefully scrutinized by the censors. Goncharov had been critical of Pisarev's articles in <u>Russian Word</u> because of his division of society into decrepit (vetkikh) and new people.[70] Pisarev's reference to the continual struggle between reason and religion also caught Goncharov's attention. Another article praising natural science and its ability to explain creation without reference to the supernatural was also criticized by Goncharov. An article condemning the European bourgeoisie and another attributing crime to social conditions drew Goncharov's attention.[71] But Goncharov was prepared to allow the propagation of scientific ideas so long as no direct issue was taken with the Bible. For this reason he allowed a description of the evolution of the earth to circulate[72] and despite the fears of the censor, favored publication of a book by the philosopher Lotze as a refutation of materialism.[73] Goncharov clearly feared the impact of scientific thought and its philosophical offshoots on Russia despite resounding phrases in his survey of periodical literature early in 1867 that socialism, communism and nihilism were completely alien to Russia. But even if he firmly believed that these alien and radical ideas could never be of more than slight influence in the Empire, his obligation as a censor required him to watch carefully for these ideas whenever they appeared.[74] Moreover, other censors and indeed, the Council were less liberal than he.[75]

The government's resistance to radical ideas is well illustrated by its treatment of the effort to publish Pisarev's essays in an uncensored work. Part I appeared in 1866 and was attacked by the censors for its negative comments on marriage, religion, and the family. But the censorship decided to await a more suitable occasion to prosecute. The opportunity, provided by a more systematic grouping of "positively harmful" atheistic praise of scientific knowledge came with publication of Part II.[76] F. Pavlenkov, the publisher was vindicated at the trial but was forced to exclude from the volume the article "Poor Russian Thought" although it had been printed with the permission of the censorship only a few years before.[77] Part III passed Goncharov's examination despite its "sophisms" and Part IV also passed, primarily because the government feared another defeat in the courts. Only with Part VI did the Council decide it had a strong case, based on two articles which it accused of blasphemy. The prosecutor however did not agree that materialistic views constituted blasphemy or immorality and he complained that no violation of a specific article of the press law had been cited by the Council. Valuev responded with the argument that the work could be cited for violations analagous to those stated in the law. But his effort to manipulate the law failed.[78] Another, final part of Pisarev's works appeared despite Pisarev's contention, according to the censor, that human society was built on the exploitation of the weak.[79]

The censorship's concern with reading matter for children and the common people was sometimes excessive. Goncharov could not agree with the Moscow committee's proposal to prosecute a children's book for its unfavorable description of the life of the common people. He argued that the book contained nothing reprehensible and moreover, describing the life of the common people as joyous would make the book absurd to children.[80] But in his report on a Russian translation of Carlyle's History of the French Revolution, he expressed fear that a "half educated and even a completely uneducated audience" might be affected dangerously by the work. His particular concern was the section describing the alienation of Louis XVI from the people and those describing popular rebellions. He urged immediate prosecution of the work.[81] The uneducated or young reader was not a mythical figure and frequent citation by censors of this reader indicates the great concern of the censorship. The Murav'ev Commission, in 1866, had encouraged even greater concern because in the course of its inquest into the Karakozov affair, it had come across two popular readers, one by I. Khudiakov and the other by A. Suvorin. As a result of the Commission's recommendations the Minister of Education, Count D. Tolstoy, proposed to supplement the existing censorship with a new examination by an Academic Committee of his ministry.[82] Tolstoy was interested in increasing the number of popular books. From 1866 to 1877, the Academic Committee passed about 55% of the 2,838 works it examined.[83] Tolstoy's monopoly over the examination of popular works was not achieved without a challenge by the ministry of interior. Tolstoy won this battle although he had lost out on an earlier effort to wrest the censorship of some inexpensive school books from the regular censorship.[84] The government's concern for reading material for the common people, always great, increased in the course of the 1870's as the "to the people" movement of young radicals became more important.

The censorship of foreign works continued on the basis of the old 1828 code while the 38 censors of foreign works were placed under the jurisdiction of the Chief Board. From September, 1865 to the end of 1866, the censors examined 7,132 new foreign works and banned about 3% unconditionally and forced revision of about the same percentage of works.[85] In 1867 the percentage of unapproved works was about the same, 5½% but it rose to 8% in 1868.[86] The foreign censorship maintained two categories of forbidden works, those forbidden for the public but available to a privileged group and those forbidden unconditionally. This last category was usually miniscule and forbidden books did circulate among scholars and others with special permission. Thus the order of May, 1866 that advised foreign censors to give special attention to democratic revolutionary propaganda that might appear in foreign works had little effect on scholars. Nevertheless, this order, a product of the Karakozov affair, led the censorship to forbid a number of scholarly works in foreign languages that had previously been permitted: Gervinus' history of the 19th century, and the histories of the French Revolution by Mignet, Thiers, Carlyle, and Lanfrey.[87] Despite the limited size of the audience for foreign literature, the number of imported titles remained high exceeding the number appearing within the Empire. Thus, from September 1865 to the end of 1866, over 7,500 new titles and over 1.8 million publications entered the Empire from abroad after examination by censors.[88] The taste of this small audience ran first to German and then to French publications.

A different view of the censorship is provided by the statistics of the Chief Board. From September, 1865 until the end of 1866, the Council heard 245 reports, (61 of which were prepared by one member, V. Fuks), 30 briefs prepared by the censorship committees and 39 petitions and complaints from authors or publishers. Seven reprimands and 17 warnings were issued to censors and 11 circulars were sent to the committees.[89] In 1867 only 127 reports of Council members were heard and only six reprimands were issued.[90] Undoubtedly the Karakozov episode and the initiation of the new press legislation explains the greater activity during 1866. The censorship establishment had 87 employees plus part-time censors and inspectors and was supported by a budget of 298,945 rubles in 1866.[91] By 1867 Valuev had succeeded in pruning the censorship establishment to a total of 73 full time employees.[92] The nine censors in the St. Petersburg committee read a total of 9,853 sheets for periodicals and 14,004 sheets from 1599 publications in the period from September, 1865 to the end of 1866.[93] If we assume that each sheet produced 16 pages in <u>octavo</u>, then each of the censors read an average of 2,650 pages monthly. In Moscow, the four censors read an average of 2,211 pages each. By 1868, the St. Petersburg censor was reading an average of 2,864 pages monthly and the Moscow censor 2,361 pages. Although the censors read more censored than uncensored titles, in St. Petersburg, about 2/3 of the censors' reading was of uncensored material; in Moscow, the figure was 3/4. Uncensored works had to be large, over 160 pages, to be free of censorship. In the provinces, in 1868, censors read an average of 892 pages monthly of censored material.[94]

This concentration of publishing activity in the capitals occurred despite the fact that the capitals had only 1/3 of all the presses in the Empire: 85 in St. Petersburg in 1867 and 29 in Moscow. Further, only 1/3 of the bookstores and libraries in the Empire were located in the capitals.[95] The growth in the number of presses and bookstores was carefully supervised by the government and restricted to district and provincial cities where inspectors were available.[96] Caution and watchfulness were a byword in the censorship.

Indeed, the caution was excessive considering the size of the threat that dangerous writings constituted. One statistic of importance is the proportion of uncensored to censored works. From September, 1865 to the end of 1866, 3,549 works were published in the Empire excluding periodicals; only 707 of these works were uncensored,[97] and more than half of these, 417, issued in St. Petersburg in 1866.[98] Of the 1,681 censored manuscripts examined in St. Petersburg in 1866, 87 were prohibited or approximately 5% of those examined. The St. Petersburg censors examined 317 uncensored works and began prosecution of 15, or about 5% in 1866.[99] The Moscow censors prohibited about 3% of the censored manuscripts they examined.[100] Another statistic that confirms the apparent insignificance of the "enemy" is the fact that the St. Petersburg censors prohibited only 60 articles for the large number of censored periodicals in 1866. Of these, 24 were to appear in the satirical periodicals and 18 were to appear in The Deed (Delo), a radical periodical started by the publisher of the Russian Word just after that journal was banned. With respect to uncensored periodicals, the St. Petersburg censors took note of 69 articles, 15 from the St. Petersburg Reports, 16 from News (Vest'), and 20 from The Voice.[101] The full force of the censorship was felt by a comparatively small percentage of printed works. Moreover, it is worthy of note that the 18 articles that were prohibited in The Deed in 1866 came from about two monthly issues since the first issue was permitted only in September, 1866 and did not issue until November. Further, the censors forbid about 20 sheets or half of the material designated for that first issue.[102]

An index of the impact of the censorship might be the percentage of works in which censors forced revisions or excluded passages. Unfortunately no figures are available. But the theatrical censorship which examined plays before their performance and was also under the Chief Board does offer some statistics on exclusions. In 1866, the Chief Board forbid about 10% of the plays it examined and forced revisions in an additional 13%. Moreover, in examining previously banned plays which were now presented to it in a revised form it forbid about 11% and forced additional revisions in about 13% before permitting them.[103] In 1867, it banned 9% of the new plays it examined and forced revision of about 13% and banned 1% of previously banned plays and required additional changes in 27%.[104] In the theatrical censorship, the percentage of works that required revision by order of the censors was usually slightly greater than the percentage of plays forbidden. Because the theatrical censors were particularly concerned about impressionable lower class audiences for plays, one might guess that ordinary censors were more lenient towards printed works; therefore the proportion of printed works that had to be revised or rewritten before publication was probably not much higher than the proportion of forbidden works. To measure the self-censorship that writers exerted even before presenting their works to censors would be impossible. All of these factors would constitute statistical measures of the impact of the censorship.

If only a few writers felt the full and harsh impact of the censorship, all were impeded in the expression of their ideas. But the censorship was not an impenetrable obstacle to those who aimed to purvey critical ideas. The obvious call to revolt was impossible but the harping on the discontents of Russians and the undermining, in a cautious way, of traditional beliefs could appear. The educated Russian could come across dangerous ideas not only in Russian works but also in foreign works. Perhaps it was the very possibility of reading dangerous foreign works either in Russia or during journeys abroad that forced censors to permit critical ideas to appear in periodicals accessible to the educated audience. In any event, censors did not keep the educated Russian in childlike ignorance of ideas that circulated freely in western Europe and they allowed uncensored works more freedom than censored literature. Although more censored periodicals were published, uncensored periodicals had with few exceptions the largest circulation of any periodicals in this period. On the other hand, censored publications were published in larger editions than uncensored works. The system Valuev established was plainly geared to preventing the masses of Russians from reading dangerous works. A small group of educated Russians was however, permitted some restricted freedom.

By November, 1867, Valuev did not expect more from the censorship. At that time, he advised the Chief Board of his aims: to permit all that did not weaken the integrity of the Empire; to eliminate all that might shake the authority and dignity of the government or stimulate hostility among the peoples and regions of the Empire.[105] This emphasis on the preventive function of the censorship showed the change in Valuev's views since 1865. Then he had believed he would be able to control the press and extirpate evil. Now he was less optimistic and more modest in his expectations.

In general, Valuev's policy towards the press and public opinion represented a mix of force and conciliation. In October, 1866, he suggested that the government appease opposition groups and at the same time concentrate its repressive measures against those who disobeyed the laws.[106] His attitude towards the press showed the same discrimination. His continuous efforts, which included articles for the Northern Post, to mold public opinion through subsidized and inspired periodicals displayed an awareness of the power and importance of the press and literature. If in February, 1868, he acknowledged that the Chief Board had not been able to influence the press [107] while in 1865 he had been more sanguine about his power, nevertheless he showed a consistent appreciation of the importance of the press and public opinion.

In his use of both force and conciliation, Valuev's policies after 1865 showed his increasing irritation at the limits the press law imposed on the government. He criticized the courts and especially the prosecutors and in the course of his administration showed a greater willingness to make use of administrative methods. This preference for administrative methods was to be carried on by his successors. On balance, however, Valuev was more willing to use the law and the courts than his successors.

Chapter IV   Censorship Legislation and the Courts, 1865-1872

In March, 1868, A. E. Timashev, former director of the Third Section, now Minister of Post and Telegraph, replaced Valuev as Minister of Interior. Valuev's departure is attributed to the hostile attitudes of the Third Section chief, Count P. Shuvalov, and the Heir to the throne. The occasion for his retirement was an accusation that he had been negligent in measures to avert a famine in two provinces. But perhaps his discriminating and flexible attitude towards public opinion and politics antagonized some conservatives. Timashev was a more conventional conservative and his appointment represented a break with the spirit of the Great Reforms. D. Miliutin noted this break in his memoirs. After citing Timashev's opposition to Emancipation and his criticism of Alexander's liberal reforms, he said that his appointment "was a new triumph for the Shuvalov party."[1]

With respect to the censorship, Timashev came into office with a proposal to hand the censorship back to the ministry of education, a suggestion the Emperor rejected. Timashev's distaste for the task of regulating the press was associated with a negative attitude towards the press, best conveyed by some remarks he made to St. Petersburg editors about 1870. Then he criticized the press for arrogance and expressed the usual conservative view that in Russia, unlike western Europe, the periodical press molded public opinion instead of reflecting it. By magnifying the role of the journalists, Timashev diminished the significance of public opinion. In effect he implied that control over a small number of journalists would give him control over so-called public opinion. Linked to this view was his argument, in a memorandum to Alexander in August, 1869, that a large group of journalists argued for the necessity of limited monarchy. He believed that the courts protected this group and punished the smaller group of defenders of autocracy.[2] Another characteristic view of the conservative camp shared by Timashev, was a dominating preference for administrative measures and suspicion of the courts. These attitudes influenced Timashev's handling of the censorship. They explain why the government failed in its promise, in 1865, to replace the Temporary Press Law of 1865 by a more permanent code of laws. The tale of this failure begins in 1866.

In April, 1866, Valuev expressed confidence that precise fulfillment of the press law could restrain the press from the propagation of materialistic and egalitarian ideas, if the courts cooperated with the censorship.[3] But Valuev's confidence apparently disappeared after the Karakozov affair. Count Peter Shuvalov, the new head of the Third Section after Prince Dolgorukov's retirement, criticized the censorship in an April, 1866 memorandum. He argued that freedom of the press was possible

45

only in a constitutional state where it served as a concomitant to freedom of speech. Where the latter was absent, a free press was dangerous in that it required the government to enter into a debate with its opponents.[4] Shuvalov recommended forceful measures to end the attacks on the government that he discerned in the press and literature. His recommendations were considered by a special committee led by the Prince P. Gagarin and including Valuev, Count V. N. Panin, head of the Second Section and D. Miliutin, the Minister of War. The Gagarin committee worked out a few sweeping proposals that adhered to the spirit of Shuvalov's recommendations: the permanent suspension of The Contemporary and Russian Word; and revision of the press laws to fill "gaps" in procedures for prosecution of violations of the press laws. By May 28, 1866, Gagarin was delivering to Valuev an instruction to proceed to the supplementing of the press law especially those sections dealing with judicial prosecution of press offenses.[5]

Valuev first pushed through some revisions on December 12, 1866 without elaborate investigation:[6] the prosecutor would have to accept the accusation of the censorship authorities or "officials" except in especially difficult cases when he might ask the minister of justice to consult with the minister of interior; works might be arrested by the courts as soon as prosecution began (in contrast to the original law which allowed arrest by the court only after it pronounced sentence); press cases would be heard in the sudebnaia palata, a higher court, without a jury, instead of the lowest circuit court which was a jury court. Then in June, 1867, the Chief Board presented a project which was distributed to a few ministers. The Minister of Justice, Count C. Pahlen, in his comments of July, 1868, noted that the proposed penalties for the incitement of hostility between classes, and criticism of the obligatory force of laws and the ideas of family and property were too low in comparison with the French laws of 1848 and 1849. He suggested the addition of monetary fines or personal punishment on the grounds that the Russian press was less mature than the French. He also wanted to exclude from the laws all mention of the author's intention because motive would be difficult to prove.[7] But by this time Valuev had been replaced by Timashev. Although it was Timashev who presented the final project to the State Council in April, 1869, the project was really the product of Valuev's administration.

The project included a few sections dealing with press crimes that the State Council had eliminated from Valuev's 1864 project. At that time the State Council had reasoned that the press laws were temporary; moreover it had remarked that Valuev's project did not accord with the Penal Code of 1845. The 1869 project would punish the printing of a manuscript which disputed the truths of Christianity or Orthodoxy or undermined faith in these dogmas and subjected them to disesteem. Penalties would be imposed also on those printing or spreading remarks or allusions weakening faith in Christian writings or propagating teachings opposed to them. The spread or printing of abuse or ridicule of other Christian faiths would be subject to penalty. (The 1845 Penal Code punished criticism or abuse of Christianity and works aiming to corrupt morals or offend decency). Timashev explained the need to supplement this article by the experience of the censors who had encountered in their work propaganda for atheism or materialism parading under the mask of works of natural science. He argued that the Penal Code punished gross blasphemy, not sly and subtle attacks by materialist writers; and since faith and God were not susceptible to logical analysis or experience and yet composed the basis for morality, these must be protected from both open and "roundabout" attacks. Indeed, he added, ridicule was more dangerous than criticism because it appealed to a larger audience. As an example of a "subtle" attack, Timashev offered Antonovich's "Intellectual Development in the 18th Century" and his "Superstitions of the Day", both published in The Contemporary in 1865. He complained that existing laws made prosecution of such works impossible and forced the government to use administrative measures against periodicals. To end this problem, Timashev proposed measures that would allow punishment of morally corrupting books. Timashev also proposed to defend non-Orthodox Christian faiths because, he said, atheists used the device of attacking Catholicism. As an example Timashev cited an article in The Deed (Delo) which had argued that Europe suffered because the Moslems were defeated by the Catholics. Timashev noted that writers intentionally did not distinguish the particular features of Catholicism from those it shared with other Christian faiths. Nevertheless, he recognized that the prohibition of polemic against other Christian churches would hinder scholarship. To avoid this difficulty Timashev proposed to punish "caustic ridicule"; he cited the harsh penalties imposed on insults to Christianity and the spread of atheism in Austria.[8]

Other provisions that Timashev included would penalize those who printed works insulting to past Russian rulers from the mid-18th century onward and also works whose aim was to shake public trust in the government's laws. Despite the desire of the minister of justice to avoid all mention of aims, the Chief Board retained this wording based on its singular reading of the word "aim." For the Chief Board, the word meant "impression" and thus was an easily verifiable concept. Timashev also proposed to supplement the Penal Code which penalized the instigation of disobedience among soldiers and sailors; he wanted to punish the stimulation of such instigation. Works "directed against the unity" of Russia would be punished as well as works in which hostility between classes was stimulated. The latter provision would replace the existing crime of preparing proclamations. The denial or disputing of the ideas of property or family would be penalized; here, unlike the old wording, there was no mention of intention. The detailed presentation of court cases and government inquests prior to official publication would be forbidden.

The Minister of Justice, Count C. Pahlen, recommended harsher penalties and Timashev agreed, especially in specifying maximum and minimum fines. Also Timashev would allow the courts to confiscate a work even when the courts found the author or publisher innocent of criminal intent. (The existing law implied that confiscation accompanied the punishment of the author while Timashev's version would allow an author to go unpunished but not the work.) The Penal Code, which penalized secretly published works aiding the corruption of morals, was to be supplemented by wording that made all works contributing to the corruption of morals punishable. Timashev would also require personal punishment for most press crimes. Finally, Timashev proposed to establish the non-jury court the sudebnaya palata, as the court of first instance for most press crimes.[9]

The minister of justice criticized the project chiefly because the changes would affect the Penal Code. He also made the damning comment that he saw little advantage to the project.[10] Prince S. N. Urusov, head of the Second Section argued that the project would require changes in the Penal Code.[11] He also made the erroneous comment that most of Timashev's changes had originally been excluded by the State Council from Valuev's project in 1864-1865. Despite these negative judgments, the Chief Board stood behind its project.[12] But apparently Timashev wavered. This seems to be the implication of Valuev's statement in his diary that Timashev sought to avoid unnecessary conflicts. In the Council of Ministers, Timashev criticized the penchant of journalism for establishing itself as a "higher court" judging the government. At the same time he apparently argued in the State Council that it was unsuitable for him to ask for an increase of his own power since he was a partisan of the application of power. Accordingly he recommended that the examination of the press laws be given to a new commission. On November 2, 1869, the Emperor established this special commission under the leadership of the head of the Second Section, Prince S. Urusov.[13] Alexander's letter noted that "laws cannot always serve as a sufficiently positive guide for judicial prosecution." Further, Alexander advised the commission to equip the administrative and judicial authorities with enough power to eliminate "the harmful influence which may occur from lack of restraint and moderation of the printed word."[14] The implication of Alexander's letter was clear. He was rejecting the notion that the courts and the law alone could restrain the press. In the light of Timashev's criticism of the courts in August, 1869 and his subsequent actions, it is very likely that he persuaded Alexander that the preparation of positive laws would not be a sufficient deterrent to press crimes.

Nevertheless, the new Commission of Urusov began its work of subordinating the press to law. The Commission included four representatives of the Chief Board, three from the ministry of justice and a few other representatives of the Second Section and other offices. It met first in November and next at the end of February, 1870. The Commission decided to use Valuev's proposed code of 1864, which in fact had been the basis for Timashev's project, as its own base for discussion. Frequent plenary sessions of the Commission did not begin until May, 1870.[15] The Commission's willingness to change the laws so that these could be used against press crimes is clear. It considered a memorandum which favored the supplementing of the existing laws penalizing blasphemy and abuse by provisions that would strike at the materialistic and physiological investigations that were being published. The Commission also believed that laws were needed that would penalize indirect attacks on the autocracy. But consideration of separate features of the press law ended in May, 1870 when Senator M. Turunov, a member of the Chief Board presented his project for consideration.[16]

Turunov's main interest was to increase the power of the Council of the Chief Board so that the minister would have the power to make decisions only when a two thirds majority was absent; otherwise the minister's power would be restricted to revisions of the Code and permission of new periodicals. During discussion of the project a member of the Chief Board, F. Elenev presented a long discourse on the censorship. He noted the restraint that the censorship imposed on journalism but argued that the influence of the uncensored press had increased. He contended that the censors could only modify the sharpness with which views were expressed but not end the power of harmful periodicals; these, he said, could carefully select articles, use allusions and juxtapositions and by their negative attitudes and even silence convey their tendency or direction. As an example he argued that The Contemporary and the Russian Word had been enormously influential even when censored, while in the United States, a free press had no influence. He concluded with a recommendation for a free press except for cheap newspapers; the minister should however retain the power to permit a periodical and to inflict administrative penalities.[17] Thirty years later, Elenev was equally pessimistic but he was no longer prepared to recommend an end to the censorship.

Elenev doubted that his proposal would be supported. He was right. But it is noteworthy that even his advocacy of a free press was conditional on retention of administrative penalties. Clearly the Commission understood that the retention of administrative measures was incumbent on it. When the Commission took up the question of administrative penalties, it decided that elimination of these penalties was not within its authority; it also decided that elimination was inappropriate because the

Russian public was not mature enough.[18] In particular, the Commission decided to maintain the penalties for a "harmful tendency" but to restrict the effectiveness of a warning to 15 months.[19] The Commission's desire to increase the government's ability to suppress dangerous literature is further indicated by its decision to establish a four day instead of the existing three day interval between presentation of uncensored works to the censorship and their distribution.[20] In defining the character of the act of printing a criminal work and presenting it to the censors, the Commission decided, by a majority, to call such acts an attempt (pokushenie) at a crime instead of a preparation, a lesser violation, despite the contention of some members that this interpretation was equivalent to penalizing dangerous thoughts. The Commission divided equally on the question of the Council's power vis-a-vis, the minister's.[21]

Clearly the Commission could not dispense with the administrative powers of the minister. Accordingly, although it included within the project a section devoted to defining crimes and misdemeanors that would be punishable by the courts, its project did not constitute a real break with the past. Moreover, against the advice of Elenev, the Commission incorporated into the project a provision that allowed the courts to punish crimes analagous to those specifically mentioned in the law.[22] The majority also agreed to allow the minister to disregard most decisions of the Council if he chose.[23] The Commission did split four ways on proposals for the permanent banning of a periodical; the variations would allow such only on decision of the Committee of Ministers or the consultation of the Senate.[24] Real innovations in the project were the recommendation that the separate clerical censorship be abolished,[25] and that the government permit uncensored publications and periodicals to appear in other cities besides St. Petersburg and Moscow. That there was some effort to innovate is indicated by a proposal in the Commission to exempt all periodicals except satirical and humorous periodicals from the censorship.[26] It is also indicated by Urusov's statement, in the Commission's summary of its guidelines, that the Commission could not acknowledge that any printed work should be excepted from the jurisdiction of the courts, but that if the government could not accept this principle, then the Commission was powerless to do anything.[27] That the Commission saw little hope of liberalizing the project is indicated by its inclusion of a provision that allowed the censorship to arrest any publication subject to prosecution; the existing law gave the courts the authority to arrest publications against which the censorship had initiated prosecution.[28] Further, the project empowered the courts to forbid the editor of a guilty periodical from editing another periodical for at least a year.[29]

In June, 1871 the Commission reported to Alexander on its

work and received from him the admonition to bring its work to a conclusion.[30] This was done in October, 1871, and the Commission went out of existence at the end of the year.[31] On February 4, 1872 a special convocation for consideration of the project was established and a more formal presentation was made in May, 1872.[32] After examination by the special convocation, the project died. The last cryptic reference to the Commission's work is a note in the archives to the effect that the work of the commission ended "for special reasons."[33] Once Timashev had secured additional authority over the press, as he did in 1872, he had no further use for the Commission.

Indeed, one might argue that it was the intention of Timashev and the new head of the Chief Board, M. Longinov, to sabotage the Commission's work. Thus, on January 19, 1872 a proposal was prepared in the ministry to allow Timashev to confiscate a work on his own authority, simply informing the Committee of Ministers of such decisions.[34] The stimulus for this proposal was the court decision of November, 1871 in favor of V. V. Bervi-Flerovskii's "ABC of Social Sciences". When the Emperor was informed of this decision by the Third Section he ordered the supplementing of the law to prevent such works from being published with impunity. Timashev's proposal was in fulfillment of the Emperor's order. His rationale was the fact that books were not subject to administrative penalties and the courts were restricting the administration's power and giving publicity to harmful works. The proposal was first considered in the Council of Ministers where the Emperor clearly indicated his support of Timashev by asking the ministers to support the proposal in the State Council. But the proposal was amended by the Department of Laws to require the Committee of Ministers to bring particular cases to the attention of the Emperor in case the Committee disagreed with the decision of the minister of interior. In March, in the State Council, the former Minister of Education, Golovnin, opposed the measure, while Valuev, the former Minister of Interior supported it in the belief that all ministers must stand behind Timashev in press affairs and that the measure would prevent complaints about the action of the minister from reaching the Senate.[35] The State Council decision did not become law until June 7, 1872 when Alexander confirmed the decision but even before, on April 29, 1872, the Emperor ordered suspension of all judicial prosecutions of books until approval of the new law.[36]

The State Council decision acknowledged the difficulty of perceiving culpable expressions which aimed at "shaking the foundations" of the state and social order. But it also noted the difficulty of prosecuting dangerous uncensored works and their availability to students at only 1/3 or ¼ of their price. On these grounds, Timashev was given the authority to arrest such uncensored works and to prosecute them. But the Council gave the

Committee of Ministers, and not Timashev alone, as he requested, the authority to confiscate and destroy harmful uncensored books and periodicals. To facilitate the examination of such works, it ordered that uncensored works be presented to the censors seven instead of three days before issuance; in the case of uncensored periodicals, except newspapers, a four day period instead of two days was adopted.[37] The new power was used eagerly by Timashev. Prior to the order, the ministry had begun prosecution of 25 uncensored works. From June 1872 to about November 1873, Timashev did not prosecute any work but instead asked the Committee of Ministers to examine about 40 works.[38] A further indication of the impact of the law was given to the chairman of the Moscow committee in July, 1872 when he was advised that henceforth there were to be no reservations expressed by censors to the effect that despite "the harm of a work, the law did not include punishment for its contents".[39] The new law meant that the government was abandoning its effort to use the courts against press crimes. To judge whether the government was correct in accusing the courts of constricting it, the history of court cases must be examined.

Certainly the Chief Board believed that the courts were not useful to it. In 1876 the Chief Board noted that after the 1872 rule became effective, the courts were used only when a "completely formal and external infringement" of the press laws was noted; in 1876 only four such cases occurred.[40] In 1879 the St. Petersburg committee began prosecution of only two periodicals but applied the 1872 law to nine works.[41] Even before the 1872 law, the press authorities had found that the courts were more prone to support prosecution of censored rather than uncensored works mainly because accusations against the former were often purely formal and entailed minor penalties.[42] As early as 1870 the Chief Board complained that the courts usually found in favor of the defendants and for this reason, the Board had left some violations without prosecution fearing the loss of prestige.[43] The following year the Chief Board reiterated the complaint adding that the existing methods of punishing violations would paralyze the effort to restrain harmful works.[44] If indeed the courts were not effective, the fault was not theirs alone; in three of the eleven cases for 1870-71, the prosecutor refused to support the accusation of the censorship.[45] But in fact it would seem that the Chief Board's complaints about the leniency of the courts were not true even though the Chief Board was convinced of the laxity of the courts.

One important case began in July, 1866 and involved the publisher of Pisarev's works, Pavlenkov. Part II of the uncensored work, which simply compiled works that Pisarev had published earlier in censored journals, was accused by the censors of exhibiting a "positively harmful" praise of scientific knowledge. The publisher won a victory but was forced to exclude from the volume the article "Poor Russian Thought".[46] The censorship avoided prosecution of Part IV primarily because it feared another defeat in the courts but in Part VI, the Chief Board decided it had a case. The guilty articles were "Process of Life According to Vogt" and "Physiological Essays of Moleschott" which the Council accused of blasphemy. The prosecutor disagreed; for him materialistic views did not constitute blasphemy or immorality, and further, he noted that the Council had not cited any particular article of the press law. Valuev responded in July, 1867 that the Council believed that the work could be cited for a violation analagous to that stated in the law. The Council's effort to evade the law was useless and Pavlenkov was allowed to release the work.[47]

In the case of the one volume that was actually heard in court, the lower court which first dealt with the case exonerated Pavlenkov for printing Pisarev's "Poor Russian Thought" and his "Russian Don Quixote." The court held that the article, 1001 of the Penal Code, under which the publisher was charged, was not applicable since it referred to the secret and illegal spread of works opposed to morality. As for the second essay, charged under article 1035, the court held that it did not undermine trust in the laws. The government appealed the case to the Senate where the prosecutor argued that since the law punished the secret printing of indecent works, it could not leave the overt printing of such works unpunished. The chief prosecutor however took a slightly different position from his subordinate and argued that Pavlenkov's action was only the preparation for a crime since the volume was arrested and did not circulate. Pavlenkov's very capable defense attorney, K. K. Arsen'ev, reluctantly accepted this last contention but said the law imposed no penalty for preparations for a crime. If preparations were punished, then in some cases a lesser crime would entail more severe punishment. Arsen'ev argued, further, the destruction of an article was sufficient punishment for an author or publisher. Both the prosecution and the Senate admitted the strength of Arsen'ev's argument, that there was a gap in legislation. But the Senate went on to hold that the words "to print" had a narrow meaning, to set in type and print, and a wider meaning, to circulate. The legislators had used the wider meaning. Therefore Pavlenkov could only be charged with preparation for a crime, an action not punishable by law in this case. In 1869, three years after the case began, the Senate vindicated Pavlenkov but ordered the essay "Poor Russian Thought" which it believed might have a harmful influence, destroyed.[48]

The Senate's Solomon-like decision disappointed the censorship. But in fact the decision confirmed the censor's power to exclude from uncensored works material that might have been excluded from a censored work. The authorities might well have been satisfied with the Senate decision to prevent the culpable work from appearing.[49] But in fact the government was not satisfied because authors were not punished, the courts were slow and

moreover gave undesirable publicity to authors. Certainly the
courts made the authorities aware of gaps in legislation which
the Chief Board tried to eliminate. Thus, the law freed original
works of more than ten sheets or 160 pages from preliminary censorship. To prevent evasion of the law by publishers using large
type and generous margins, the government ruled that a book in
octavo must have 240 spaces on a line and 22½ lines on a page as
a minimum.[50] But not only omissions in the law restricted the
censorship. Sometimes the letter of the law encumbered the
censorship.

In the case involving the anthology Light (Luch) the censorship showed its unwillingness to be bound by the letter of the law.
On the other hand, the prosecutors stubbornly insisted on adherence to the law. The two volume anthology, was prepared by G.
Blagosvetlov, the publisher of the Russian Word after February,
1866 when the journal was banned for five months. However, the
anthology was not presented to the censors until after the
permanent ban on the journal in May, 1866. At that time the
publisher proposed to compensate subscribers for the missing
issues of the journal. The censors found six articles in the
second volume to be culpable but the prosecutor would agree only
to prosecute one, "Psychological Studies," for immorality and
blasphemy. The censorship committee did not agree and argued
that the connection between the anthology and the banned journal
as well as the "not well intentioned tendency" of the anthology
should be grounds for prosecution. Two years after the decision
to begin prosecution, the minister of interior complained to the
minister of justice about the prosecutor's recalcitrance. He
argued that the goal of the press laws would never be achieved if
the courts were limited to the formal application of the letter
of the law and avoided the question of the general tendency or
intention of a work. He insisted that the separate indiscretions
of an author were not as important as the "systematic and stubborn
propagation of an immoral or anti-governmental tendency." But he
agreed to the prosecution of only one article with the reservation
that the whole article and not separate pages in it be prosecuted.
In July, 1868 the prosecutor was instructed to begin prosecution.[51]
Three years later the courts decided to force the exclusion of a
few pages from the article but rejected a request for destruction
of the whole article. The government appealed the decision and
the Senate ruled that a new trial should be conducted in the lower
courts. The trial had not yet taken place when the Committee of
Ministers took up the case on the basis of Timashev's 1872 law.
In October, 1874 the Committee decided to destroy the anthology.[52]

Here the main complaint of the censorship authorities was
the willingness of the court to exclude separate places from a
culpable article. The article, by E. Kolonn, was accused by the
censorship committee of materialistic views. The censors said
that the author rejected innate ideas and called the notion that

there is a knowledge inaccessible to reason theosophical. In
criticizing the belief that there is a knowledge beyond reason,
the author discussed hallucinations involving sex and attributed
the visions of St. Catherine to sexual stimulation. He argued
further, according to censors, that the insane often imagine
themselves to be pregnant after copulation with the devil.
Another example of hallucination offered by the author concerned
a young girl who tried to convince a doctor that she was a man;
on another occasion she imagined herself to be the Duchess of
Berry. In all these places, the censors saw a materialist
direction and a negation of the Christian dogmas of immortality
of the soul and life in the future. The prosecutor agreed that
the article contained blasphemous and immoral judgments but
thought that exclusion of about six pages from the article would
eliminate these places. The minister of interior however argued
that exclusion would be an act of leniency which might encourage
publishers and authors. This case illustrates the complaints the
censorship had against the courts: the delay; the insistence on
citation of laws; the refusal to indict a "tendency;" and the
reluctance of the courts to impose severe penalties. But it is
clear that the courts and the prosecutors were not rejecting the
government's case. Further, the work never did reach the public.

In one of the earliest cases brought by the censorship, the
author P. A. Bibikov was brought to a jury court for his work
Critical Studies. The Chief Board, without arresting the work,
charged that the author denied the principle of marriage with the
intent of weakening or destroying this institution. The charge
was based on the author's criticism of the family as a unit
dedicated to struggle with the environment and his argument that
monagamous marriage was simply a custom. The authors' argument,
in his defense, was that he was not advising man to model his
life on that of animals and that the law permitted the analysis
of laws so long as no instigation to disobedience of the laws was
present. The court found the charge to be justified but decided
that the work would have no serious effect. It sentenced the
author to arrest for seven days, instead of the six weeks that
were the maximum permitted by the law.[53]

Another case involved I. Sechenov's Reflexes of the Brain
which had been prohibited for publication in The Contemporary
(Sovremennik) in 1863; at the same time the censors ruled to
permit it to appear in scientific journals if the author wished.
In 1866 the work was published and the Chief Board decided that
Sechenov's insistence that external stimuli are the source of
thought would corrupt morality and undermine Christian dogma,
especially since the work was written popularly and printed in an
inexpensive edition. The prosecutor demurred, saying that
Sechenov's materialism might be erroneous but not criminal.
Prince Urusov, then directing the ministry of justice, added, in
his letter to Valuev, that a court case might spread Sechenov's

ideas.[54] Valuev reluctantly agreed and the case never went to trial.

One curious case showed the divergent views of the prosecutor and the censorship. The case, which was tried in 1868 involved a criticism of the courts for their decision in another press case. The criticism was in the periodical News (Vest') and was to the effect that the courts had not prevented the defamation of the class of landowners. The defense attorney argued that the publisher was merely expressing a personal opinion. The accused himself insisted on his loyalty to the monarchy. The court found the accused innocent but the prosecution appealed to the higher court. The higher court also rejected the prosecution's contention on the interesting grounds that the criticism was merely an expression of the tendency of the publication and not an insult to the court.[55] The clear import of this decision was that good intentions exempted one from punishment. Such good intentions obviously were not found in the publisher of the scandal sheet Petersburg Leaves (Listok) in 1867 who was accused of a similar crime and ultimately sentenced by the Senate to three months imprisonment and a fine of 500 rubles.[56] The courts were clearly willing to accommodate themselves, within limits to the needs of the government.

From the inception of the new press law until mid-1868, the government prosecuted 15 cases. The defendants were punished in nine of those cases with penalties ranging from a minimal fine of 25 rubles to sixteen months imprisonment in a fortress.[57] But this record clearly displeased the censorship. The courts for example rejected the censorship's argument that Louis Blanc's criticism of the French monarchy in his Letters about England constituted an implied criticism of the Russian autocracy.[58] The prosecution itself refused to honor the censorship's accusation of blasphemy against J. S. Mill's Utilitarianism in a Russian translation.[59] Nor would it support the censorship's charges of subversion against H. Spencer's Scientific, Political and Philosophical Essays in Russian.[60] The Senate overturned two lower court decisions that upheld the censorship in its charges against Spirit of Man and Animals by the German psychologist Wundt.[61] And because the prosecutor refused to esteem the censorship's charges against the first volume of Hugo's Les Miserables in Russian since no law was cited in the accusation, the censorship dropped the charges.[62] The censorship had some important successes. N. Sokolov, author of the work The Renegades (Otshchepentsy) was sentenced to 16 months imprisonment for criticizing Christianity, attacking property rights, and questioning the autocracy, even though the book had not been distributed.[63] But even the successes of the censorship in the courts did not entirely please the government.

For example, there is the case involving the work Anyone

(Vsiaki) by A. Suvorin, who later became the conservative publisher of the powerful newspaper New Times (Novoe Vremia). The censorship accused the author of expressing sympathy for ill-intentioned people in this work, most of which was reprinted from the St. Petersburg Reports; thus, a favorable description of the young generation; an allusion to government subsidies to editors; a criticism of government officials. The prosecutor charged that the work exhibited a negative attitude towards the gentry and a sympathy towards law breakers and asked for destruction of the book and two months imprisonment for Suvorin. The defense attorney, K. K. Arsen'ev, argued that the remarks of characters in the work did not necessarily express the author's views, that a class could not be insulted since it was not a person, and that in any case, the work had not circulated. The lower court supported the prosecution. On appeal, Arsen'ev protested against the effort to penetrate the motives of the author. He insisted that if a concealed motive was to be considered by the court, it must be one most favorable to the author. Further, he argued that only in cases of insult to the Emperor was the mere fact of preparation a crime; the present case was merely a preparation since the work had not circulated and therefore did not constitute a crime. The appeals court apparently honored this argument for it sentenced Suvorin to three weeks in the guardhouse and destroyed the book. At the same time, the court rejected the position of the prosecution that the publication of criticism composed a social violation.[64]

In the light of these cases, it is clear that the courts cooperated with the censorship in the prosecution of press crimes. Further, had Timashev succeeded in pushing through his amendments to the press law in 1869 which would have made the propagation of materialism and the ridicule of religion punishable offenses, the courts might have become even more cooperative. Despite the slowness of the courts, their insistence on legal grounds for charges, and their refusal to bend the law for the convenience of the censorship, the courts might have been very effective in restraining the press. Even the publicity that trials gave to accused works might have aided the government in its aims. But the government was not willing to abandon its customary reliance on administrative measures.[65]

K. Arsen'ev, in an article in Messenger of Europe (Vestnik Europy) in 1869 presented the issues squarely when he argued for changes in the press law. He pointed out that the role of opposition journals in Russia was limited and that the courts, although slow, were as competent as censors in defining the tendency of a journal. He contended that the definition of harm varied frequently and that in the past warnings had in fact been given not for a tendency but for a particular article. Accordingly a warning did not avert specific evil actions, because these were not designated, but simply inspired fear. He noted too that the retention of administrative penalties for periodicals and the certification of publishers by the minister were superfluous; they expressed "a spirit of distrust and indisposition to the press." He also suggested that since the large majority of books were written for a narrow audience and published in only 2000 or 3000 copies, the government could well concentrate its attention on cheaper and smaller works. Most importantly, he argued that an author is not responsible for the impression his work produced unless he desired to produce it. Further, the courts should not concern themselves with the consequences of the printed word since these depended on the notoriety of the author and other circumstances. Accordingly, authors should be punished only for what they had said if their remarks were criminal. After contrasting the severe penalties of Russian law to those in Prussian and French law, Arsen'ev repeated his belief that the conduct of the periodical press did not justify the suspicions of the censorship and its excessive precautions.[66] Arsen'ev's argument clearly presented the issue and constituted an excellent defense of the use of the courts.

But the government in fact wished to inspire fear in writers and desired to punish authors for the impression their works produced. It did fear the incalculable consequences of the printed word. Administrative measures offered the government little publicity, and the prevention of possible evil. The price to the government was acceptable: a measure of arbitrariness and the consequent lack of sympathy of the educated public. Use of the courts was as speedy as administrative measures since a book could be arrested when prosecution was initiated; after the December, 1866 law, the court also was empowered to arrest a work prior to its decision. That same law transferred cases to courts without juries and so allowed the government to prosecute cases with less publicity than before. But trial before any court entailed some publicity since cases could be discussed in the press, unlike administrative decisions. Further defense attornies could find defects in the arguments of prosecutors and censors. And the courts might not uphold the government in its mistakes. The government's own fears, its penchant for secrecy, and its demand for complete control led it to abandon the effort to use the courts for press crimes.[67]

Chapter V   Censorship 1868-1881

   Timashev's accession to the post of Minister of Interior in March, 1868 began a regime that was notably more severe towards the press than Valuev's. The suspicion of the press and literature that characterized his ministry continued into the regime of L. S. Makov, Timashev's replacement in 1878. Only with the appointment of Count Loris-Melikov as dictator and later as Minister in 1880 was there a break in the pattern of hostility and suspicion. By then the government had decided that its general policy of force towards radicals and revolutionaries of which press policy was a part had to be modified. All through the 1870's the government faced the threat of radicalism which took the form of the "to the people" movement in 1873 and again in 1877. The Russo-Turkish War which followed the Serbian uprising of 1876 halted for a time the growth of revolutionary groups. At the same time it encouraged the government to relax the press regulations somewhat to accommodate the flood of patriotism that affected Russia. But the war's end and the subsequent appearance of revolutionary terrorism led to a renewed crackdown on dissent that affected the press. This chain of threat and counter-threat was interrupted by the appointment of Loris-Melikov as head of an Extraordinary Commission, early in 1880. Loris-Melikov's effort to revive a selective policy, combining leniency and some effort to further legality, with force against the disloyal was short lived. It ended soon after the assassination of Alexander II in March, 1881.

   The harsh policy characteristic of Timashev's regime was implemented by the issuance of amendments and supplements to the 1865 press laws. More fundamental changes, in the form of a new press law, were discarded as indicated in the previous chapter. The bureaucracy's distrust of law and the courts and its desire to retain discretionary authority for itself destroyed efforts at legal reform. Occasionally these administrative efforts were supplemented by efforts to persuade and influence the public. Thus, in 1869, a new newspaper The Government Messenger (Pravitel'stvennyi Vestnik) replaced the Northern Post.[1] And in 1875 the ministry supported the publication of a monthly Russian Worker (Russkii Rabochii) which sought to preach the proper values to the working class.[2] But in the 1870's such attempts to mold opinion were less significant than the general policy of repression.

   About a month after he became Minister, Timashev sought the first of his supplemental and restrictive amendments to press legislation. He asked the Committee of Ministers in April, 1868 to allow him to ban the public sale of separate issues of any periodical at street stands or on railroads. He explained that such power would allow him to influence periodicals whose harmful attitudes might not justify harsher measures. Although the ministers decided that such a rule should be temporary until the adoption of new laws concerning the retail sale of books and periodicals, and although they believed that Timashev should have presented his proposal to the State Council, they agreed to the request. Timashev did not heed their advice and frequently presented his requests to the Committee of Ministers.[3] The order, ostensibly issued to preserve public order, could have a large economic effect on a periodical. In 1869, The Voice estimated that an eleven day prohibition of retail sale might cost a newspaper more than 500 rubles in lost sales, and in four months, 5,000 rubles. By 1870, retail sales accounted for about thirty percent of The Voice's total sale, and in 1875, about 15%. The measure therefore represented a well conceived effort to apply financial pressure to periodicals.[4] Timashev was to use this penalty frequently in subsequent years. About 1/3 of the penalties that the ministry imposed on periodicals during the period from 1870 to 1879 prohibited retail sale of separate newspapers. By 1885 this method had come to supplant administrative warnings as the major penalty imposed on periodicals.[5]

Another major change in the regulations came on June 7, 1872 after Timashev abandoned his half-hearted effort to revise the press regulations by means of the November 1869 Commission. This measure, which the State Council approved under the pressure of Alexander II, gave the Committee of Ministers the authority to ban an uncensored work or periodical on the request of the minister of interior. The regulation also lengthened the period between presentation of a work to the censors and its issuance to allow time for examination. With some deference to the 1865 law, the State Council admonished the Minister to prosecute those works in which crimes appeared. Clarifying orders followed directing authorities to either burn or turn into pulp the banned works and requiring censors to report on uncensored works almost immediately on their receipt.[6] The impact of this change was huge. Censors were now advised that henceforth they need no longer decide the harmfulness of a work on the basis of law; that is, they were no longer to use the expression "despite the harm of the work, the law did not include any punishment for the offense."[7] Publishers, fearing the financial loss entailed by confiscation of a work, began unofficially to ask for preliminary examination of the uncensored works they were preparing. The procedure became so widespread that in April, 1874 the Committee of Ministers ruled that to be considered an uncensored work, the publication had to be printed in its complete edition. Otherwise it would be treated as a censored work, and, to use the Committee's words, subject to the rigorous examination that censored works received since those appealed to a less educated and more gullible audience.[8] Despite the ban, publishers, especially of periodicals, continued the practice of having trusted censors examine an issue prior to publication. The Chief Board was aware of this practice and allowed it to continue.[9] Thus, either through confiscation or prior censorship of uncensored works, Timashev could assure himself that literature and the press remained obedient.

Immediately after the 1872 law went into effect, Timashev arrested a work of Ferdinand Lassalle, the German socialist and another by the French socialist, Louis Blanc.[10] Within a short time, the Committee of Ministers was asked to consider forty cases, of which twenty five involved works that the ministry had already begun to prosecute. Further, from the time the June, 1872 rule went into effect until November, 1873 not one of the questionable works was prosecuted despite the admonition of the State Council.[11] Under the rule, from 1872 to 1904, works by George Brandes, G. Hauptmann, E. Haeckel, Diderot, Zola, Lecky, Renan, and Thomas Hobbes, all in Russian translation were banned and destroyed.[12] The censorship vigorously defended the new procedure noting, in 1877, that without the law, it would have found it difficult to prevent the appearance of periodicals that pandered to the coarse tastes of the crowd or attracted youth to a purportedly better political and social structure.[13] Timashev could well congratulate himself on restoring the discretionary authority of the ministry.

However, Timashev did not rest content with these changes. In 1873 the Committee of Ministers took up a new request by the Minister to allow him to bar editors from their position if they violated injunctions against printing forbidden information. The Committee balked at this request and turned it over to the State Council. The latter agreed in June, 1873 to Timashev's request in a modified form. He could issue circulars excluding sensitive topics from consideration by the press and penalize violators by a ban on the publication of up to three months. Although the State Council thought that only extraordinary circumstances would dictate such circulars, Timashev and his successors issued 200 circulars from 1873 to 1895. In the period up to 1881, "extraordinary circumstances" impelled ministers to forbid: advertisements of the London Society for the Insurance of Losses in Horseraces, articles about a few suicides and legal cases, articles about the murder of Peter III, and discussions of bankruptcies and poor harvests.[14] The list of circulars is long and some deal with topics that might legitimately be called sensitive, such as military information, or expressions of doubt about the government's solicitude for the welfare of Russians.[15] The penalty for infraction of these circulars was so severe that Timashev tried, unsuccessfully, in 1875, to win approval for the imposition of fines instead of stoppage.[16] One additional weapon in the hands of the censorship was won in 1879 when the censorship was empowered to forbid private advertisements in any periodical.[17]

This profusion of administrative supplements should have been sufficient to forestall infractions by writers and journalists. But in fact the government remained extraordinarily sensitive to the printed word. This sensitivity, more than extraordinary circumstances, explains the government's precautions. The government had in fact not accepted the principle of a punitive censorship. It continued to believe, as stated in one warning to censors, that censored articles were to be considered not only as permitted but as approved by the government.[18] Since even uncensored works appeared only after prior examination by censors, in effect censors were being enjoined to make sure that everything printed was approved by the government. Despite the immensity of the task, the censors performed this task with great efficiency even though they sometimes erred.

With these supplements to the press regulations, Timashev felt no need to pursue the revision of the press laws and the codifying of press crimes that had been considered from 1866. The new rules also ended the need to prosecute dangerous works. The Chief Board noted in 1876 that after issuance of the 1872 rule, it prosecuted cases only when a "completely formal and external infringement" of the press laws was noted. In that year there were only four such cases.[19] In 1879 the St. Petersburg committee began prosecution of only two periodicals but applied the 1872 law to nine works.[20] Even before 1872, the press authorities had found the courts more sympathetic to the prosecution of censored than uncensored works, mainly because the accusations against the former were often purely formal and the penalties minor.[21] This was the source of the Chief Board's complaint in 1870 that since the courts usually found in favor of the defendants, the Board had decided to avoid prosecution in some cases fearing the loss of its prestige.[22] In the following year the Chief Board reiterated this complaint adding that the existing methods of imposing penalties would paralyze the effort to restrain the appearance of harmful works.[23] Despite the effort of the Board to blame the courts, the fault was not completely that of the courts. In three of the eleven cases for 1870-1871, the prosecutor refused to support the accusation of the press authorities.[24] Timashev himself in 1871 refused to prosecute Notes of the Fatherland despite the request of the head of the Chief Board. Instead, he accepted the alternative of exclusion of the offending article.[25] As was pointed out earlier, it was not the failure of the courts that led the censorship to turn to administrative measures but the predilection of officials for unrestricted and discretionary authority. With Timashev's supplements to the press laws, the censorship had the license it desired.

Timashev's changes accompanied a spurt in the growth of the periodical press during the 1870s. A large audience for periodicals had appeared in the Empire, as in western Europe. In December, 1870, 374 periodicals were being issued in the Empire, of which 101 were uncensored.[26] By 1879 505 periodicals issued,

115 of which were uncensored. In St. Petersburg alone, 61 daily newspapers and 151 weeklies were being published.[27] The most popular periodical in 1870 was Son of the Fatherland (Syn' Otechestva) with 13,000 subscribers; the most popular "thick" journal was the new Messenger of Europe (Vestnik Europy).[28] By 1876, the newspaper The Voice had 17,000 subscribers, and by 1880, the figure had risen to about 23,000 to 25,000. By that year the most popular periodical was the illustrated The Field (Niva) which sold, on occasion, 50,000 copies.[29] The wide audience for periodicals with which the government had long concerned itself now existed.

The number of administrative penalties imposed on periodicals also grew. In 1872, the number was 18; in 1876, more than 30; and in 1878, 36. Only with the appointment of Count Loris Melikov as dictator and later Minister of Interior did the number of penalties decrease, to 11 in 1880.[30] Warnings remained the penalty most often imposed although the prohibition of retail sale was a very close second. In the period from 1870 to 1879, these two penalties composed from 78% to 85% of all penalties imposed on periodicals.[31] In 1879 alone 15 warnings were issued and five periodicals suspended as a result. Retail sale was forbidden seven times.[32] From 1870 to 1878 twenty-four periodicals were banned twenty-five times for a total of over 108 months. Those public penalties were supplemented by private warnings given to editors of eight periodicals. Moreover, the censorship noted for future reference 34 articles as "tendentious" but not deserving of punishment.[33]

Despite these actions a perceptible change in the attitude of the censorship towards periodicals occurred in this period, a change from general suspicion to more selective suspicion indicative perhaps of the gradual acceptance of journalism within the Empire. Thus, in 1871, the Chief Board reported that periodicals had remained faithful to their "negative attitude to power, family, and faith." Even ostensible supporters of the government were accused of trying to entice the government and society beyond the limits of reform established by the government. The Board explained that these dangerous periodicals were popular and, without explaining the reasons for the public's perversity, added:

> The presence of a selfish element in journalism is proved particularly in St. Petersburg...by the fact that there are many Jews among the publishers and editors and these Jews print little on the basis of conviction but turn to journalism as an object of exploitation.[34]

By 1874, the Moscow committee noted, with respect to the conservative periodicals published by Katkov and Giliarov-Platonov that some periodicals have the "positive task of serving society."[35] In 1880 the same committee commended Moscow periodicals for fulfilling their tasks "with full consciousness of direct obligations", none more outstandingly than Katkov's.[36] The change in attitude should not be exaggerated. Even in 1868 the Chief Board had noted that journalism had become a social force molding public opinion and putting pressure on the government. At the same time it described journalism as more restrained and businesslike, less concerned with utopias than with particular reforms.[37] And Timashev remained extremely critical of Katkov's pretensions.[38] Nevertheless, with perhaps some reluctance, officials came to recognize that journalism had become an established institution, one that could be used for good or ill.

Kraevskii's The Voice had some defenders in the censorship. Indeed, it was correctly rumored at the time that Valuev, when Minister, had subsidized the publication.[39] A censorship official referred to the newspaper in 1869 as an opponent of the radicals and a "partisan of severe order and esteem to the law."[40] These words were crossed out by some superior who did not feel kindly towards the newspaper. But Kraevskii's friend, a member of the council of the Chief Board, F. Tolstoy, was able to help the newspaper in 1871 when he allowed it to publish an account of the Nechaev affair a few days before other newspapers received this privilege. Tolstoy was apparently too friendly and indiscreet here because other newspapers attacked this favoritism.[41] If The Voice had friends, it also had enemies. Thus, a reference to the newspaper in 1873 as "serious" was omitted in a final report signed by the head of the Third Section, Count Shuvalov, which condemned all uncensored periodicals as distinguished by "coarse curiosity" and a taste for scandal.[42] Apparently enemies of The Voice outnumbered friends.[43] Certainly, Count D. Tolstoy, the Minister of Education, whose espousal of a classical gymnasia was criticized by The Voice, was one of the more powerful enemies of the newspaper. The net result for the newspaper was that from 1863 to 1877 it received eleven warnings, three temporary suspensions, and was deprived of the profitable right of retail sale eleven times for a total of 461 days, a prohibition which the newspaper estimated cost it 150,000 rubles.[44] The offenses of the newspaper which brought about these penalties included criticism of the government's educational policy or high officials,[45] and the spread of rumors about a cholera epidemic.[46] In 1876 alone, The Voice was required to print twelve refutations of articles it had printed.[47] Despite warnings, the newspaper remained popular and important in this period. But in 1882, Count Tolstoy, now Minister of Interior pushed through new legislation that was soon after applied to The Voice. The newspaper did not survive long.[48]

The monthly, The Deed (Delo), founded by the publisher of

the defunct Russian Word, Blagosvetlov, as a successor to his banned journal, not only survived but flourished as a censored journal. In 1869 it had about 4000 subscribers and in 1879 subscriptions had risen to from 5000 to 5500.[49] Rumor had it that Valuev tolerated the journal and had charged censor V. Lazarevskii, a reputed admirer of Chernyshevsky, with its supervision. In 1867 a Third Section report that recommended the banning of the journal was simply ignored.[50] The Soviet scholar, Teplinskii, suggests that Valuev and a few other officials, convinced that an opposition press could never be completely suppressed, adopted a policy of allowing a few radical journals to appear under close supervision. Such was the conviction of censor F. Tolstoy in 1871 who suggested that complete suppression might force radical writers into underground literature.[51] In any case The Deed was subjected to very close supervision and the whole committee was required to pass on articles for the journal until 1877, a very unusual procedure.[52] As a result, 18 articles were forbidden for the journal in 1869,[53] 13 articles and 23 poems in 1873,[54] 5 articles and 5 poems in 1876,[55] and 2 articles and one poem in 1880.[56] Fourteen of the articles forbidden in 1870 were considered to be threats to religious feeling, family, property or the state structure; the remaining ten were forbidden because they were "expose" articles attacking abuses and unnamed officials.[57] Despite this rigor of the censors, they attributed harmful socialistic tendencies to the journal in 1871[58] and accused it of propagating negativistic ideas, mocking old literary authorities and pandering to youth.[59] Not only the censors were circumspect. Blagosvetlov, the publisher, instructed writers on what subjects to avoid. He advised the writer N. V. Shelgunov, for example, to be as sly as a serpent and innocent as a dove in his writing.[60] Apparently the slyness of the authors was a match for the censor's caution because the journal retained its reputation for radicalism through the 1870's. Moreover, the figures indicate that by the end of the 70s, a smaller number of articles were being forbidden. Editors and writers had learned to live within the limits of the censorship.[61]

The most important radical journal in the 70s was Notes of the Fatherland, an uncensored journal which Nekrasov purchased the rights to in 1868 to replace the banned Contemporary. The redoubtable Nekrasov assured himself of support in the censorship office with discreet bribery of Council members F. M. Tolstoy and V. M. Lazarevskii. Tolstoy's payment was a position as music critic of the journal.[62] Often Nekrasov and his successor, Saltykov-Shchedrin, would consult with the former's official friends about the propriety of particular articles and the practice continued despite its illegality and despite the loss of friends in high positions.[63] Nekrasov's diplomacy was rewarded. In 1869 censor Lebedev called the journal a "progressive liberal" publication whose moderation was explained by its monthly agreements with the censorship.[64] A censorship report in 1870 referred to the "same moderate liberal tendency" of the journal noted earlier and suggested that its progressive views were presented "decently and moderately."[65] In the following year a report by censor Lebedev remarked that the journal continued its attack on what was backward in social life, the sciences, and legislation.[66] A list of articles that had attracted the attention of the censorship in 1871 was crossed out in a censorship report, probably by the journal's protectors. The list included two articles by N. K. Mikhailovskii---"Theory of Darwin and Social Science" and "Philosophy of History"---and two works by Saltykov. But even protectors like F. Tolstoy could not always forestall punishment. Occasionally, however, he succeeded in having the Council accept exclusion of an offensive article or simply note an article for future reference, or give an oral warning to the editor.[67] Despite a number of warnings, fewer than some other periodicals, the journal was able to survive the 70s. Only in 1884 was it banned despite the strong efforts of its protector, Lazarevskii.[68]

Why did the government tolerate this radical journal? Teplinskii suggests that the reputation of the journal and the support it had in the public explains its survival. He argues, additionally, that censors were public figures, often professors, obliged to justify their activities to educated society; this desire for standing among their colleagues and in society sometimes conflicted with their duties as officials. Moreover, he points out that officials like Valuev and censors like F. Tolstoy and Lazarevskii did not consider the censorship simply as a repressive device. Sometimes they thought of using it to manipulate and control journalists and sometimes they responded to special situations. Tolstoy in particular seems to have held a liberal view towards literature and the press. The evidence Teplinskii offers is important. Tolstoy wrote to the publisher, Kraevskii in July, 1869 referring to "our general business, the gradual and serene development of the free Russian word." It is true that Tolstoy went on to say that this goal required him to eliminate the "superfluous" irritating phrases he found in Notes of the Fatherland.[69] His remark may simply have been an apologetic attempt to put the best light on his job rather than the expression of conviction. But his statement does suggest his awareness that censor and journal must cooperate, if not to promote the free development of the Russian word, then simply to avoid punishment of both. Teplinskii and Evgen'ev-Maksimov both suggest that in 1876 and 1877 the government decided not to apply punitive measures against the press because of the impending Russo-Turkish War and the consequent desire not to antagonize society.[70]

In support of his suggestion that Valuev wished to manipulate journalists by selective concessions and threats, Teplinskii quotes from a report of Valuev on February 8, 1868. Valuev there noted that the task of the censorship should be to keep the press within limits while encouraging, through privileges, the more moderate press.[71] Certainly Valuev's policy, privileges in conjunction with repression, conformed to this statement. But Teplinskii's argument, that the result of Valuev's practice was to encourage the concentration of radicals in one journal in order to facilitate the task of observation and restriction, is plausible, not conclusive. Greater confirmation of Teplinskii's argument can be found in statements by Lazarevskii and Tolstoy, perhaps self-serving in that they justified their fruitful and profitable collaboration with Nekrasov. In 1868, Lazarevskii, Council member, argued that in the hands of Nekrasov, the journal Notes of the Fatherland was tolerable because the poet valued his position in society and could moderate the position of his writers more than another editor, who, perhaps less esteemed in society, would be less restrained.[72] Tolstoy, in an October, 1871 meeting of the Council argued that restraint of the journal was preferable to forcing its writers into the underground. Moreover, he argued that it was impossible to completely suppress the tendency the writers represented. As an alternative he offered his own practice, advice to publishers on what to print and especially what was unprintable. On this particular occasion Tolstoy was not convincing enough. Timashev rejected Tolstoy's argument on the grounds that without Tolstoy's ministrations, the journal would soon be banned, a fate he clearly thought desirable at the time.[73] Further, Valuev himself expressed a position similar to Timashev's in 1868 after hearing F. Tolstoy defend The Deed. Valuev argued that the Council was not an intermediary between the press and the government. If a work, intentionally or not, was harmful, he said, either because of its tendency, influence, or impression, the censorship did not have the authority to be lenient. On another occasion, the head of the Chief Board, then V. Grigor'ev, scolded the chairman of the St. Petersburg committee for excluding an article from the journal The Word (Slovo) because the printing of the article might have led to the banning of the journal.[74] But Grigor'ev added that the kind of assistance the chairman provided should be reserved for "well intentioned" periodicals, not such as The Word. Thus, control through manipulation was not an established method of treating radical periodicals. Still, Teplinskii's evidence indicates that some censorship officials did consider the muzzling and muting of radical writers more useful to the government than complete suppression.

Teplinskii supplies some good evidence for his other arguments. Grigor'ev, who headed the Chief Board in 1876, created a minor scandal by treating Saltykov-Shchedrin abruptly and impolitely. As a result, Grigor'ev, who was also a professor at St. Petersburg University, felt the disapproval of his university colleagues. To evade this disapproval, Grigor'ev was forced to lie and say he had never met Saltykov and so, of course, could not have been impolite to him.[75] The reputation of Notes of the Fatherland may also have saved it from a ban. The official Northern Post commented soon after the 1865 Press Law went into effect that the decision to impose a warning was determined not only by a particular article but by the inconvenience and talk a warning might produce.[76] The inconvenience might include a negative public reaction but it might well include the financial loss to a publisher because of a ban. Teplinskii does not present this argument. But the investment a periodical represented was quite sizeable. Business interests spent 68,500 rubles on Aksakov's Moscow (Moskva) from 1866 to 1868 and another publisher, M. Cherniaev, spent 34,000 rubles from 1871 to 1874 on his unsuccessful periodical which closed for lack of an audience. In 1874, V. A. Poletika purchased the important newspaper, Market Reports (Birzhevye Vedemosti) and its press for 200,000 rubles.[77] The Voice spent in 1867 about 11,160 rubles for press and paper but by 1877 its costs had risen to 99,188 rubles. Honorariums for its contributors rose from 24,070 to 101,382 rubles during those years.[78] The closing of a periodical that represented such a substantial investment would be an important decision. It is notable, in this light, that the permanent ban on The Contemporary in May, 1866 occurred when its subscriptions had fallen from over 4000 to about 2,100 in January, 1866.[79] Of course, The Voice was closed eventually as was Notes of the Fatherland, and most likely The Contemporary would have been banned even if it had maintained its audience. But it is probable that the size of a journal's audience, the investment a journal represented, as well as the dissatisfaction harsh actions might cause were factors the censorship considered before it issued warnings to a journal or banned it.

In general, it would appear that the continued existence of Notes of the Fatherland, despite its radicalism, was not a result of the ineptness or stupidity of the censorship. It testifies instead to the self-imposed limits under which the censorship acted. The government did not want to appear to the public solely as a policeman and oppressor and so chose to tolerate some dissidence in print as the price of popular acceptance. Further, it is clear that the censorship did not try to isolate Russia from Europe or from dangerous ideas. Such a task was impossible at the time because travel abroad, with the resulting direct access to foreign works, was possible. The government would always measure the threat posed by a radical journal against the discontent and inconvenience severe measures would bring. Moreover, some censors were prepared to tolerate a moderate radicalism; this seeming contradiction is understandable as a radicalism couched in a respectful rather than an angry tone, and perhaps adjusted to tolerable limits by censors such as Tolstoy and Lazarevskii.[80] But to achieve this exalted state, a radical periodical had to secure, through luck or skill, a following large enough to inspire respect, and perhaps a little fear among officials. These "fittest" periodicals survived in the harsh conditions created both by the censorship and the competition among journals for subscribers and readers.[81]

Another radical periodical that learned this secret was the newspaper The Week (Nedelia). It did not escape the censorship unscathed; the 16 warnings it received after 1865 made it second only to The Voice.[82] But considering a censor's evaluation of the newspaper in 1870, this was mild punishment. He called the newspaper "an organ of nihilism, extremely hostile to the whole order" in Russia and "continuously condemning the present situation in Russia" by concentrating attention on disorders, backwardness and abuses within the Empire.[83] Examples of such a tendency may have been a defense, in 1871, of student treasuries and a sympathetic description of the plight of students, calculated, a report said, to stimulate dissatisfaction.[84] Apparently the stragegy of The Week was to suppress its radicalism temporarily after every squabble with the censorship. The suspension imposed after the above articles was followed by an "improvement" in the behavior of the newspaper according to the censors.[85] The improvement was only temporary and warnings came again. Despite, or perhaps because of these warnings, the circulation of the newspaper grew from about 2,400 in 1873 to from 7,500 to 10,000 in 1878.[86] How can the government's tolerance be explained? Certainly its following was very small in the early 1870s; a ban would not have been a weighty issue. The sources are not helpful. Valuev is reputed to have favored the original publisher, N. P. Munt, but by 1868, when the newspaper was launched on its radical career, it had a new publisher.[87] A Soviet historian suggests that The Week was subsidized by the government but offers no evidence in support of this statement. Perhaps the anti-semitic and anti-liberal point of view of the newspaper combined with its populism was acceptable to the government.[88] In any case the newspaper was treated more like a nuisance than a major threat to the government.

The government's attitude towards a liberal journal like the Messenger of Europe (Vestnik Europy) was even more tolerant. In 1871 censor Bogdanov referred to the journal as a leading periodical; in the previous year a censor had noted articles of "serious literary content" in the journal by the best contemporary writers.[89] The implied admiration for this "serious" journal, which Timashev himself read, did not prevent notation for reference of an article on the Franco-Prussian War, a sympathetic account of the French Republic, and a critique of the government's use of preventive measures against crime. However, the only article that led to a significant penalty, a warning, was by K. K. Arsen'ev, a discussion of the Nechaev affair which the censors thought contained a suggestion that the government's measures might stimulate further political opposition.[90] On one occasion, the minister of interior proposed

confiscation of an issue, the December, 1879 issue, fearing its
dangerous impact on students. But the Committee of Ministers
rejected his request.[91] In 1876 the journal avoided arrest by
excluding an article entitled "Reform and System". The article
spoke of the need for reforms such as the participation of
zemstvo men in provincial and central government.[92] The journal
received some warnings and threats but remained a tolerated and
even admired journal. It could be argued that the journal was
allowed to present the position of the "legal" opposition in
Russia.[93]

The "serious" liberal newspaper was the Russian Reports
(Russkie Vedomosti), published in Moscow and called the "professors"
newspaper because of its contributors in the early
1870s. By the beginning of the 20th century two thirds of its
readers were people with higher education.[94] The influence of
its readers and its editors did not save it from warnings and
other penalties but did help to establish its standing with
censors. In January, 1881, a censorship report called it a
worthy but extremely liberal publication.[95] In earlier years the
censorship had been less generous; the newspaper was called
"extremely unselective", tactless, and lacking seriousness in
1871, and in 1874 it was accused of "consciously" stepping beyond
the limits of the law.[96] The rise in esteem was accomplished
despite the dedication of the staff in the 1870s to constitutionalism.
It was achieved by a muting of the staff's views, but not
complete suppression. The publishers learned to write for the
censors just as the censors learned to live with the newspaper.[97]

The satirical press also survived but under more strenuous
conditions. It had incited the particular suspicion of the
Murav'ev Commission after the attempt on the Emperor's life in
1866. The ensuing Imperial order on May 28, 1866 which enjoined
special caution for The Spark (Iskra), Alarm Clock (Budil'nik),
Diversion (Razvlechenie), and other satirical and humorous
publications because of their anti-government tendencies and
their circulation among the common people, was carefully observed
by the censors.[98] Alarm Clock was characterized by the censorship
in 1871 as democratic and egalitarian in its tendency; that
year censors prohibited 31 articles from the censored periodical
while 32 were prohibited during the previous year.[99] The periodical
survived even though, according to Chekhov, the censorship
would eliminate about 400-800 lines in each issue.[100] "Expose"
articles that verged on defamation were the rule in the periodical
as was true of The Spark, a satirical journal that was uncensored.
One section in The Spark entitled "Isn't it True" was
devoted to "exposes" but was discontinued by the publisher after
a warning.[101] Censor Iuferov described the periodical in 1870
as presenting material of an "extreme socialistic, communistic,
and materialistic character." Warnings, prohibition of retail
sale, even prosecution in the courts bedevilled the publisher

until, in 1873, he had the misfortune to require the approval of the Chief Board of a new editor. The Chief Board rejected the publisher's choice and for lack of a suitable editor, the periodical ended publication that year. By this time subscriptions had fallen to 2000.[102] Satirical journals, closely watched by the censorship, increased in number in the mid-1870s.[103]

"Expose" articles were the largest category of forbidden articles in the censored provincial press during this period.[104] Of 75 articles for provincial periodicals rejected by the Moscow censors in 1878, "expose" articles were the single largest category. The next important group included criticisms of the government's measures against the increasingly active revolutionaries; next was criticism of the police.[105] Description of some unpleasant aspect of Russian life or of the situation of the peasants, or antagonism between teachers and students, also led to prohibition.[106] Subject as they were to different standards than the uncensored capital press, provincial newspapers might be prevented from reprinting articles extracted from the capital newspapers.[107] In the Baltic area, the censorship concerned itself with the quarrel between German and Russian nationalism. While trying to stem this rivalry without striking too hard at Russian nationalism, the Chief Board showed some favor towards the Estonians and Latvians. In 1870 came an order that publications in these languages were henceforth to be censored by a non-German and non Lutheran censor in Riga, technically subordinate to the Riga German censor but actually subordinate to the Chief Board.[108] But even Latvian nationalism had to be restrained from criticizing Germans.[109] In general, the provincial press was strictly controlled by the government. Concessions were rare: in 1871 official provincial newspapers were permitted to include history and ethnography in their unofficial sections and to publish scholarly or scientific articles. But as far as politics were concerned, until the late 1870s, the government made few concessions. Perhaps the growth of the revolutionary movement explains the decision to allow <u>Village Reading</u> (Sel'skoe Chtenie) to present its conservative social and political ideas in the provinces from 1877-1878.[110]

The most formidable local nationalism within the Empire was Polish and the censors carefully prohibited works that catered to the "fantastic interests" of Polish nationalism, to quote the Warsaw censors.[111] As noted before, Valuev had preferred moderation and harmony to the expression of vigorous and divisive nationalism. Still in exceptional cases, the government took a partisan stand, especially with respect to Ukrainians and Jews. In August, 1875, the government established a special committee to consider the question of Ukrainian or "Little Russian" publications. In the committee the representative of the Third Section took issue with the anti-Ukrainian arguments of other members. He noted that no anti-government works circulated in the language.

Nevertheless, the committee decided that "Little Russian" publications encouraged separation and so proposed counter measures such as the surveillance of teachers and libraries, subsidies to Russophile newspapers, and the curtailment of all "Little Russian" publications except for historical works. Fictional works in the language might appear only with the permission of the Chief Board, and then only in the Russian alphabet. Alexander II agreed to this regulation. His son, Alexander III, extended the scope of the ban, encouraging the performance of Russian plays in the Ukraine in 1884, and forbidding translation of Russian works into Ukrainian in 1892.[112]

A similar break with the policy of harmony and moderation towards nationalism explains the decision in April, 1874 to establish a commission to consider the censorship of Hebrew works.[113] Apparently this commission, like the Ukrainian committee, decided to restrict publications in Hebrew. At any rate, in 1876, the Chief Board rejected a petition to publish a Hebrew newspaper in Odessa on the grounds that approval was incompatible with the government's views on the spread of Hebrew.[114] Whatever language they used, however, Jews were prevented from describing their condition "in dark colors" or from defending an extension of civil rights to Jews too sharply.[115] A sort of even-handedness ruled in the censorship however. Thus, a work by Liutostanskii that claimed to disclose the deep hatred towards Christianity in the Talmud had to be expurgated before printing. Ironically, the censor feared that the work might spread "absurd" traditions among Russians about Jesus.[116] But a current of anti-semitism ran through the censorship establishment. A passing negative reference to the presence of Jews in St. Petersburg journalism appeared in a report in 1870.[117] A report of the Foreign Censorship in August, 1880 referred to the "Judaizing" (zhidovstvuiushchaia) foreign journalism to which it had given increased attention in the previous years.[118] The spirit of nationalism, of which this anti-semitism was an offshoot, was undoubtedly at odds with the picture of harmony and peace that the censorship tried to cultivate in literature and the press. But the government itself during Timashev's regime was choosing to sacrifice harmony for nationalism.

Politically and morally dangerous works might also shatter the illusion of harmony. Accordingly censors tried to prevent such works from appearing, or confiscated them after they did appear. Most of the 26 articles or works forbidden by the Moscow censors in 1879 were banned because of their immoral, vulgar, or "expose" character.[119] Only three were forbidden because of their politics. That same year, the St. Petersburg committee banned 49 works. However, most of the 14 works the Chief Board chose to cite in its annual report dealt with politics.[120] The Board's attention was probably a reflection of its own preoccupation with politics and not that of authors.

The literature of the 1870s did however exhibit a growing concern with politics in Russian society. The movement "to the people," the rebellion of youth against tradition, and the growth of radicalism among them, the Russo-Turkish War, the rising sentiment in favor of representative institutions, and finally the growth of terrorism in the late 1870s affected literature and hence the censorship. For example, in the early 1870s, the political work the censors handled was very likely to refer indirectly to politics. Moreover, the work might often be large and hence free of censorship because of its size. An off-print from an article by A. Koshelev in the periodical Conversation (Beseda) was forbidden in 1871. Its crime was a vague reference to the need for new ideas with respect to zemstvos, the press and law.[121] Another work was prosecuted in 1871 for using the poetry of N. Nekrasov and G. Uspenskii to depict the oppression of the lower classes.[122] By 1877 the vagueness of Koshelev's article had disappeared. A forbidden pamphlet that year talked of the spread of revolutionary propaganda through 37 provinces and blamed its spread on the disappearance of the landlord's influence over the peasants.[123] In 1876 censors excluded from the Messenger of Europe a gently worded internal survey which alluded to the need for representatives of zemstvos to participate in future political reforms.[124] In 1878 the St. Petersburg censors banned a study of Russian society for suggesting that the participation of the public in government affairs was a necessary consequence of emancipation of the serfs.[125] By 1879 the censors were forbidding a pamphlet that attributed political murders in Russia to Poles and Jews and advised their exclusion or limited access to higher education and high official positions as a remedy.[126] Another forbidden tale that same year was translated from the Italian and anti-revolutionary in tone. In parable it argued that successful revolutionaries soon re-establish much of what they rebelled against.[127] The allusions of the early 1870s were being replaced by less veiled references to revolutions and constitutions by the end of the 70s. An evolution had occurred in literature.

Teplinskii argues that the spread of the "to the people" movement of young students after 1873 led to greater harshness in the censorship. A break with this policy came during the Russo-Turkish War when the government decided to offer some concessions to the press. The visible sign of this change was the revocation of all prior warnings to periodicals after the successful siege at Plevna in late 1877. When the press began to use this freedom to suggest Russia's need for a constitution, the government demurred. At the end of 1877, Timashev convoked the more important editors and publishers to warn them against issuing calls for "freedom in the European sense."[128] The evidence here confirms Teplinskii's argument to some extent. There was greater harshness. But by the end of the 70s censors were dealing with efforts to publish political ideas in pamphlets of a comparatively few pages and low price that would be accessible to more readers. Clearly the political activity of the 70s had changed the level and content of political references in printed works.

It is also clear that the government's attitude towards political references vacillated in the late 1870s, proferring leniency on occasion and then quickly withdrawing concessions as writers overstepped the desired limits. For example, in 1879, the minister of interior tried to ban Bezobrazov's Collection of Political Knowledge, volume 8, an uncensored work, because it suggested that constitutions were necessary for correct governance. The Committee of Ministers rejected the proposal and the work was issued in 1879.[129] Censors recommended prohibition of Mackenzie Wallace's Russia in translation, and a critique of the history of socialism by Lorenz Stein. But the works appeared when the censors were overruled.[130] On the other hand, censors were willing to allow publication of Finley's History of the Byzantine and Greek Empire but a minority of the Committee of Ministers, joined by the Emperor, decided to ban the work for its improper remarks about autocratic power.[131]

The vacillation among censors and officials apparently ended as Teplinskii argues, with a decision in favor of repression. Statistics bear out this contention. The largest percentage of warnings to periodicals and bans on retail sale for any five year period from 1865 to 1904 occurred in the years from 1875 to 1879. Moreover, this period was also notable because during it periodicals received the largest number of penalties for any five year period; the next highest five year periods were 1870 to 1874 and 1895 to 1899.[132] It would appear then that the changes in literature made the censorship's task of curbing the public's interest in politics more difficult. References to politics became less veiled and authors might try to present these in works designed to appeal to a large audience that would inevitably include members of the lower classes. But the censors remained a mighty obstacle to this effort, trying to stem this interest.[133]

"Expose" literature, as earlier, remained an important concern of the censorship. An attack on judges in the St. Petersburg Reports led to a warning to censors to eliminate such articles in the future.[134] In 1878 the periodical Russian Survey (Obozrenie) was closed, according to its editor, because it had disclosed details of a financial scandal.[135] Political considerations explain the negative attitude of censors towards the description of peasant life in "very dark terms."[136] The fear that stark descriptions or commentary would stimulate discontent also explains the censors' rejections of "dark" portrayals of the life of workers, clergy, and the poor.[137] More extensive and abstract disquisitions on society and life were also examined carefully to ban socialistic and sometimes "cynical" points of view. One description of contemporary Russian society by Bibikov was accused of undermining Christianity, authority in general and "shaking the foundations" of the moral and social order. The work was destroyed in 1874.[138] A more cautious work, a play whose heroine talked of her willingness to struggle for her rights against powerful oppression, was forbidden in 1876.[139] A work exhibiting a fatalistic philosophy of life was also forbidden that year.[140] The censors also forbade a patriotic but pessimistic work that complained of German and Jewish exploitation of Russians.[141] This work, and a few similar works, were rejected as having no literary worth or as ungrammatical. A new audience, less educated but nevertheless interested in political and social affairs, had appeared.

The censorship noted the appearance of this new audience very quickly. As early as May, 1872 censors were warned about the special requirements for works that would be accessible to the masses because of their cheapness.[142] Censors guarded against material capable of inspiring dissatisfaction[143] or presenting the wrong moral examples to the common people.[144] Tales from Russian history had to be edifying[145] and even an attack on revolutionary ideas was banned because a censor thought the work would do more harm than good.[146] Positive means of countering dangerous ideas were also contemplated by the government. Early in the 1870s it considered the publication of a popular handbook of law; from 1875 the newspaper <u>Russian Worker</u> tried to oppose dangerous ideas and inculcate the proper attitudes towards religion and the Tsar.[147] At the request of the Emperor, the future Alexander III investigated the question of reading material for the common people. His report advised the publication of inexpensive loyal works. To that end the ministers of interior and education as well as the head of the Third Section were charged with supervising the publication of such works by private publishers.[148] Reading matter for children was required to adhere to similar exemplary standards.[149] In practice, this meant the prohibition of a story that depicted a serf shooting his master,[150] and the story of Luther's struggle against the Catholic Church.[151] One reckless author presented to censors a tale of a school rebellion in which the students established a constitutional republic. The tale was of course prohibited.[152]

Morality, a traditional concern of the censorship, was carefully defended. Censors prohibited stories of moral corruption[153] and carefully examined manuals about sex to see whether the author's aim was scientific or simply entrepreneurial.[154] Zola's novel <u>Nana</u>, in translation, was forbidden[155] as well as works listing magical incantations, the latter because of the fear of spreading superstitions.[156] To protect religious beliefs from popular superstitions, the censors forbade a work that referred to the discovery of holy relics.[157] Spiritualism and mysticism were also hounded by censors who forbid a work that set forth these ideas. Another work, that contended that Scripture permitted only spiritual cohabitation, was also forbidden.[158] Thomas Hobbes' Leviathan was purged of its anti-Catholic ideas, interpreted as being anti-Orthodox, before it was allowed to be published in translation. Even then the publisher was prosecuted and the book was destroyed in 1874 on decision of the Committee of Ministers.[159] Darwin's Origin of Man and Sexual Selection was also prosecuted.[160] A study of the Schismatics was destroyed because it presented the ideas of the various sects.[161] But censors maintained the traditional hierarchical system denying circulation among the masses to ideas that they permitted in works with a more limited and educated audience.[162] The Protestant beliefs of one author were noted by the censorship as it decided that because its audience would be the educated reader, the work might be permitted.[163] The corollary of this attitude was that works designated for the common people had to meet exemplary standards, often standards of good grammar as well as "serious" worth.[164]

Historical works were also judged in the light of their potential audience. The common people were not allowed to read of the bloody deeds of Ivan the Terrible,[165] nor of the court intrigues around Peter the Great.[166] Even an educated audience could not read Karamzin's unexpurgated memorandum About Ancient and New Russia when it was printed in the scholarly periodical Russian Archive (Russkii Arkhiv). The work was printed with exclusions as were the Letters of Joseph De Maistre, the Sardinian ambassador to the court of Alexander I.[167] La Croix's history of Nicholas I's reign was banned.[168] Both Russian Archive and the similar Russian Antiquity (Russkaia Starina), scholarly periodicals devoted to Russian history, had difficulties with the censorship. On occasion they were forced to expurgate articles to see them published.[169] Sensitive topics such as the murder of Paul I and the coup by Catherine II were likely to meet difficulty. By 1880 however the Moscow censorship was describing Russian Archive as "calmer"; at the same time, the journal was publishing less significant material, said the censors. Perhaps for the censors there was a correlation between "significance" and danger.

The educated reader was not confined to Russian language works. In fact, the Russian educated class was probably more likely to read works published abroad than Russian works. In 1876, the number of titles imported was five times greater than the number of titles, excluding periodicals, published in Russia. Moreover, since two thirds of the Russian titles that year were either textbooks or spiritual works, it is very likely that the typical reader from the educated class would read a foreign rather than a Russian work.[170] The Russian's appetite for foreign works increased during the period from 1868 to 1880. In the former year, the number of foreign titles examined by the Foreign

Censorship was 4,000.[171] By 1874, the number had grown to 9,391[172] and in 1880, it reached 14,712.[173] During this period the percentage of new foreign titles forbidden varied from a high of about 12% to a low of about 6%. Most often the percentage was about 8% to 9%. French and German works predominated among imports with English works third in importance. About 4% of French titles were forbidden in 1875-1876 while the figure for German works was 6%. Polish imports were most often forbidden; about one in three titles were banned in these years.[174] By 1897, the Catalog of Forbidden or Expurgated Foreign Works prepared that year by the censorship listed about 3,000 French titles and 4,540 German titles. Among the authors named in the list were Lecky, Morley, Renan, Comte and John Stuart Mill.[175] What drew the foreign censorship's attention most by 1879 were periodicals which, according to censors, had become particularly anti-Russian. Most of the prohibitions imposed that year were of periodical works.[176] On the average each foreign censor that year examined 93 issues of periodicals and 19 separate titles each month. The appearance of an anti-Russian bias in the foreign press undoubtedly added to the labors of the foreign censor.

The size of the censorship establishment did not grow in proportion to the increase in its work. The budget for 1868 provided 221,709 rubles while in 1879 the figure was 254,333 rubles,[177] a figure somewhat smaller than the budget in 1870. The number of Council members grew from six in 1868 to nine in 1871 and then fell to eight in 1879. The total personnel of the establishment was 90 in January, 1868 excluding chancery personnel and 111 in 1880.[178] In the course of this period the Council's work diminished; in 1868 it prepared 380 conclusions, in 1874, 208 and in 1879 only 114.[179] The complaint of one council member, Lazarevskii, in 1872, that the Council met only to hear decisions of the minister explains the decrease in the number of decisions.[180] The Council was becoming less of a consultative body than a corps of examiners. To improve its ability to supervise the press and literature, the Chief Board was reorganized in 1871 to create a special division within it for surveillance of periodicals. A third division was created in 1878 when the surveillance of provincial periodicals was separated from that of the capital press.[181] Disagreements between the minister and the Council were infrequent; indeed, disagreements within the Council were rarely maintained up to a final vote since the overwhelming proportion of Council decisions were unanimous. About half of the Council decisions ensued after the initiative had been taken by some member of the Council.[182] An additional task assumed by the Chief Board in 1871 was a daily review of newspaper articles and opinions, each review containing extracts from about four or five articles. The survey probably became a regular task thereafter.[183]

Another important duty of the Council was to pass on

petitions to establish periodicals. In 1876 the Council considered 112 petitions and agreed to permit 45 periodicals, of which six were to be freed of censorship.[184] Rejections came for a variety of reasons, from the absence of local censors, the character of the petitioner, or his lack of education to his literary reputation.[185] Some petitioners were rejected for clearly arbitrary reasons: there was no need for a special publication for women; or the proposed editor was Jewish. But arbitrariness was inherent in the system Timashev and other ministers maintained. And despite rejections, the censorship did permit the growth in the number of periodicals published during these years.

The censorship's carefully measured generosity increased the burden of the censors. Moreover, despite prohibitive regulations, writers and publishers were able to persuade censors to read their works before publication although their size would have exempted them from prior examination.[186] This added to the tasks of the censors. In 1868 the average censor in St. Petersburg examined about 2,151 sheets a year, over half of which was uncensored material. If we assume that each sheet produced 16 pages in octavo, then the average censor was reading about 3000 pages monthly,[187] or over 34,000 pages a year. By 1875 that St. Petersburg censor was reading over 4,400 sheets a year, close to 40,000 pages in octavo or about 3,333 pages monthly.[188] Of the manuscripts and proofs that censors read, they rejected usually not more than five percent and often only about two and a half percent.[189] The record of the theatrical censorship of the Chief Board in 1879 shows greater severity. Although often it prohibited no more than ten percent of the plays it examined, it forced revisions and exclusions from about as many plays as it permitted unconditionally.[190] For his labor, censors often received admonitions and occasionally reprimands but sometimes rewards.[191] The government did provide the censor with good salaries and high status. For example, in 1879, a State Councillor was appointed censor in St. Petersburg. This position, rank five in the official hierarchy, placed the censor in the upper middle rank of the hierarchy in the bureaucracy. The "younger" censors in the Warsaw committee were in ranks VII and VIII which also placed them in the upper middle ranks of the bureaucracy.[192] The censor's job was an important one for the government. But in return for status, the censor found himself subject to the vagaries of government policies.

Timashev broke with Valuev's selective mix of repressive and conciliatory measures against the press. His administration of the censorship was marked by a more consistent policy of repression and an end to efforts to base the censorship on the law and the court system. But during his regime, the radical movement developed and changed its goals from propaganda to terrorism. The government's attitude towards the press reflected the changed situation. After January, 1878 when Vera

Zasulich shot General F. Trepov, the head of the St. Petersburg police, and inaugurated the terrorist campaign that eventually led to the assassination of Alexander II, the government became increasingly concerned about the dangers of radicalism. By the time Timashev retired as Minister in 1878 to be replaced by L. S. Makov, it was clear that ordinary precautions were insufficient. Russia had entered what Soviet historians call a "revolutionary situation." The political tension inevitably affected the government's policy towards the press and literature, inspiring experiments and expedients. A break with the policy of repression that Timashev conducted was a mark of the new period.

Chapter VI   The Crisis of Alexander II's Reign 1878-1881

During the period from 1878 to the assassination of Alexander II in March, 1881, the monarchy came under serious attack from the radical movement. The radicals in the course of the 1870s had devoted themselves to propaganda in favor of socialism and against the government. By the late 1870s, in the wake of the failure of propaganda to stimulate peasant discontent and uprisings and in the face of repressive measures against them in the form of long internment and elaborate trials of propagandists, the radicals turned to violence. The turn to violence began with the attempt by Vera Zasulich on the life of the police chief of St. Petersburg, F. Trepov, in January, 1878. A series of violent attacks on government officials began, justified by the radicals as retaliation for official brutality. But the radicals, organized since 1876 in the group called "Land and Freedom", soon moved from a defense of terrorism as retribution to the espousal of terrorism as a means of bringing the government down and precipitating a revolution that would bring socialism to Russia. Not all radicals could accept this transformation. In 1879, the advocates of terrorism created an independent organization, "The People's Will", while their radical opponents, the "villagers", opposed to terrorism but not to violence as retaliation, retreated to a group that called itself the "Black Repartition." This latter group soon disintegrated while the "Will of the People" decided to concentrate its energies on the task of assassinating Alexander II. Despite counter-measures by the government, the terrorists succeeded in their efforts on March 1, 1881. But the government did not topple. Instead with Alexander III's accession, a period of sharp repression began.

Terrorist attacks did not topple the government but they did precipitate feverish activity in the government. The censorship felt the impact of this activity. Officials like the Minister of War, D. Miliutin who wished to root out the sources for the radicals' success and those like Timashev whose automatic response to radicalism was repression could agree on the need to elicit the support of the public at large in the government's fight against radicalism. The great test of the public for officials was the jury trial held for Vera Zasulich after her unsuccessful attack on General Trepov. Despite the obvious guilt of Zasulich, the jury found her innocent on March 31, 1878. Leaving the court rapidly, she avoided arrest by the police and was quickly hidden and eventually smuggled abroad to safety. A special meeting convoked by Alexander II on the day of the verdict included within its recommendations some proposals about the press and the censorship. From that time until the murder of Alexander II, the government's war against the radical terrorists invariably included some proposals dealing with the press, literature, and the censorship.

At the end of 1877, at the request of the Emperor, Timashev summoned the more important editors and publishers to a meeting at which he warned them against publishing statements calling for "freedom in the European sense."[1] The warning clearly did not bring about the results the government desired because a special meeting convoked by Alexander on March 31, 1878 issued a bitter indictment of the press. The group, headed by the former Minister of Interior and then Minister of State Domains and chairman of the Committee of Ministers, Count Valuev, attacked the press on various counts: for challenging religious ideas in scientific articles; using articles on politics and economics to incite antagonism among classes; and challenging accepted political traditions.[2] Valuev was also involved in other special meetings dealing with the threat of the terrorists. From one such meeting came a recommendation that the censorship take measures to prevent the appearance of systematic criticism of police institutions in periodicals.[3] The terrorists continued the attack and in August, 1878 succeeded in murdering the head of the Third Section, General Mezentsov. A new effort to kill the Emperor on April 2, 1879 led Alexander to order Valuev, General Drentel'n, successor to Mezentsov as head of the Third Section, L. S. Makov, the new Minister of Interior, and D. Miliutin, the Minister of War, to consider a proposal to establish temporary military governors in a few large cities of the Empire to counter the terrorism.[4] Valuev was the author of the April, 1879 regulations that emerged from this meeting. The regulations established temporary military governors and equipped them with extraordinary powers, among which was the right to ban any printed work which could be interpreted as supporting the terrorists.[5] Makov's role, in coordination with this measure, was to summon about 18 to 20 representatives of the press to him for a scolding. He criticized the press and warned that any periodical which dared to violate his decrees would be closed immediately.[6] M. I. Semevskii, the editor of Russian Antiquity (Russkaia Starina) confided to his diary that the episode reminded him of some half-drunk policeman terrorizing some indecent girl. The threat was nevertheless a real one.

Valuev's group was also the source of another proposal in April, 1879 to counter the threat of radical ideas. The group acknowledged that general dissatisfaction gripped the country and that if educated society disapproved of terrorism, it was also critical of government measures. To win over society, the minister of interior was instructed to draw up new rules concerning monetary fines for periodicals. The group produced a proposal to subsidize the publication of a new daily newspaper, as an unofficial spokesman for the government. The result of this deliberation was the periodical Echoes (Otgoloski) which began to issue in January, 1879. Valuev, whose brainchild this was, received 21,000 rubles from the Third Section for the publication of the newspaper. But he personally involved himself in the success of the newspaper and wrote 40 articles for the 15 issues to April, 1879. By the time the periodical ceased publication in December, 1881, Valuev had written more than 200 articles for it.[7] The government's efforts to present its views to Russians, especially the masses, led the Third Section to publish a number of pamphlets in editions of 100,000 copies. The author of one of these pamphlets was V. V. Kardo-Sysoev, the editor of the subsidized Village Conversation who received 5000 rubles for his editorial work. Another subsidized periodical was the Popular Sheet (Narodnyi Listok) published by I. Batalin who received a subsidy of 1500 rubles.[8] Finally from March, 1880 another semi-official publication The Shore (Bereg) began to appear.[9] In the tense situation caused by the efforts of the terrorists, officials no longer discussed whether or not "public opinion" existed in Russia. Valuev's argument that the press should be controlled and manipulated in order to direct public opinion had clearly triumphed at least temporarily over a policy of pure repression.

Temporarily the tension within the government diminished while the terrorists unsuccessfully tracked Alexander in the effort to kill him. Then, early in February, 1880 an explosion planned and executed by one of the terrorists nearly killed the Emperor. Agitation within the government was the background of a special meeting on February 8, 1880 at which the Heir suggested the formation of a supreme inquest commission into the explosion. Despite objections, Alexander decided to create a Supreme Executive Commission and appointed the former Kharkov governor, General Loris-Melikov to head the Commission.[10] The Commission, which assumed almost dictatorial power over the campaign against the terrorists, soon produced a program of action. In the meantime, the head of the Chief Board of Press Affairs, Grigor'ev, summoned editors and publishers of St. Petersburg periodicals to warn them to avoid discussion of the school system and German foreign policy. This policy of threatening the press, bitterly noted by Semevskii, was soon to change with the appointment of Loris-Melikov.[11] Perhaps a memorandum, prepared by about twenty liberal-minded public figures in March, 1880, to Loris Melikov influenced the General. The memorandum argued that to counter the rise of the revolutionary movement, the press should be free to discuss politics. In fact, the authors saw the root of the current terrorism in the suppression of public debate which had turned what ought to have been a struggle of ideas into a political and social struggle. In any case, they suggested that freedom for the press would end the tendency of the public to regard praise of the government as hypocrisy and self-aggrandizement. Further, they expected that freedom would end the habit of seeking hidden meanings in a prose that was intentionally made obscure in order to pass through the censorship.[12]

Loris' attitude towards the press and public opinion shows some evolution from a basically conservative position, contemptuous of public opinion and the press, to a willingness to accommodate the press and even to conciliate public opinion. In his memorandum to Alexander in April, 1880, Loris expressed a view that Timashev would have agreed with, that in Russia, the press formed public opinion while in the west, the press expressed the variety of opinions. But unlike Timashev who had concluded that repression of errant and unruly journalists was the sole means of control necessary, Loris proposed to guide or direct the press.[13] Like Valuev, he was prepared to make the effort to mold and direct the press and public opinion. In effect he acknowledged the significance of the press and public opinion.[14] Instead of scolding and frightening writers into cooperation, Loris was willing to make some concessions to win the support of journalists. In the course of his administration, Loris moved in the direction of more and more leniency towards the press. The public accepted Loris' policies as conciliatory and by August, 1880 rumors spread that restrictions on the provincial press would be eased as part of a general revision of the press regulations.[15] The rumors were fed not only by Loris' conciliatory attitude but by the proposal of Valuev and the Minister of Interior, L. S. Makov, to revise the press laws.[16] The vanity of Valuev, repeatedly noted by Miliutin in his diary, may have inspired this proposal. But whatever the cause, the promise of a more relaxed censorship was being made by mid-1880.

In August, 1880 Loris ended his role as leader of the Supreme Executive Commission and replaced Makov as Minister of Interior.[17] By September, Loris was prepared to convoke representatives of St. Petersburg periodicals. His address to them, later printed as a communique, reprimanded the press for vainly agitating the public with the aim of winning legislative and administrative responsibilities for it. He advised those assembled to discard such illusions. But on the other hand he suggested to them that his program was meant to integrate the zemstvos and municipal dumas into the existing administrative system. As a concession to the press, Loris offered to allow periodicals to deal with government actions so long as they avoided advocacy of illusory proposals. This was Loris' program, expedient concessions to win the support of the press instead of the return to the 1865 press law which was desired by liberals.[18] The policy was however generous in comparison with the repression that had characterized censorship policy prior to Loris' regime. A series of new periodicals, mostly liberal, began to appear and the number of warnings and penalties imposed on periodicals diminished. From April 1, 1880 to January 1, 1881 only one warning was issued to a periodical. Ivan Aksakov received permission to publish his Russia (Rus') and the liberal publisher of the Messenger of Europe (Vestnik Europy) was permitted to publish the newspaper Order (Poriadok). If Kavelin was not permitted to publish in <u>Messenger of Europe</u> an article favoring representative bodies, still Loris did read the article himself.[19] The word "constitution" could not be printed but the conservative <u>New Times</u> (<u>Novoe Vremia</u>) was allowed early in 1881 to allude to a <u>zemsky sobor</u>, the Slavophile concept of an assembly of popular representatives with no legislative power.[20]

According to Zaionchkovskii, quoting the diary of State Secretary E. A. Perets, Loris-Melikov was rushed into the decision to end his Supreme Executive Commission by the intrigues of Valuev and Makov who had proposed revision of the press laws and the zemstvo laws.[21] To counter their activities, Loris himself took over the position of Minister of Interior. Nevertheless, his program, as announced to the editors in September, 1880 and as carried through in the autumn of 1880, appropriated elements of Valuev's and Makov's ideas. In particular, the replacement of V. Grigor'ev by N. S. Abaza as head of the Chief Board was made only after Abaza had insisted, as the price for his appointment, on the revision of the press laws with the purpose of subjecting press crimes to the courts.[22] Yet once the deliberations about a new press law began, Valuev, who might justly have claimed credit for initiating the idea, expressed a vindictive and hostile attitude towards Abaza, the work of revision, and Loris-Melikov. Loris' program also met opposition from liberals. In the October and December issues of the liberal <u>Juridical Messenger</u>, (<u>Iuridicheskii Vestnik</u>) the liberal S. A. Muromtsev, noting Loris' comment that his program, to extend the rights of the zemstvo and duma organizations, unite the police and gendarmerie, and to extend some leniency to the press, would take from five to seven years to implement, commented that such a lengthy period was not necessary for these changes. Muromtsev argued that simple observance of the law could restore privileges to the zemstvos and a simple stroke of the pen would revoke all these supplemental decrees which ensued after issuance of the 1865 press laws.[23] The creation of a special group to revise the press laws implicitly recognized the justice of Muromtsev's position. For the first time since Timashev abandoned the effort to subject press crimes to the courts in 1869, the government, under the leadership of Loris and the stimulus of N. S. Abaza was attempting to replace administrative control of the press and literature by express law and the courts.

A preliminary meeting of the special group on revision of the press laws was held on October 23, 1880. Present were Valuev, Loris-Melikov and his aide Kahkhanov, Makov, the Ministers of Finance and Justice and the head of the Second Section, Prince Urusov as well as K. Pobedonostsev, the Over-procurator of the Holy Synod. At the first full session of the group on October 30, Abaza argued for the establishment of court imposed penalties on the press. Valuev at this time refrained from attacking a proposal that he did not favor. In November, the group heard a number of publishers and editors on the subject. One publisher was Stasiulevich who insisted that administrative penalties be eliminated.[24] Valuev, outnumbered by Loris' partisans, and unhappy at the direction the group was taking, was nevertheless given the task of chairing a subcommission to work out a new project of press laws. Although he thought that the aim of establishing a free press was already ordained, he decided that in the subcommission he would try to minimize the harm freedom would create. His letter to N. Abaza in December, 1880 indicated his distaste for the task. There he wrote that newspapers in the capitals were filled with articles incompatible with the interests of the government but which the government, under the present state of press legislation, could neither eliminate nor restrain. He went on to note that the intended changes were meant to establish an exclusively punitive system based on the courts, a system that would be more severe than the existing mixture of administrative and judicial penalties.[25] Legality rather than leniency was to be the aim of the subcommission. But in the light of the history of the censorship, legality itself would have constituted an act of leniency.

An early proposal of the subcommission was that the appeals court, or sudebnaia palata, become the court of first instance in press crimes. These courts, without juries, had been made the courts for press crimes in the decrees of December, 1866. The Senate would decide disagreements between censors and prosecutors about the charges which would be brought by censors. Perhaps in an effort to sabotage the project, Valuev insisted that the court of first instance should be the lowest circuit court, that is a jury court, even though the appeals court had been established as the court of first instance during his tenure as minister.[26] The remainder of the project left a number of powers to the censorship: permission of periodicals and confirmation of editors; issuance of special prohibitory circulars after informing the Committee of Ministers; the right to arrest a work before it was issued; the initiation of charges against printed works; and the obligatory receipt of copies of each printed work prior to issuance. Administrative penalties for periodicals would end; the banning, temporarily or permanently, of a periodical or the destruction of a printed work would henceforth be permitted only after a court finding. In deference to the split in the group on the issue of the court of first instance in press crimes, two variants of this part of the project were prepared.[27]

A second part of the subcommission's project imposed a maximum penalty for press crimes of three years confinement in a prison or five years of arrest in a fortress or a fine of 3000 rubles. A statute of limitations was established of six months for periodicals and one year for other works. The project listed as crimes the stimulation of hostility between classes, nationalities, or separate parts or classes of the population such as owners and workers. Other crimes stated were blasphemy and mockery (glumlenie) of Christian or non-Christian religions of states recognized by Russia and the printing of offensive information or judgments dealing with the Imperial Family for the period after 1762. Offensive remarks about existing laws or about foreign heads of state were also included in the list of press crimes. A final part of the subcommission's project exhibited the habitual caution of the bureaucracy. The existing mixed prior and punitive censorship would remain in effect pending further experience. The punitive system would be extended gradually at the discretion of the minister of interior to those localities where the judicial system had been established. In the capitals and in cities where judicial institutions existed, editors of all periodicals would be freed of the preliminary censorship at their request. Only publications designated for "popular reading" were excluded from this privilege. Liberated periodicals would pay a bond of from 5000 to 8000 rubles in the captials and half of that in the provinces. Original books containing more than five sheets (80 pages in octavo) and translations of more than ten sheets (160 pages in octavo) were to be freed of prior censorship. Finally, the clerical censorship, heretofore separate from the secular censorship, would become part of the regular censorship. The Foreign Censorship would continue.[28]

    Analyzing the project, Zaionchkovskii notes that the project increased the existing penalties for press crimes. But, he adds, the end of administrative penalties would have had a "positive significance" since it would have ended the reign of government arbitrariness. His judgment, that the project contained few essential changes aside from the establishment of a system of judicial penalties for press crimes is correct. It is however worth emphasizing that the project would have marked a major change in government policy. It would have represented a return to the principles of the original press law with its cautious but optimistic hope that the system of administrative penalties could soon be replaced by a punitive system relying on the courts. Further, it would have explicitly listed those infractions which would bring penalties. Reliance on the laws and the courts had been the hope of liberal reformers in the 1860s. Despite
the government's reversion to administrative measures, this remained an essential part of the program of reformers at the end of the 1870s. The government, in its search for public support against the terrorists, had returned to the spirit of the Great Reforms.

    The project was considered by a special convocation composed of Loris-Melikov, the Minister of Finance, A. A. Abaza, Kakhanov, Pobedonostsev, the Minister of Justice E. Frish and his Vice Minister, Prince Urusov the head of the Second Section, the former Minister of Interior L. S. Makov, and the head of the

Chief Board, N. S. Abaza. According to Valuev's biased recollections, at this meeting of February 28, 1881, Pobedonostsev alone protested vigorously but "indecisively" against the project. According to Valuev, no participant really thought the project would become law. Valuev's diary entries from later in the year imply that Loris himself had doubts about the project. Perhaps these doubts were about Alexander's agreement to the changes. In any case, the assassination of Alexander II on March 1, 1881 ended all discussion of the project.[29]

The possibility of the project becoming law was not really as far-fetched as Valuev suggests. Certainly Alexander, even if reluctantly, had agreed to Loris' proposal to include some representatives of the zemstvos and some cities in the preparation of reforms in local government and other areas of government concern. This proposal, which Zaionchkovskii says was less radical than earlier projects of Valuev, and others in the 1860s, had been agreed to by Alexander on March 1, 1881. Even Valuev, despite his offended vanity, was prepared to support this proposal at the Council of Ministers' meeting of March 4, 1881.[30] Considering the very important proviso that the press reform was to be introduced piecemeal at the discretion of the minister of interior, it is possible that Alexander would have agreed. Further, it is notable that Loris-Melikov insisted, in April, 1881, to the new ruler, Alexander III, that the best solution to the problem of literature and the press was greater legality and more leeway to the press to consider social questions.[31] In this light, an opportunity was lost in March, 1881 with the assassination of Alexander II. A truly punitive regime might well have been in the offing for Russian writers. Instead, they had to wait another twenty five years for that freedom. Alexander III, at first hesitantly and then with more conviction, rejected the advice of Loris and instead chose to adopt a policy of increased repression.[32]

Chapter VII   Censorship in the Reign of Alexander III
1881-1894

The murder of Alexander II on March 1, 1881 frightened and shocked government officials. For over a month the new ruler, Alexander III, hesitated before choosing a new policy towards the terrorists. During that period, the liberal proposals of Loris-Melikov were being debated by higher officials. Finally Alexander made his choice and after the resignation of Loris-Melikov and other liberal officials, a period of reaction began that was to last through his reign. The reaction was marked by the establishment of "Exceptional Regimes" imposing martial law on areas of the Empire, the creation of gentry Land Captains to control the peasants, the restriction of admissions to the universities, and a strict and harshly repressive policy towards the press and literature. The ministers of interior who presided over these policies and indeed contributed to their harshness were Count N. P. Ignat'ev to 1882, Count D. Tolstoy, former Minister of Education and Minister of Interior from 1882 to 1889, and I. N. Durnovo. It is notable that, according to Zaionchkovskii, the greatest success of the reaction was in censorship policy.[1]

That the periodical press should have received this special treatment is not surprising in the light of Alexander's special dislike for the "mangy" Russian press which he accused, in a letter to Pobodenestsev on April 21, 1881, of popularizing the idea of representative government. Pobedonostsev, Alexander's former tutor and now Over-Procurator of the Holy Synod, answered Alexander on April 23 that the main reason for the popularity of representative ideas was the press.[2] This tribute to the Russian periodical press, which expressed a widespread feeling among Russian conservatives who believed that the poor Russian public was victimized by a partisan journalism, was echoed by State Secretary, E. A. Perets. He accused the press of "sowing dissension and dissatisfaction (and) burning passions" among Russians.[3] A similar reproach of the press appeared in a memorandum by the liberal historian Boris Chicherin in a memorandum to Pobodesentsev that was prepared for Alexander. He suggested that the press in Russia served as a corrupting force, an "element of decomposition" that yielded slander, scandal, and half-baked thoughts instead of light. But he qualified this condemnation by noting that this condition occurred when an unrestrained press existed in a society without an active political life. In a more practical vein, he argued against a policy that would deprive the government of the right to issue warnings to periodicals, since its abandonment would only promote the socialist cause. However, Chicherin's memorandum was not simply a distribe against socialism or perhaps an anguished reaction to the assassination. He called for the invitation of representatives of the gentry and zemstvos to the State Council and contended, with perhaps some regret, that Russia was condemned to move in the direction of a constitutional government.[4] Chicherin's angry comments about the press were not representative of Loris-Melikov's attitude. Certainly Loris was more watchful of the press after the assassination. But his policy remained moderate although less generous than before.

On March 4, 1881 Loris Melikov secured Alexander III's approval for official warnings to The Voice and The Country (Strana) for articles that suggested that Alexander II had disagreed with some of his reactionary advisors, and that blamed the death of the Tsar on their repressive policies. In addition to the formal warning, Loris orally warned the editors to show moderation or risk suspension in the future.[5] Loris' caution is attested to by his efforts to keep the Emperor closely informed of his treatment of the press. On March 12, Loris, independently, allowed the Chief Board to begin prosecution of the St. Petersburg Reports for an editorial that accused officials of busying themselves solely with corruption.[6] But on March 16, Loris again turned to Alexander with a request to agree to the closing down for one month of Rumor (Molva) and the St. Petersburg Reports, the former for its extreme liberalism and the latter for its extreme reactionary position. Loris, while also condemning the liberal Russian Courier (Russkii Kur'er) asked permission to limit its punishment to a personal reprimand. Alexander agreed with the comment: "It was about time".[7] In this action, Loris again showed a great desire to appease Alexander; his action by passed the Chief Board as is indicated by the source for Zaionchkovskii's information: the archives of the Emperor. Moreover, Loris' action showed an effort to be even handed in dispensing punishments even as he gave Alexander evidence of his vigilance.

This even handed vigilance, again after Alexander's agreement, was apparent in the banning of retail sale of Order (Poriadok) and the suspension of the Smolensk Messenger (Vestnik) for eight months. The first periodical had published news of a peasant uprising. Loris took the opportunity to warn all editors against printing such delicate news.[8] The offense of the provincial and censored newspaper was more subtle. On the reverse side of the sheet bearing an Imperial Manifesto the editors had printed an advertisement for the publication Laughter and Sin (Smekh i grekh). The governor of the province asked for the penalty because he thought the impropriety was not accidental; he noted that the editors had refused to attend a requiem for the dead Emperor and that the newspaper had contained, a few days later, a printing error in a telegram about Alexander's funeral which changed the words "martyred father" into "father of martyrs." Both periodicals, according to the public communique, were penalized for their "harmful tendencies" but the cases were quite different. In punishing the censored newspaper, Loris made use of an 1862 law unused from 1865 to 1879. That law, used in 1862 against The Contemporary and Russian Word allowed the government to ban a censored periodical for a period up to eight months.[9] Loris' action here became a precedent for future instances of imposition of this unjustifiably harsh punishment on a censored and therefore approved periodical.

Clearly Loris' position in the weeks after the death of Alexander was a difficult one. He hesitated to act independently and yet tried to convey to Alexander III his own determination to restrict the press. Thus, in addition to the actions detailed above, on March 4, he warned editors against making "improper judgments" about the necessity for political changes or imputing lack of patriotism or concern for the people's needs to high officials.[10] Loris' moves were most likely dictated by the hesitation he felt about the fate of his reform proposals, approved in principle by Alexander II just before his death. At a meeting on March 8, 1881, Pobedonostsev had attacked Loris' proposals suggesting that they were a step in the direction of a constitution which in turn would mean the end of Russia.[11] While Alexander postponed any final decision at the time, Loris prepared carefully for the impending decisions on his program. On April 12, 1881 he prepared an extended memorandum for Alexander III which summarized his program for Russia in detail: administrative reform, economic improvement of the condition of the peasants; an end to the poll tax; reforms of the school system and the encouragement of literacy; the election of public representatives to participate in legislative projects; and the establishment of unity of policy among ministers, in effect, the establishment of a prime minister. With respect to the press and literature, Loris proposed revised press legislation that would put the rights and obligations of the press on a legal basis. He would allow publicity and commentaries on social questions while restraining the stimulation of emotions and attacks on personalities.[12] As Zaionchkovskii points out, Loris here repeated much that he had proposed earlier to Alexander II but in greater detail and with some important changes, in particular the recommendation of a united ministry. Clearly Loris was taking up the challenge issued by Pobedonostsev and preparing himself for the imminent denouement.

A special convocation of ministers and advisors was called by Alexander III on April 21, to consider the proposals. Alexander refused, despite the urging of Loris, to allow Valuev and Prince Urusov to be present at this meeting. Loris, in turn, tried to concert his actions with War Minister D. Miliutin and Finance Minister A. Abaza prior to the meeting. At the meeting, Pobedonostsev, to Miliutin's surprise, spoke more moderately than he had at the March 8 meeting. Still, Alexander postponed decision on Loris' proposals. But that same evening, he wrote to

Pobedonostsev indicating his distaste for Loris' policy of pressing for "representative government."[13] Alexander was clearly retreating from his earlier indecisive position, perhaps, as Zaionchkovskii suggests, because he had discovered that the terrorists were small in number and that their violence against his father had been the policy of energetic leaders. In any case, at the next convocation of ministers on April 28, when Alexander himself was not present, Loris and his supporters learned of the imminent publication of a royal manifesto prepared by Pobedonostsev without the knowledge of Loris.[14] Understandably, Loris and his colleagues expressed their dissatisfaction about this act of Alexander, since it indicated Alexander's unwillingness to accept the advice of his ministers. On April 29, Loris offered his resignation; Miliutin deferred his resignation in order to avoid the appearance of a public defiance of the Emperor, but retired in May, 1881 when the Emperor asked him to become governor-general of the Caucases.[15] The manifesto itself, greeted by the Moscow Reports with enthusiasm and by liberal periodicals with unjustified optimism, stated Alexander's devotion to the autocratic principle. It was silent about any of the reform projects Loris had advanced. The enthusiasm of the conservative Moscow Reports was justified. Alexander had chosen his course; he had repudiated the last acts of his father. Ironically, one signal of the new policy was a press circular that prohibited comment about the resignations of Loris, D. Miliutin, and A. Abaza.[16]

Despite the comparative harshness of Loris' treatment of the press in the weeks after Alexander II's death, it is clear that an important element of his program was the effort to establish a government policy towards the periodical press and literature based on law. A memorandum prepared by N. S. Abaza, the head of the Chief Board, dated March 29, 1881 reaffirmed Abaza's preference for "severe legality" over the rumored alternatives, which, he stated, were administrative measures or bribery.[17] The new governors of the press and literature, after Abaza, were not as inclined to abandon the government's administrative authority. Abaza was replaced by Prince P. P. Viazemskii as head of the Chief Board in April, 1881 and then in 1883 the erstwhile liberal of the 1860's and now ardent conservative friend of M. Katkov, E. Feoktistov became head of the Board.[18] Alexander III's mentor in reaction, K. P. Pobodonostsev, the Over-Procurator of the Holy Synod became an important maker of policy towards the press. Reading the press assiduously, even the advertisements, he continually harassed the censorship, insisting upon vigilance and trying to keep the press and literature within desired limits. His reputation is that of an intelligent and certainly articulate critic of representative institutions and the press. Yet Feoktistov, the recipient of many of his incessant denunciations of the press, characterized him as essentially negative in his thinking, a man capable of criticism but not able to offer useful alternative policies. Feoktistov is probably correct in attributing Pobedonostsev's attitude to fear of an inevitable revolution.[19] Another important spokesman of press policy was the Minister of Interior after 1882, Count D. Tolstoy, whose policies as Minister of Education had led Loris-Melikov to ask for his resignation in 1880. Tolstoy replaced Count N. P. Ignat'ev as Minister of Interior; Ignat'ev, who had served under Loris as Minister of State Domains from March, 1881 had replaced Loris after the latter's resignation in April, 1881.[20] Under Ignat'ev, a series of prohibitory circulars began to appear that restricted press comment on delicate subjects, such as pogroms and peasant disturbances.[21] Even Katkov protested bitterly to Pobedonostsev about these restrictions.[22] Under Ignat'ev, sixteen administrative penalties were imposed on periodicals, with Pobedonostsev playing an important role in prodding the Minister. Moreover five publications were banned without any previous warning. Katkov's complaint was correctly addressed.[23]

Ignat'ev was however not content simply to enforce existing restrictions on the press. In the spring of 1882, he worked out a project for a high commission on press affairs that would take charge of the struggle against the "harmful tendency" of the press. He argued that the law allowed only the Senate to close down a periodical permanently and then only after three warnings. To replace the Senate as the supreme judge in such cases, Ignat'ev proposed a commission made up of the ministers of interior, education, invited members as well as the Over-Procurator of the Holy Synod, Pobedonostsev. The Commission, he proposed, would have the power to permit new periodicals as well as the power to ban existing ones. He reasoned that the decisions of this collegiate body would have a greater impact on society than those of the minister of interior alone. While Ignat'ev had secured the approval of Pobedonostsev to this project, he feared opposition in the State Council. Accordingly he was prepared to introduce this project as a temporary measure. But before he could accomplish this task, he was discharged and replaced by Count D. Tolstoy. It is notable however that the new law, confirmed by Alexander on August 27, 1882, was never presented to the State Council in accordance with Ignat'ev's advice. Instead it became law after approval by the Committee of Ministers. In the Committee Tolstoy argued that existing weapons neither forced periodicals to change their tendency nor curbed their popularity. This was the aim of the new rules.[24]

The new rules, known as the Temporary Press Rules, required uncensored periodicals to disclose the names of authors of articles at the request of the government. A second feature of the rules established a special procedure for suspended periodicals that resumed publication. Newspapers (i.e. periodicals issuing more than once a week) would have to present their completely printed edition to censors by 11 P.M. of the evening before issuance. Issuance might be prevented by the censors if they noted anything harmful; they would not have to initiate prosecution. Thus a harsh preliminary censorship was restored for uncensored periodicals that had the misfortune to be suspended. A third provision of the Temporary Rules created a special convocation made up of the ministers of education, interior and justice with the addition of Pobedonostsev. This new body might ban a periodical, censored or freed, for an indefinite period and further, might prohibit an editor or publisher from practicing his profession. These rules, which diverged seriously from the 1865 Press Laws, gave more unrestricted power to the administration than it had ever had before. They serve as evidence of the great threat officials perceived from the periodical press. The authority this law gave officials supplemented the powers under the "Exceptional Laws" of August, 1881, to ban periodicals indefinitely whenever an emergency situation of "extraordinary protection" existed within their locality.[25] The government had responded to the request of publishers for greater legality with an increase in arbitrary power. Certainly Chicherin had not contemplated a regime in which a publisher or editor might be deprived of his livelihood indefinitely without benefit of a court trial.[26]

These measures were supplemented by additional restrictions. From 1881 to 1893 inclusively, 227 circulars were sent to censors and publishers restricting comment on sensitive topics. Outbreaks of violence or the details of the arrest of political criminals might not be referred to in the press.[27] A number of circulars dealt with the great famine of 1891-1892 and forbade the appearance of requests for assistance unless these had been approved beforehand by the local police.[28] One circular prohibited remarks on the 25th anniversary of the 1865 press laws in 1890.[29] Political questions such as the implications of the Franco-Russian trade treaty had to be treated with extraordinary moderation, to use the jargon of the censorship.[30] One circular, in 1884, would allow only that information published by a government department about its measures to be printed, a throwback to the preliminary censorship under Nicholas I.[31] The government supplemented these restrictions with efforts to purchase the services of periodicals and publishers, against the advice of the head of the Chief Board from 1883, E. Feoktistov. According to Feokstistov, Tolstoy received authority from Alexander III to spend up to 20,000 rubles yearly on such efforts. Sources indicate that in 1883 Alexander authorized Tolstoy to spend up to 6,000 rubles a year for secret expenditures relating to the press.[32] In addition, in 1881, Alexander agreed to subsidize a newspaper through the local government administration. By 1892 the newspaper, primarily for the peasantry, had achieved a circulation of 30,000[33] The "Black Cabinet" of the Postal Department continued to open private mail; folios containing secretly opened letters

94

number sixteen for the years 1883-1884 and even the letters of a member of the State Council were secretly opened by officials in 1891.[34] All these measures were rooted in the government's fear of radicalism.

The aim of the restrictive press legislation, according to Feoktistov, was to end the "leniency" towards the press which had appeared in the late 1870s.[35] Feoktistov's comment is perhaps more accurately a description of the mood of officials than it is of the circumstances that produced their antagonism towards the press. The government was frightened and thought that a restrictive policy would help secure the autocracy. In fact, their plans did tame the press. Even if Feoktistov's argument is rejected, as well as his contention that during his tenure as head of the Chief Board, "really serious" literature was unaffected by the censorship's campaign against malign influences in journalism, it is clear that writers and journalists had to exercise extreme caution during the period from 1881 to 1894.

Nevertheless, journalism continued to grow in importance during these years. The circulation of Russian periodicals grew as did the number of periodicals, despite the sizeable investment of from 400,000 to 500,000 rubles required to begin a newspaper, and their dependence on advertisements and sales for income. Suvorin, the enterprising publisher of the conservative New Times, used his newspaper as the basis for the establishment of a publishing empire that made him a millionaire. An innovator, he was the first newspaper publisher to use illustrations and in 1877 he imported the first high speed rotary press into Russia. He was also the first to introduce the use of a press run by electricity.[36] The annual expenditures of the liberal Russian Reports grew from 186,000 annually in the period from 1883 to 1887 to 246,000 from 1888 to 1892.[37] These signs of growth were paralleled by a growth in circulation; in 1881, the illustrated popular Field (Niva) had a circulation of from 59,000 to 62,500 while the most popular uncensored newspaper was The Voice with a circulation of from 18,000 to 26,000.[38] By 1884 Field was reaching over 110,000 readers.[39] In fact the new, so called, "boulevard" or "yellow" press that catered to public interest in scandal and gossip, a new mass circulation journalism, was appearing during these years. By 1886, the most popular uncensored newspapers were these "yellow" journals represented by the Petersburg Gazette (Peterburgskaia Gazeta) with a circulation of 22,000. The New Times, which its critics described as a "yellow" sheet had a circulation that year of from 20,000 to 26,000. Thick journals like the Messenger of Europe trailed behind with 6,100 although the new thick Russian Thought (Russkaia Mysl') had a circulation of over 10,000 that year.[40] By 1888 the "yellow" newspaper Moscow Leaves published by the self-taught entrepreneur N. I. Pastukhov, had reached a circulation of from 30,000 to 35,000. The uncensored periodical Light achieved in

1889 a circulation of over 60,000.[41] The government was very concerned by what a censorship report in 1894 called the "extraordinarily powerful" growth of the periodical press. The report implied that the reason for the government's displeasure was the abuse of freedom by the press and actions "contrary in the majority of cases" to the government's expectations.[42] What these actions were is indicated by a circular of June, 1881: the invention or distortion of news and the failure of ensuing corrections to undo the harm; the "systematic" appearance of sharp criticism and unfounded news or rumors that were intended to stimulate dissatisfaction with official measures.[43] But even without these "abuses," the government would have been concerned. A publishing revolution was taking place as a new larger audience for journalism was appearing in the Empire during this period.

The publishing revolution affected books as well. In 1882 the number of censored non-periodical works issued was 5,158 in close to 15,000,000 copies. A decade later, the number of works published was 8,535 in close to 22,000,000 copies. In both St. Petersburg and Moscow the increase in censored titles was greater than that for uncensored titles, an indication that the growth affected mostly shorter books accessible to a less educated audience.[44] Moreover, the number of titles published in Russian grew 80% from 1882 to 1891, a percentage exceeded only by Hebrew publications and those in Eastern languages.[45] The new audience was indeed a mass audience, a conclusion verified by the increase in the number of reading rooms from 640 in 1882 to 850 on January 1, 1892.[46] The old bugbear of the censorship, the impressionable reader from the lower classes was becoming fact during these years. This mythical reader had justified repression of literature and the press in past years. But just as the old myth was becoming reality during Alexander III's reign, a new myth appeared to justify the repressive policies of the censorship. This was the myth that the government had maintained a lenient policy towards the press during the late 1870s, and that in turn this leniency had helped produce the terrorist attacks that led to the death of Alexander II. In fact, as has been shown, leniency was an exception until the administration of Loris-Melikov. Whatever the justification, the government tried to restrict the growth of the press and control its content from 1881.[47]

One method of obstruction used by the government was to permit fewer new periodicals. In 1882 new periodicals composed almost 8% of the periodicals published; by 1891 the percentage had been reduced to 5½%.[48] Another method used was to encourage the reduction in the number of periodicals of "general" interest while permitting more specialized periodicals to appear. In 1881, 153 of the total of 531 periodicals published in the Empire were general. By 1890 the number of general periodicals had dropped slightly to 149 but now 697 periodicals were being published.[49] These general periodicals were most likely to suffer penalties;

Rozenberg noted that 173 periodicals received a total of 715 penalties during the entire period from 1865 to 1904.[50] Another weapon against the uncensored periodical press was the temporary ban, a penalty which after 1882 Temporary Press Rules, might lead to subjection to preliminary censorship. During Alexander III's reign fifteen periodicals ended publication. Eight publications closed because they were subjected to preliminary censorship after being temporarily banned; seven were banned completely as a result of a decision of the special convocation of ministers. Nine of these closings occurred during the years 1883-1885.[51] Moreover, from 1882 to 1894, eighteen censored periodicals were temporarily banned for their harmful tendencies, as the government made use of the power given it by censorship rules of 1862, unused after 1865 until 1879.[52] Even though the number of administrative penalties imposed on periodicals declined from 94 in the period 1880 to 1884 to 60 in the following five year period and 48 from 1890 to 1894, the threat to journalism was indeed a formidable one during Alexander III's reign.[53]

The means used by the government to control the periodical press were ingenious and various. It prevented the advertisement of lower subscription rates for students and school teachers.[54] It supervised the personnel and book lists of free reading rooms from 1884. By 1894 it had banned from these institutions all issues of Notes of the Fatherland from 1867 to 1884, Russian Thought from 1880 to 1881, The Contemporary from 1856 to 1866, and the Russian Word from 1857 to 1866.[55] Apart from its examination of every uncensored periodical before issuance, the government might penalize a periodical in any of the following ways: it might delay or destroy an offending issue, an infrequent practice with newspapers; it might prohibit retail sale for an indefinite period, a very costly and serious penalty;[56] it might prohibit the publication of private advertisements for two to eight months, again a costly punishment;[57] it might suspend a periodical for up to three months for violating prohibitory circulars; it might issue warnings to uncensored periodicals, three of which could bring about suspension for up to six months; it might issue oral warnings to editors; or after 1882, it could ban an uncensored periodical indefinitely without any prior warnings and without specifying the offending article, or prevent an editor or publisher from pursuing his career, and subject a suspended publication to an onerous preliminary censorship for an indefinite time after it was renewed.[58] The censored press, particularly the provincial press, might be required to send their issues to Moscow for examination before publication if there were no local censorship committee; and has been indicated, under the authority of the Temporary Censorship Rules of 1862, a censored periodical might be suspended for up to eight months for exhibiting a harmful tendency.[59] An additional threat to periodicals was the power given to local governors in provinces under "reinforced protection" to ban a periodical temporarily without explanation.

Finally, apart from the authority of the Committee of Ministers under the June 1872 law, the residual authority of the Emperor to ban any periodical was available to the press authorities. Indeed this was a formidable array of weapons against the press. Yet the press survived and grew in importance.

Prince Meschcherskii, publisher of the ardently pro-government The Citizen (Grazhdanin) often came into conflict with the censorship despite the subsidy it received from the government.[60] In fact, Mescherskii's newspaper was banned five times in the period up to 1904, a total surpassed only by The Voice.[61] In part, Meschcherskii's difficulties stemmed from intra-governmental intrigues, and in part from his vulgar and scandalous articles. Thus, in 1881, Ignat'ev asked him to compose an article on the zemskii sobor, an institution which Ignat'ev admired; this article led Pobedonostsev to reprimand the publisher soon after. Meshcherskii apparently also assumed that his personal standing with Alexander III exempted him from the requirements imposed on other periodicals; indeed, Mescherskii quotes the Emperor as having advised him to write whatever he wished so long as it was proper. These vague limits were violated frequently by the publisher.[62] Another periodical systematically harassed by the censorship was the illustrated Newspaper of Gatsuk which had a circulation of about 12,000 in 1886.[63] Warnings, admonitions and arrests abounded in its history and in 1887 the authorities noted that this uncensored newspaper had been forced to revise practically every issue before it was allowed to circulate.[64]

The fate of The Voice was even less pleasant. Distinguished by the fact that during its twenty years of existence, it received more warnings than any other periodical, 20, its destiny was decided by the Temporary Press Rules of 1882. By 1882, it had already received two warnings after a suspension in 1881.[65] The next occasion for a penalty was the appearance of three articles which in passing criticized the government's excessive precautions against unreliable groups and defended the principle of zemstvo control of elementary schools. Pobedonostsev, an advocate of clerical control of elementary schools, was of course antagonized, and Count Tolstoy, new Minister of Interior, was reputed to harbor an old grudge against the newspaper for its attacks on his educational policies in the 1870s. Now these two high officials were members of the special convocation empowered in 1882 to subject banned periodicals to prior censorship. The unfortunate newspaper soon after received a third warning and when renewed was required to present its complete edition to the censors on the evening before the day of publication. Kraevskii, the publisher, found this condition intolerable for a daily newspaper, as one must suspect it was intended to be. He closed the newspaper in 1883.[66]

The radical Notes of the Fatherland also ceased publication

in this period. Indeed, Feoktistov's wife is reported to have said that her husband had been appointed to head the Chief Board for this express purpose. But she spoke figuratively; Feoktistov's mission was the more general task of establishing order and decorum in the periodical press and in the process he restricted the collusion between the editors and censors that had allowed the periodical to maintain its existence. In 1881 censors had noted incriminating articles in a number of issues and one censor had even recommended arrest of an issue for expressing, in a novel, a pro-worker and anti-employer attitude. In this case however the official patrons of the journal saved it.[67] A censor described an article by Krivenko in the October, 1882 issue as presenting the view that the rural bourgeoisie were treating the common people cruelly. The censor also saw in the article a criticism of the prosecution of sedition for involving innocent people. The censorship committee decided that the article was not extremely harmful but forwarded a report on the case to the Chief Board as an indication of the journal's direction.[68] The journal continued and although it received warnings, it was often allowed to exclude offensive articles. But by 1884 the number of subscribers was falling. Further, Saltykov-Shchedrin decided to halt the printing of his "Contemporary Idyll", a satirical section he had been printing in the journal.[69] And, early that year, the government discovered proof that a few of the regular contributors to the journal had some connection with emigres. One of the contributors in fact was arrested in January, 1884.[70] The combination of events proved fatal to the journal. At this juncture, Tolstoy's Director of Police, V. K. Pleve, prepared a memorandum for the Minister naming the journal as a prime example of the hostile press which he regarded as a threat to the government. Tolstoy, as Feoktistov notes with disgust, was fearful of public reaction, but was persuaded and in April, 1884, the special convocation closed the journal.[71]

This action had some aspects of a vendetta, of a vengeance, long postponed either for lack of opportunity or will. Tolstoy recognized the challenge he was issuing to educated society and hesitated before closing to the journal. It is important to note that the journal was in fact losing its audience and thus its authority just before the government acted. The weakness of the journal did not necessarily precipitate the government's action but it certainly was a factor in persuading Tolstoy to strike. In this period, the censorship, equipped with the special powers conferred by the Temporary Press Rules of 1882 and urged on by Pobedonestsov, struck out at many periodicals, especially liberal periodicals. The liberal Country (Strana) was placed under preliminary censorship after it was suspended.[72] Moscow Telegraph Moskovskii Telegraf) was a particular devil for Pobedonostsev. It caught the attention of censors twenty times in 1881. But in 1883, soon after censors reported on an editorial that called for a renewal of public life and an article about the struggle against reaction, the special convocation moved. The newspaper was banned in March, 1883.[73]

On the other hand, a few liberal periodicals survived this repressive era and the penalties. The liberal newspaper Russian Courier (Russkii Kur'er) published by the champagne manufacturer Lanin, was accused in 1881 of favoring representative government and criticizing arbitrariness in the censorship.[74] In 1883 censors reported on articles on seven occasions. Among these articles were discussions of peasant resettlement, a criticism of the police, and a description of Turgenev's funeral that expressed, the censors thought, dissatisfaction with government decrees.[75] In the course of its harassment by the government, the newspaper received six warnings including one in 1881 for suggesting that zemstvo representatives should be consulted in deciding the problem of the peasant's redemption payments.[76] Despite a number of suspensions, the newspaper lived on until 1889 when it finally ceased publication after being subjected to preliminary censorship.[77] No suspensions but frequent changing of articles to avoid warnings characterized the history of the liberal Messenger of Europe in this period of reaction. Twice in 1881 the journal was allowed to exclude offending places in articles, and again in 1882 and 1883. In the latter cases, censors proposed arrest of the volumes but the articles ultimately appeared.[78]

The independent but progressive periodical Russian Thought (Russkaia Mysl') had even more difficulty with the censorship. The police described the editor, Professor V. A. Gol'tsev of Moscow University as an "extreme radical" and in 1885 accused the journal of seeking political changes through criticism of government actions.[79] Indeed, the publisher was aware of this suspicion especially after the journal became in 1884 a legatee of Notes of the Fatherland and picked up 4,500 of the 7000 subscribers to the radical journal after it was banned. To allay suspicion the publisher sent more important articles to the Moscow chairman in proof, thus turning the formally uncensored journal into a censored journal in fact.[80] This procedure, adopted in 1884, merely regularized a policy that had been in effect before. Exclusions or revisions had been forced on the journal in 1881 and 1882; in 1884, 1886 and 1889 the journal went through the same experience.[81] The journal survived however.

Survival was of course not sufficient to produce an independent journalism. But in the light of the government's successful effort to control the press in this period, to create what Zaionchkovskii describes as a uniformity of thought in literature and the periodical press, the survival of independent journals was important.[82] Zaionchkovskii acknowledges that in the short run the government's efforts were successful; Russian writers were tamed.[83] But even a tamed journalism managed, by

100

its discussions, to bring about modifications in the 1890 zemstvo reform, changes which made the law less unpalatable than the original proposal of the minister of interior. In fact, the original proposal for reform of the zemstvos was posed by A. D. Pazukhin in 1885 in an article in Katkov's Russian Messenger (Russkii Vestnik).[84] This success of journalism may have been the result of Tolstoy's sensitivity to public opinion, a sensitivity attested to by Feoktistov. In general, journalists muted their critical attitudes towards government policies during this period. The dangers of openness were too great.[85]

What threats to the government and society did the censorship discover during this era of repression? Political violations uncovered by censors were for the most part concerned with foreign policy,[86] educational policy and school disorders,[87] and claims on behalf of the zemstvos for a greater role in the making of policy.[88] In 1888 the Moscow committee considered reports on 28 articles that had appeared dealing with political questions such as German policy in Poland, the policies of the ministry of finance, and zemstvo legislation.[89] A censor's report in 1893 noted that a comparatively significant number of works had been forbidden because of their tendentious criticisms of the government.[90] Public interest in politics had been stimulaged by the assassination of Alexander II and as a result short popular tracts that blamed the Poles, the Baltic Germans, the Jews, the former War Minister D. Miliutin, and Loris-Melikov for the Emperor's death were being submitted to the censorship and forbidden.[91] The increased interest kept alive old problems for the censors such as the depiction of the peasant's condition in "dark colors". Censors forbade such descriptions, and circulars in 1882 and 1883 banned discussion of resettlement of the peasants or redivision of the land.[92] New problems for the censors appeared also: in particular, the tendentious depiction of the condition of factory workers and the description of the famine of 1891-1892.[93] The evidence is clear that the repressive policies of this period required perpetual vigilance by the censors.

Another old concern of the censorship was the rivalry between Baltic Germans and Russians,[94] as well as the expression of Polish nationalism.[95] The new Estonian and Latvian nationalism which produced works attacking the Germans and sometimes Russians also occupied the censors.[96] Another new nationalism was Armenian; in 1886 the censors reported that the government's decision to close Armenian schools in the Caucases had stimulated a large number of Armenian publications which had been forbidden because of their sharp tone.[97] The policy of Russification pursued by Alexander III's government produced new enemies for the government which now began to abandon the image of impartiality it had cultivated in earlier years. Old enemies remained. From 1882 to 1892, the St. Petersburg censorship rejected over 32% of the 696 Ukrainian manuscripts it examined. The reasons were either the glorification of the Ukrainian past or the presentation of an unfavorable picture of the Ukrainian present.[98] With respect to another old enemy, the Jews, censors protected the status quo. They prohibited a number of works that justified anti-Jewish pogroms;[99] at the same time, they banned works that defended Jews against various charges or sought full citizenship and greater rights for Jews.[100] Jewish chauvinism was prohibited[101] but the periodical The Sunrise (Voskhod), devoted to the Jewish question, was allowed to appear despite seven warnings, a temporary ban in 1891, and the censor's judgment in 1891 that it represented an unreliable tendency.[102] Nevertheless, in Warsaw and Odessa in particular, censorship officials clearly showed an anti-Jewish bias; in Warsaw, the committee noted that the anti-Jewish newspaper Rola was being condemned by other Polish publications for presenting a "clear" picture of Semitic influence in Warsaw and expressing ideas familiar to Poles acquainted with Jews;[103] the Odessa censor suggested that the New Russian Telegraph (Novorossiiskii Telegraf) deserved lenient treatment because it was devoted to the state and opposed to the Jews.[104] The development of this attitude among officials made the task of censorship more difficult. Anti-Jewish attitudes might produce turmoil and destroy the appearance of harmony that the government desired. However, the promotion of Russian nationalism clearly took precedence in this period.

Nationalism, even Russian nationalism, threatened the stability of Russian society. The censors considered rationalism a major threat also. In 1894 the censorship reported that it had prohibited 24 works in the previous year for their rationalism, their belief in evolution, or their challenge to religious and ethical ideas.[105] A translation of Lester Ward's Dynamic Sociology was destroyed by the censorship in 1891 for propagating materialistic and non-religious views of man.[106] Brandes' Main Currents of Literature was also destroyed, in 1888, while an exposition of Schopenhauer's philosophy was expurgated before publication.[107] Socialistic works such as John Stuart Mill's Chapters on Socialism and an exposition of Karl Marx's teachings were banned, the latter possibly because it was to be published in the provincial city of Odessa.[108] But the government was more ambivalent in its treatment of less overt and more indirect criticisms of social conditions. It permitted volume II of the radical Shchegolev's History of Social Systems after the work had been arrested and considered by the Committee of Ministers.[109] Censors took note, but no more, of Zola's "cynical" undermining of the family, in their opinion, in his "Pot-bouille".[110] Their reaction to the appearance of Zola's The Village and Gleb Uspenskii's Power of the Land and The Mother of the Land was to advise editors against reprinting these stories in their newspapers after a few had already reprinted the works.[111] Thus even the very repressive censorship regime under Alexander III had difficulty preventing the appearance of critical works on politics and society.

This evidence makes it difficult to accept the contention of the Soviet author Baluev that the periodical press confined itself to trivialities during this period and avoided the discussion of important contemporary problems. He himself notes that articles on the peasants appeared as well as articles dealing with the zemstvos, the universities, and factory workers.[112] Even the nationality question was presented in the press with a slant opposed to extreme Russian nationalism.[113] The criticism was muted and indirect; the fabled "Aesopian language" had to be used and allusions remained a substitute for open statements. But Russian journalists were used to these circumlocutions even though they thought them unjust and criticized them.[114] Contrary to Baluev, it appears that the press did deal with important political and social questions, and that the censorship did not suppress all such discussions. Certainly the censorship was more restrictive than it had been under Loris, and even under Timashev. But the Russian reader, skilled in reading "between the lines" did receive some pale image of the problems in Russian society.

Censors remained vigilant guardians of sexual morality[115] and "exposes" of wrong-doing by public figures were carefully restricted.[116] In fact, "exposes" of officials virtually disappeared from the censorship documents, a notable byproduct of the repressive atmosphere of the period. But the government was resilient in the face of international and national fame. Leo Tolstoy was allowed to publish Kreutzer Sonata, his tale of adultery and murder, in his Collected Works although the tale was forbidden in Odessa. Pobedonostsev himself regretfully wrote to Feoktistov that it would be hypocritical to forbid the work because it reflected life.[117] That Tolstoy's fame rather than his verisimilitude saved his work is indicated by Alexander's reversal of his judgment on the author's work Power of Darkness which he wanted to forbid. Although the work could not be performed as a play, it was ultimately permitted as a printed work.[118] In 1893 a censor noted that if the article by Tolstoy he had examined were forbidden, it would circulate in lithograph. For this reason, and because of its comparative innocence, he proposed to permit the article.[119] The less famous writer N. Leskov was less fortunate and in 1889, volume 6 of his Complete Works was destroyed because it dealt with corruption in the lower clergy.[120] Spiritualist works and expositions of Schismatic beliefs were forbidden,[121] as well as a historical sketch of the Old Belief by A. S. Prugavin. Some parts of Leo Tolstoy's professions of his unorthodox faith were also forbidden despite his fame.[122] In general it would seem that the special force of the repression during this period was directed at political and social threats to the status quo rather than threats to religion and public mores.

The concern with politics appeared most important in the censorship of historical works. Gibbon's <u>Decline and Fall of the Roman Empire</u>, was permitted in translation in 1883 although the censors considered it to be a destructive work.[123] Morley's work on Diderot and the Encyclopedists was permitted even though censors noted its rationalism and atheism which they believed subverted monarchy.[124] Michelet's study of the Directory was permitted in Russian although with exclusions, and Fyfe's history of the 19th century Europe was permitted with only a comment by the censors that it showed "deep esteem to the French Revolution."[125] When a work dealt with Russia, the censors were less tolerant. Volume II of Bilbasov's <u>History of Catherine II</u> was forbidden after the first volume had been permitted with expurgations. His volume on Diderot in Russia was eventually permitted although it was first threatened with arrest.[126] An article in <u>Russian Antiquity</u> (<u>Russkaia Starina</u>) on L. V. Dubel't, a Chief of Staff of the Gendarmerie under Nicholas I was expurgated before it was printed as was the <u>Diary</u> of his contemporary, the professor and censor A. Nikitenko, and the recollections of the former Minister of Interior, P. A. Valuev.[127] A short historical note in the <u>Russian Archive</u> (<u>Russkii Arkhiv</u>) about Katkov led to arrest of the issue in 1890 and another issue that same year appeared only after exclusion of an article on the coup that brought Catherine II to the throne.[128]

The Foreign Censorship continued its defense against foreign works that either presented a secular ethic or expressed an unfriendly attitude towards Russia, tendencies it noted in foreign literature.[129] The work of the Foreign Censorship grew in this period as the number of titles as well as volumes imported grew. In 1892 the Foreign Censorship examined 15,138 titles including periodicals, in over 7 million volumes.[130] This number of titles, which exceeded the number of titles published within the Empire, diminished during the following year to 12,336 including periodicals, but the number of volumes imported rose to 9 million.[131] About 6% of the titles examined were prohibited in 1892; if expurgated works are included as rejected works, the percentage is just over 10%. The rejection rate was highest for Polish works, 50%, but only about 10% for French and German works. German works, composing over 40% of the titles examined, constituted [132] the single largest language group of imports that were examined. The rejection rate dropped to 3% in 1893 as the number of titles imported decreased; if expurgated titles are considered as rejected titles, the rejection rate dropped slightly from that of the previous year to just under 10%. Again Polish works predominated among rejected works. German titles remained the single largest group of imports and the rejection rate for these, 7%, was slightly lower than the 7.9% for French works.[133] What seems especially significant about these figures is that the number of foreign titles imported into the Empire had not increased significantly from the 1880s. Neither had the number of copies imported. The rejection rate for this period was high, higher than during the most of the 1870s. But even during this most repressive period the educated class still had available to them most foreign works.[134]

The great growth in the reading public was reflected however in the publishing figures for the Empire. The number of copies of censored works issued in Russia, excluding periodicals,[135] rose from about 15 million in 1882 to about 22 million in 1891. The number of uncensored titles published also grew; in St. Petersburg in 1891, 1624 titles, excluding periodicals, appeared while ten years before, only 947 titles had appeared. During the decade from 1882 to 1891, a total of 16,476 uncensored titles were published in the Empire, apart from periodicals.[136] The average censored work was published in more copies than an uncensored work but it was shorter. In 1884, the average censored title in St. Petersburg appeared in 2,977 copies while the uncensored work appeared in about 1,115 copies.[137] By 1888, the average for censored titles in St. Petersburg had fallen to 2,899 while the average for uncensored titles had fallen to 864.[138] To generalize about these figures, is difficult. Nor can the reading audience for these books be described precisely. On the basis of a study made in 1900, cited by B. Esin, which showed that about one third of the literate workers in a Moscow factory read newspapers, it may be estimated that about 8 million of Russia's literate 26.6 million in 1897 constituted the potential audience for these works.[139]

The increase in the number of publications of course increased the work of the censor. In 1884, the St. Petersburg censor, on the average read a total of 4,034 sheets a year; this total was made up of 513 sheets for censored and 1,167 sheets for uncensored periodicals and 727 sheets for censored and 1,627 sheets for uncensored works.[140] By 1886 the average total had increased to 4,703 sheets,[141] by 1890 to 4,841 sheets,[142] and in 1892 to 5,391 sheets.[143] Of the censored manuscripts and proofs that the St. Petersburg censor read, he rejected a small percentage. In 1881, he rejected less than 2%;[144] in 1882 the rate of rejection was about 2½%[145] in 1884, the rejection rate was 2%;[146] in 1888 the rate was about 2½%;[147] and in 1890 the rate was just over 2%.[148] The rate of rejection in Warsaw and in the Caucases was about the same.[149] In the ten years from 1882 to 1891, the St. Petersburg committee examined 37,496 manuscripts and rejected 759 or 2% while the Moscow committee rejected 5.2% or 456 manuscripts out of the 8,754 it examined in that period. The Warsaw Committee rejected about 2% or 346 manuscripts of the 17,987 it examined.[150] This general rate of prohibition had some exceptions. Thus, over 32% of the 696 Ukrainian manuscripts examined in that period in St. Petersburg were rejected. Moreover the figures on prohibitions do not give the precise number of works, either censored or uncensored, that censors returned to publishers with the advice that they be revised to pass the censors. In 1892 a report noted that publishers of a number of books had easily acceded to the persuasive arguments of the censors. The report listed about eight works including Skabichevskii's *History of Recent Russian Literature*, Tarde's *Law of Imitation*, and Paul Bourget's *Physiology of Contemporary Love*.[151] It is very likely that the censors could be even more persuasive with publishers of censored works. But the statistics do make it clear that the overwhelming majority of the manuscripts and proofs that censors read during this period of extreme repression passed the censorship. Of course, both authors and publishers prepared their works knowing that censors would have to pass on them. The radical Shelgunov complained bitterly in 1888 that the editors of the journal *Russian Thought* were more severe than the official censors.[152] Cautious editors and writers undoubtedly served as unofficial aides to censors in the task of making Russian literature innocent. Nevertheless it would be wrong to ignore the fact that the overwhelming majority of works presented to censors passed official examination.

The new audience for literature was a less educated audience. The fact that the greater increase came in censored volumes would support this conclusion. Other confirmation comes from the fact that in 1886 the largest group of forbidden works were those designated for the common people. Prohibition came for a variety of reasons ranging from tendentiousness, socialism, obscenity, to slander or immorality.[153] During the period from 1882 to 1891 the number of public reading rooms grew from 640 to 850 and the number of bookstores from 1204 to 1684.[154] Despite the government's caution about permitting the opening of presses and bookstores, presses and bookstores multiplied. Apparently there were so many "reliable" people around to run these establishments that the government found it impossible to reject their petitions.[155] Still the government maintained a close watch on these purveyors of books. It maintained a special censorship for works performed in the popular theaters and from 1884 it maintained a list of works that could not be included in public libraries.[156] As indicated the work of the average censor increased during the period from 1881 to 1894. The government made some effort to increase the complement of the censorship office to accommodate the increasing burdens of censors. In 1882 the number of officials in the Chief Board was 16 with ten additional persons directly working with them and 75 officials in organizations subordinate to the Chief Board, a total of 101. By 1891 the Chief Board included 13 officials, 12 additional personnel and 89 officials subordinate to the Chief Board, or a total of 114. But the Chief Board, instead of attributing the increase to the increased number of publications, felt called upon to offer another explanation of the increase: the subordination in April, 1883 of the Caucases censorship to the Chief Board and the establishment of inspectors in Vilna, Kiev, Odessa, and Riga.[157] In fact, the size of the censorship establishment had increased slightly over 10% in the ten year period while the increase in the number of censored non-periodical works was over 60% in that same period.[158] To these figures for censorship personnel should be added the numerous provincial officials whose task it was to censor provincial newspapers. In general an overworked censorship establishment was faced with the enormous task of supervising an ever growing quantity of printed material.

How successful were the censors in their performance? The evidence is convincing that the censors were very effective. Still, all they could do was muffle writers, not silence them completely. For example, an article in the Russian Reports on the occasion of its 25th anniversary shows the cautious and allusive, yet understandable language that journalists used to convey their principles. In stating the goals of the newspaper, the article listed progress in culture and citizenship, the spread of education, patriotism but not chauvinism, the improvement of the condition of the peasantry through credit, the lowering of their tax burden and technological improvements, esteem to the courts, adherence to the reforms of Alexander II, and legality. The import of this statement was clear: the newspaper was an advocate of liberal reform. In 1906, after abolition of the censorship, the editors could be more explicit. At that time they proclaimed their adherence to freedom of the press, of conscience, and of assembly and popular representation.[159] But no alert reader in 1888 would have erred in interpreting the newspaper's elliptical presentation of its position. The censorship indeed merely prevented the implicit from becoming explicit. Or to use the words of Stasiulevich in a letter to Kavelin in June, 1882, all that appeared in print was translated from oral and open Russian to written and therefore censored Russian. He added that if everyone wrote what he thought, then indeed they "would always appear very original, almost genius-like."[160] But the day of frank and candid printed Russian was far off. Alexander III's repressive censorship regime was successful to that extent.

Chapter VIII   Censorship in the Reign of Nicholas II:
                                    1894-1905

In 1894, after the unexpected death of his father, Nicholas II came to the throne. His conservatism soon brought him into conflict with a part of the public which, with increasing boldness, sought political and social change. With respect to the censorship, this boldness took the form of petitions from writers, even from the Academy of Sciences, for some relaxation of the censorship. The unrest, of which these petitions, uncommon in the past, were a symbol, led the government finally to reconsider the press laws. On the eve of Bloody Sunday, January 9, 1905, a special convocation to examine the press laws was established. The convocation recommended changes. But even before it completed its work, Nicholas, under pressure of the revolution, agreed to relax the censorship regulations. Revolution extracted from him the concessions that petitions and pleas had not.

The continuity between the regimes of Alexander III and Nicholas II was not complete. Actually much change occurred in the censorship. In 1895, I. G. Goremykin replaced I. N. Durnovo as Minister of Interior and in turn was replaced by D. S. Sipiagin in 1899. Sipiagin was assassinated in 1902 and V. K. Pleve replaced him in that year. Feoktistov, who had headed the Chief Board from 1883 was replaced by M. P. Solov'ev in 1896 on Pobedonostsev's recommendation. Solov'ev lasted until 1900 when he lost his position because a newspaper incorrectly stated that the Dowager Empress Maria Fedorovna had given birth instead of the Empress Alexandra Fedorovna. The new chief was Prince N. V. Shakhovskoi who, on the basis of his experience as head of the St. Petersburg committee planned to improve the lot of the press. But within two years he lost his position and was replaced by a professor of law at Moscow University, N. A. Zverev.[1] The turnover was indicative that not all was satisfactory in the censorship office from the point of view of the government.

A clear expression of governmental dissatisfaction was a lengthy memorandum prepared by a former member of the Council of the Chief Board, F. P. Elenev. It was printed abroad by Russian emigres. Elenev had been a contributor to Notes of the Fatherland under the pseudonym Skaldin. As a member of the 1869 Urusov press commission, he had made the radical proposal to eliminate the preliminary censorship for all works except those designated for the common people. Thirty years later he was equally radical in his proposals and equally cynical about the effectiveness of the censorship. His indictment of the press and literature was based on the assumption that the right to express oneself publicly on public questions should be restricted to those certified by the government. Further, he doubted the complete effectiveness of the changes he proposed; to "compel literature to be moral, conservative, and patriotic, not to permit it to avoid by stubborn silence all that might improve morals, raise the spirit and strengthen the force of the state..requires other forces, positive ones, which would reeducate our society."[2] But although this transformation of Russian society was desirable, Elenev clearly thought the goal impossible, certainly in the near future. The ideal of Koz'ma Prutkov, the fictional advocate of uniformity of thought, remained unattainable for Tsarist officials. For this reason, the major part of Elenev's memorandum was devoted to recounting the evils of Russian literature and the remedies.

The major evil was the widespread opposition literature, and he assigned responsibility, of course, to writers, editors, and publishers but also to incapable censors. The prime culprit for Elenev was the Jew, even "fictional" converts, who to implement their conspiratorial aim to acquire dominion in Europe spread their poison secretly; they corrupted morality, and spread atheism and cosmopolitanism through literature while their brothers acquired money to further their aims.[3] True to the conventions of anti-Semites, Elenev coupled this awesome picture of Jewish power with a low opinion of the Russian public which "even in the capitals (lacked) free intellectual force to conduct good literary, political, or general educational publications."[4] But, again true to the conventions, he saw only a minority of the public as taken in by the conspiracy and the spirit of opposition. This minority, the young and those who would like to be thought young, constituted the audience for "progressive" periodicals who in turn admired these "maniacs."[5] Among the specific evils Elenev noted were the presence of publishers whose sole motive was profit and who often were uneducated;[6] the government's ill-advised treatment of the privilege of publishing a periodical as if it were a property right instead of a precious and dangerous privilege;[7] the concentration of ownership of periodicals;[8] the unsuitability of public warnings as a device to restrain the press;[9] and the low abilities of provincial censors.[10] In the course of detailing his indictment of literature, Elenev disclosed two rarely stated principles of the censorship. Bewailing the large quantity of harmful books, he noted that if the Chief Board brought to the Committee of Ministers all the harmful uncensored works that were published, the Committee would be swamped. Accordingly, the Chief Board brought only the most extreme cases to the attention of the Committee.[11] The implication of this statement was clear; the particular harm of a work was judged in the context of what was being printed. Since no fixed rule could be applied for most cases, the impermissible in one year or decade might become permissible on another occasion simply because the ideas the work expressed had become common in the interim. Another characteristic of the censorship disclosed by Elenev emerged in his negative reference to those who would protest decisions to prohibit works; "only those readers who are incorrigibly corrupted by this (evil) literature" would complain. By this remark Elenev implied that the fear of public reaction had restricted the government's use of prohibitory measures against literature and the press.[12]

Elenev's solutions combined one old idea with some new, radical proposals. He would place in charge of the censorship an individual with close ties to writers who could influence them and direct writers and publishers with private but clear admonitions.[13] He combined this old idea with a proposal to transform the right to publish a periodical into a personal and untransferable right except with government permission. Further, he would end the legal distinctions between publisher and editor and require special reliability of the former. Public warnings would be replaced by private admonitions backed by the right of the special convocation of ministers to ban a periodical. While publishers might seek monetary support from shareholders, these arrangements would not be allowed to affect the judgments of the press office. No monetary bond would be required of publishers; instead a 10% impost would be established based on the price of each copy sold. The impost could be forgiven by the government for deserving periodicals; thus governmental favor would become a direct source of profit to publishers. Further, Elenev proposed to end preliminary censorship for all periodicals, including provincial periodicals, except those published in the numerous national languages of the peoples of the Empire.[14] Finally Elenev proposed some formal changes in the administration of the censorship, eliminating the St. Petersburg committee, enlarging the Chief Board and increasing its budget for its 34 officials by 5,000 rubles, ending the censorship of foreign works except those in French and those, including German, published in languages used in the Empire, and combining the postal and foreign censorship for periodicals.[15]

Elenev's diatribe against literature and the press was surprising because his despair came after Feoktistov and Pobedonostsev had so diligently tried to restrain the press. His report had only one important consequence. In March, 1897 the Committee of Ministers gave the minister of interior the right to consent to the transfer of a periodical from one publisher to another.[16] Indeed, this curtailment of property rights and transformation of a right into a privilege was a key element in Elenev's memorandum. An already onerous press regime thus became more burdensome.

Not only the government was dissatisfied with the press regime. Writers and publishers were dissatisfied and from the beginning of Nicholas' II's reign, they became more vocal in their opposition. In 1895 seventy eight writers petitioned Nicholas for changes in the press regime arguing that the laws deprived them of the protection that other citizens enjoyed. The petition also noted the divergence between the published code and practice, the extended duration of supposedly temporary prohibitive circulars, and the harmful impact on newspapers of the Temporary Press Rules of 1882. S. Witte, the Minister of Finance, approved the petition but advised its authors not to submit it at that time. His advice was disregarded and when the petition reached Nicholas, Witte did not support it. Instead he asked Nicholas for a grant of 50,000 rubles for needy writers. Nicholas rejected the petition after the special convocation of ministers refused it.[17]

Failure did not daunt the writers and in 1898 a new petition was given to the minister of interior asking for a reexamination of the press laws. The writers complained that administrative decrees had in fact nullified Alexander II's aim in issuing the 1865 press law. In particular, they noted that two new practices of the government had made conditions worse; the requirement of government approval of temporary editors and also of the transfer of periodicals. The petitioners spoke of the sufferings of the provincial press and noted that the suppression by provincial officials of news of the cholera epidemic of 1892 had produced harm rather than good.[18] The petition had no result. But the restiveness of writers, which coincided with a growing restiveness in society, led them to continue their campaign for reform.

Easly in 1903 a special committee was created to commemorate the 200th anniversary of the Russian press. The committee proposed to sponsor a banquet which would prepare a resolution calling for freedom of the press. The proposed banquet was considered at a meeting of the literature section of the Academy of Sciences in February, 1903 at which protests against the censorship were made. But the new Minister of Interior, V. K. Pleve, at a meeting with a few members of the committee dissuaded them from holding the banquet.[19] Nevertheless, these events did produce some concrete acts. A collection of articles under the title "In Defense of the Word" was prepared in 1903 undoubtedly inspired by the discussions in the Academy.[20] The volume, confiscated in 1903, appeared finally in 1905. Aside from illegal broadsides, some sponsored by the Social-Democrats, the discussion of the issue led the Academy of Sciences to prepare a petition which, although composed in 1903, was not delivered to the Committee of Ministers until late in 1904. The petition noted that the Academy had studied the question from the spring of 1900 and now had concluded that the press regulations should be reexamined. It listed the famous scholarly works banned by the censorship such as Hobbes' Leviathan, Spinoza's Ethics, Lecky's History of Rationalism and many others. The Academy suggested that treatment such as this would discourage the translation of scholarly works and lead the public to read less solid works. The Academy also took note of the inconsistent character of censorship decisions which produced completely different decisions on the same work at different times. The petition also remarked that the administrative procedures adopted since 1865 deprived authors of the opportunity to defend themselves.

It recommended that the Senate, in camera if necessary, be empowered to confiscate a work instead of the Committee of Ministers whose decisions had to be confirmed by the Emperor. The petition, a clever appeal to dissociate the administration and especially the Emperor from unpopular decisions was in fact successful. It stimulated the government to undertake a reconsideration of press legislation.[21] But this success coincided with the strong popular movement for reform that preceded the 1905 revolution.

The boldness of writers was a product of their increasing influence and importance. The number of titles published increased rapidly as well as the number of copies issued during this period. In 1895, 8,699 titles were published in 35.5 million copies.[22] In St. Petersburg alone, in 1895, 3,711 censored titles in Russian appeared in 18.4 million copies, and 2,185 uncensored titles in 2.5 million copies, only 158 of which were not in Russian.[23] These figures for 1895 showed significant growth as compared to previous years. But growth within the next five years was phenomenal. In 1900, 24,532 titles issued in Russia in 101.1 million copies, a threefold increase over 1895. Of this large number of copies, over 90 million were in Russian (21,879 titles), 6.3 million in Polish (1,683 titles), 1.4 million in Hebrew or Yiddish (478 titles), and 2.1 million (359 titles) in Eastern languages.[24]

The circulation figures for periodicals support the conclusion that the reading public had expanded enormously in a few short years. In 1895 the most popular St. Petersburg periodical was Field (Niva), circulation about 170,000 while editions of the uncensored Market Reports (Birzhevye Vedemosti) and New Times reached over 30,000.[25] The "thick" periodicals such as Messenger of Europe and Russian Wealth (Russkoe Bogatstvo) issued in about 7,000 copies. By 1900, Niva issued in 200,000 copies and Motherland (Rodina) in 120,000; the New Times had a circulation of 50,000 while the popular Journal for All (Zhurnal dlia Vsekh) sold 62,000 copies and the government sponsored Village Messenger (Sel'skii Vestnik) 82,000 copies. The audience was nationwide and the method of reaching readers had changed. By 1900 the New Times distributed 33,000 copies through the postal service of which only 12,500 went to city subscribers. The remaining 17,000 issues or 1/3 of its press run, were distributed at bookstores, railroad stations and kiosks. Niva sent 3/4 of its issues to the provinces and most of the "thick" periodicals, such as God's World (Mir Bozhii), Messenger of Europe and Russian Wealth sent a similar percentage of their issues to the provinces.[26] The other capital, Moscow, showed a similar increase in its reading audience. In 1895, the censored Russian Leaves (Russkii Listok) issued in about 20,000 copies, Moscow Leaves (Moskovskii Listok) in over 30,000 and Russian Reports (Russkie Vedemosti) in 23,000 copies.[27] By 1901, the Moscow Leaves had 38,000 to 40,000 readers, but a rival, the newspaper Russian Word (Russkoe Slovo) issued in about 30,000 copies, and two other newspapers circulated in 20,000 or more copies.[28] In 1904 Russian Word issued in from 50,000 to 118,000 copies, Moscow Leaves in from 45,000 to 60,000 and five other newspapers including the Russian Reports issued in 20,000 or more copies.[29] A veritable explosion had occurred in the publishing industry.

The number of periodicals also grew and the growth affected the provinces. In 1890, 796 periodicals were being published in the Empire of which 149 were social and political. By 1900 the number of the latter had risen to 212 and 1002 periodicals were being published in Russia.[30] By 1910 the total number of periodicals rose to 2,391. Official figures, which differ somewhat from these, indicate that 308 newspapers were being published in the Empire excluding Finland in 1900. Most of these were censored and were published in the provinces; only in St. Petersburg did uncensored dailies outnumber censored newspapers.[31] The same list gives a figure of 294 censored provincial publications of 319 appearing in the provinces. For 1901, another official list notes that of 1,067 private periodicals appearing in the Empire, about half, or 583 were published outside the capitals.[32] Thus at the same time that the publishing industry grew in influence, the role of the provincial press was growing. The power of the press was indeed becoming nation-wide during the decade following Nicholas' accession to the throne.

The government itself followed an ambivalent policy towards the provincial press at times encouraging and most often curbing it. In September, 1881, the government had freed official provincial newspapers from the preliminary censorship. Soon after it allowed them to print domestic and foreign political news, which helped the audience for these newspapers to grow.[33] On the other hand the government discouraged privately owned periodicals in the provinces. In 1896 it rejected the petition of a Tambov publisher on the grounds that the local official newspaper took care of local needs.[34] Only in 1895 was the privilege of exemption from preliminary censorship first conferred on a private provincial newspaper, published in the Mongolian and Russian languages in Chita.[35] The Warsaw censorship suggested in 1903 that a ban be placed on all new periodicals except in science because the existing publications already overburdened censors.[36] The government's effort to put an obstacle in the way of new periodicals was half-hearted. The idea was there but the will to implement it was lacking. Feoktistov is recorded as having told one publisher of the Minister's desire to prevent the publication of additional newspapers.[37] Despite the wish, the number of periodicals published grew.

The authorities found it difficult to prevent provincial newspapers from discussing public affairs. The Kazan censor complained in 1904 that the Volga Leaves (Listok) was critical

114

of the bureaucracy and continually reported demonstrations, banquet resolutions and strikes.[38] In 1901, even before the great agitation preceding the revolution had begun, the Chief Board noted that its main problem with the provincial periodical press was the treatment of sensitive questions such as freedom of conscience, corporal punishment, the sects, the zemstvos and representative institutions in general.[39] That same year the censorship listed 40 provincial periodicals which attracted the unfavorable attention of the authorities.[40] Pleve himself, in June, 1902, complained of the tendentiousness of the provincial press and blamed the local authorities whose inconsistency allowed the appearance today of what they forbid yesterday.[41] Pleve's comment was unjust in that provincial censors were no more guilty than the capital censors of being guided by what was being presented to them; as indicated before, the character of the literature presented to the censors influenced their determinations as to permissibility. Arbitrariness and the lack of legal foundations for many decisions in the censorship produced this kind of vacillation. According to one author, it was not the local censors but rather the local police who established the conditions under which the local newspaper was published.[42] Other complaints of provincial writers testify to the high degree of arbitrariness in the provincial censorship: one local governor suspended an Astrakhan newspaper for two months and told the publisher to dismiss the "foreigners" from his staff;[43] another writer concluded that concern for the good reputation of the local administration rather than the censorship rules guided the local censors.[44] Indeed, the difficulties experienced by journalists in the capital cities were magnified in the provinces although their difficulties did not differ in kind.

But just as a greater boldness appeared among the writers in the capitals, so did provincial journalists display greater boldness in this period. Publishers in Saratov who complained that their censors were overworked and so delayed publication of their newspapers petitioned in 1896 for the right to contribute to the salary of a censor who could speed the examinations.[45] When Prince Shakhovskoi became head of the Chief Board, he made an effort to acquaint himself with the situation of the provincial press by traveling through the provinces. Two Saratov newspapers used the opportunity to request freedom from the censorship but the request was denied.[46] In 1901, the Council of the Chief Board heard and considered a number of complaints by provincial journalists on the censorship.[47] In 1903 a number of provincial journalists joined to petition for the end of the preliminary censorship in the provinces.[48] Sometimes provincial journalists were even bolder. M. K. Lemke, the noted historian of the censorship, edited a provincial newspaper around the turn of the century. Until his probationary term of three months as editor ended, he was cautious. Then he became more adventurous and as a result the censor began to receive reprimands from his superiors. Lemke effectively avoided local private denunciations of his newspaper by persuading the censors that such private criticisms would reflect unfavorably on them. Lemke admitted, in his recollections, that the charge against his newspaper, the undermining of Orthodoxy, was true. But the audience for his newspaper, he said, was mainly Jews and Schismatics. Ultimately Lemke's stratagems failed him and his newspaper was closed for eight months after he published a completely blank issue as a gesture of protest against the censorship.[49] Lemke's admission indicates that in some cases the suspicions of the authorities were justified. One provincial newspaper, the Don Speech (Donskaia Rech') was considered by the police to be a legal cover for a local illegal unit of the Social Democratic party. In fact, the publisher was sympathetic to the group.[50] But the evidence seems overwhelming that in most cases simple captiousness explains decisions by local censors.

One newspaper, the Siberian Messenger (Sibirskii Vestnik) so troubled a censor that in his report he appended an issue of the newspaper noting the incriminating articles in red pencil. One article had been forbidden by him but nevertheless appeared; it dealt with the sale of company shares. Among other articles either prohibited or cited as culpable were descriptions of a public meeting of writers to honor the literary critic Mikhailovskii, a note on the bad harvest in the Transbaikal region, an article that remarked that in England opponents "of the motherland" were permitted to assemble; and an article on the defeat of the Russian fleet at Port Arthur.[51] The censor was too [52] arbitrary; but in fact the newspaper was ready to defy the censor. Despite the explanation of the censor that the newspaper behaved as it did because a Jew wrote for it and a revolutionary served on the staff, the explanation for the daring of the provincial press is less simple. The Russian public, in the capitals and the provinces, was putting forth a claim to express itself openly on public questions. And if in 1902, a provincial censor could believe in fighting the "undesirable" tendency of, for example, the Kharkov Leaves (Listok) that this tendency was an isolated case, by 1904 as the documents show, the censors were facing a general offensive by Russian writers against the old practices.[53] The ability of the censorship to control journalism was now limited by the increasing willingness of journalists to challenge the restrictions imposed by censors.

The government's own actions contributed to the changed attitude as it moved from, at first, a tightly repressive policy, to a more lenient policy with the appointment of D. S. Sipiagin as Minister in 1899 and Prince N. V. Shakhovskoi as head of the Chief Board in 1900. The new officials presided over an amnesty issued in February, 1901 which removed all current warnings, some of which dated back as far as 1878. Also in June, 1901, the State Council conceded to persistent requests of publishers and limited the effectiveness of warnings; henceforth, a first warning would last one year unless a second warning was received in which case the duration of the warnings would be two years.[54] The period of conciliation was short but it may have whetted the appetite of journalists for more freedom; it may also have encouraged journalists to feel that continuous pressure on the government might be more successful than occasional petitions. In any case, by April, 1902, the period of concessions ended as V. K. Pleve became Minister and a new period of repression began.

According to the reckoning of Rozenberg and Iakushkin, forty seven warnings were given to periodicals in the period from 1895 to 1904; the penalties most often used during this period were the banning of retail sale and the temporary ban of a periodical.[55] An official count for the period does not differ much from this figure; it lists 178 administrative penalties as compared to the figure of 183 in Rozenberg and Iakushkin. The official report notes that while 70% of the penalties were applied to periodicals published in the capitals, provincial newspapers were closed down more often than capital periodicals, 45 to 8. In the capitals, the ban on retail sale was more important.[56] In closing censored provincial newspapers, the government made use of the 1862 censorship laws that had been neglected until renewed use of the law in 1879. Indeed, the line between censored and uncensored periodicals was often disregarded when it suited the government's purpose. Arsen'ev noted that the Chief Board penalized an uncensored periodical for stimulating hostility between classes despite the fact that the regulation on which the penalty was based seems to have been drawn up for censored periodicals. A censored periodical could no longer expect that in return for accepting close supervision, it could receive more lenient treatment from censors. Certainly the censored Russian Wealth (Russkoe Bogatstvo) suffered as much as any uncensored periodical, as it was banned for three months in 1899.[57] Additional restrictive measures came during this period. The programs of periodicals were examined to verify whether they were acting within their rights. At the end of 1896, the government began the practice of appointing only temporary editors for periodicals whose rights could be withdrawn without any explanation. Following Elenev's recommendation, the Committee of Ministers ruled, in March, 1897, as a temporary measure, to require the consent of the Minister of Interior to the transfer of a periodical to a new publisher.[58] Clearly the government was moving in the direction of establishing a semi-official privileged press as a means of controlling journalists.

Controls in the form of restrictive circulars continued as the government issued 255 circulars from 1895 to 1904. In 1905, 97 circulars were still in effect indicating that here, as in other areas of the censorship, the temporary decree was the most permanent form of law.[59] In 1902, one sizeable group of circulars restricted remarks on the excommunication of Count Leo Tolstoy; another group restricted unofficial information about disorders in schools and the army and problems involving the army; a third category concerned political and foreign affairs; a fourth curtailed remarks about court cases, scandals, or suicides of some prominent individuals.[60] Usually specific events stimulated these circulars such as the Khodynka tragedy in 1896, or a worker's assembly in 1902 to commemorate the Emancipation.[61] The government's concern here was to have the news presented in the most favorable way. The evidence is strong that the censors found this task increasingly difficult despite the formidable apparatus of penalties, licensing, and admonitions. The press was pushing against the traditional barriers and moving them.

The boldness was not always directed against the regime. Despite the fact that Nicholas II was reputed to be a reader of The Citizen (Grazhdanin), published by Prince Meshcherskii, Meshcherskii received six penalties, including temporary stoppage in 1896 for an attack on French President Faure.[62] Moscow Reports (Moskovskie Vedemosti) was more fortunate. It received only a warning in July, 1902 and still merited, in 1903, a commendation as a "protective newspaper."[63] Notovich's The News (Novosti) received six penalties from 1895 to 1905 although it received little mention in the archives.[64] On the other hand, News of the Day (Novosti Dnia) which was temporarily banned in 1901 and The Courier (Kur'er) which was banned temporarily in 1902 received extensive treatment in the censorship reports.[65] The reports went beyond a recitation of the misdeeds and included an analysis of the ideas of their publishers and staff. News of the Day was characterized in 1903 as a "purely Jewish liberal organ" edited by Efros, a Jew; the newspaper was said to disparage writers unsympathetic to Jews and to discourse on the harmfulness of nationalism in Europe.[66] In February, 1904, the Moscow committee again charged the newspaper with representing "Jewish cosmopolitanism and false liberalism." Despite the censor's dislike of Jews, which paralleled that of Elenev, he involuntarily expressed some admiration for the "educated and very experienced" Efros whose "Jewish persistence" sometimes prevented censors from curbing the periodical's "false liberalism."[67] The editors of The Courier were also Jews; the censors thus explained the newspaper's efforts to stimulate ferment in society and weaken national feeling.[68] In February, 1904, the Moscow committee described the newspaper as a representative of Russian democracy, as contrasted to constitutionalism, and tried to explain its success at propounding its viewpoint by the "tribal" qualities of "nimbleness" and "cleverness" of its writers. The committee noted that by petitions, by seemingly innocent little articles, and by stratagems such as presenting large quantities of material to censors on those days when it intended to print something impermissible, it managed to present its views to the public.[69] Unfortunately, for

the censors, the "tribal" stubbornness had infected non-Jews with
in the Empire by 1904.

"Jewish liberalism" explained the behavior of the "conservative" and "patriotic" Russian Leaves, according to the censors.
They called the editor an "anti-Semite," unfriendly to liberals
"and Jews" who had forced his exclusion from commemoration of the
200th anniversary of the periodical press. He had retaliated
with abuse that the Chief Board was forced to curb.[70] But on the
other hand, the censors' attitude towards the Russian Reports was
almost laudatory; it was called an organ of "our intelligentsia"
in contrast to organs of Jewish liberalism. A sort of familiarity
and solidarity was felt by the censors between them and the
liberal newspaper, a solidarity one might guess of old enemies
as the government faced new enemies. The censorship's sympathy
did not suppress criticism of the newspaper. The report, while
noting that Iollos' foreign correspondence, especially his
"lively and interesting sketches of the German social-democrats"
was avidly followed by readers, reported that the newspaper
tended to use silence as a means of conveying its attitude.[71]
Perhaps a comment of Pleve best conveys the attitude of the
censorship; he is quoted as saying that it was not the demands of
the left that frightened the government but those of the moderates because these could not be rejected "without violating
elementary justice." Pleve added that the moderates were growing
in power and would in the end supplant officials like Pleve.[72]
Pleve certainly did not hesitate to act against moderate demands.
Perhaps his remarks were calculated to elicit greater moderation
from the moderates; or perhaps his harsh actions against moderates
were despairing and perfunctory moves designed to carry out his
role as a defender of the autocracy when he had lost faith in the
cause he was obliged to defend. In any case, the censorship did
grant some concessions to the Russian Reports. It allowed it,
when temporarily subject to preliminary censorship, to present a
copy of its issue of the next morning at 11 P.M. without the
latest telegraph dispatches and to print the issue during the
night with the additional dispatches under threat of double
penalty for violations.[73]

The government's attitude towards the Russian Reports had
changed. At the beginning of the reign of Nicholas, Pobedonostsev
had tried to close the newspaper but failed because of resistance
by the minister of justice.[74] Moreover, the newspaper was banned
temporarily in 1899 and 1901, lost the right temporarily of
retail sale in 1895, 1896 and 1903, and was subjected to preliminary censorship from 1898 to 1901.[75] But in 1901, the censorship
gave the editors a somewhat reluctant compliment; they were
decent and did not treat censors in the "caustic" and "rash" way
other members of the liberal "mob" and the intelligentsia did.
Further, the censor called the newspaper the organ of the very
"solid and abundant" culture and literary talent of "our

119

constitutionalists." Some official replaced this latter
characterization by the term "gradualists" and added that the
newspaper was the organ of the "zemstvo and city institutions and
the leading group of merchants."[76] Both descriptions were in fact
accurate. Moreover the censorship clearly understood the aim of
the newspaper. In 1904, a censor reported at length on an article
in the newspaper. The author, he reported, believed in equal
rights for the peasants, the bringing together of classes, an end
to tutelage of the people, promotion of education and individual
initiative, and continual efforts, despite the Russo-Japanese War,
to raise the worth and welfare of Russians and spread enlightenment and culture.[77] Allusive language did not conceal the program
of the newspaper from the censors or readers. The language was
meant to maintain appearances, the appearance of decorum and
moderation. By 1904 that is about all the government could demand
of censors.[78]

Snobbery pervaded the censorship report on Russian Word
(Russkoe Slovo). It was called a "purely commercial newspaper"
whose liberalism was assumed because this attitude was popular.
After giving details of articles especially those by V. M. Doroshevich, its most important writer and eventually editor, the
report concluded that the periodical was really just a "street
sheet" and that this constituted its greatest sin.[79] A report of
February, 1904, again described the newspaper as seeking "external
success" whatever the means.[80] The apparent contempt of the
censors towards this "street sheet" led them to condemn the newspaper more than they did the journal Russian Thought (Russkaia
Mysl') although the latter was called "tendentious" on a number
of occasions.[81] Certainly a kind of snobbery pervaded the censorship. "Street sheets" were by definition scandal-hawking and
sensationalistic; they lacked conviction or substance. But the
anxiety about the Russian Word's liberalism was real because
Sytin, the publisher, and Doroshevich, editor from 1902, were
producing a serious newspaper with a mass audience. By 1905, the
newspaper issued 157,000 copies and by 1913, 325,000 copies.
Further, the publishers believed that each issue had at least ten
readers.[82] Sytin, who took five years to transform the formerly
conservative newspaper into a liberal periodical, was an entrepreneur who took advantage of the new interest in public affairs.
He paid out half a million rubles in honorariums in 1900 and in
1910, the total was 635,000 rubles. He and Doroshevich recruited
correspondents from all over the Empire and as the newspaper's
popularity grew, so did its income until it received 2 million
rubles from advertising alone.[83] The newspaper by its popularity
changed the locale for the debate between liberals and the government. Now the debate moved from the "respectable" periodicals
with a limited audience where all the advantages were with the
censorship, to the popular press with a large audience. Now
masses of people were becoming involved in political and social
questions. In this new situation, it is not surprising that

censors came to consider their traditional radical and liberal writers as less outrageous and less dangerous opponents.

That same reluctant respect for old enemies appeared in the political surveillance of the censorship. For example, in 1904, a volume of articles printed earlier in the Russian Reports and Russian Wealth (Russkoe Bogatstvo) on the peasant question was closely examined and then permitted on the grounds that the articles were moderate in tone, that they in some cases defended the commune, and they were in general useful.[84] The work by Rozenberg and Iakushkin on the Russian press passed the Moscow committee because it was thought it might be useful to future historians of the censorship and to the new government commission on the press laws.[85] Ten years earlier, the censors permitted Dzhanshiev's work on the liberal advocate of representative government in 1862, A. M. Unkovskii, because of the seriousness of the work.[86] And Boris Chicherin's Course of State Science was also permitted as a serious and useful work despite the author's occasional sympathy for limited monarchy.[87] On the other hand, the old enemies still suffered from the censorship. An article published many years before by N. Shelgunov, was excluded from a new edition of his works because it presented Russia as a land of persecution, arbitrariness, and popular protests like the rebellion of Stenka Razin.[88] Another work by another radical of the 1860s, Eliseev, was confiscated and destroyed after a censor characterized it as a series of radical judgments.[89] The old threats to the government were handled without difficulty by the censors. They forbade, for example, works that described abuses in local government.[90] A translation of S. Krasinskii's novel was banned because its tale of the conspiracy against Eleogabulus, the Roman emperor, exhibited a hatred of Rome that included a hatred of the state and Christianity.[91] But the new threats to the government required special measures and caused difficulties for the censors.

The special measures began with the government's subsidy to the Marxist journal The Beginning (Nachalo) through the husband of the publisher. The police hoped to discover the intentions of the staff.[92] In 1900 a special representative of the ministry of foreign affairs was appointed to provide capital newspapers with explanations of current political questions.[93] But the establishment of an official government spokesman did not end the government's problems. In 1904 the Chief Board overruled a committee decision to forbid D. A. Khomiakov's criticism of the Russian bureaucracy. The work, reported the censors, accused the bureaucracy of trying to subject both the State and the Church to its power. The Chief Board permitted the work but only in 100 copies instead of the proposed 200.[94] A sketch, in "dark colors" of the activities of Russian agents in the Amur area was permitted in 1904 despite an unfavorable report by censors.[95] And a work critical of the opening of private letters by officials in western Europe was ultimately permitted after the publisher complained about the negative decision of the censors.[96] By 1905, a censor, after denouncing a translation of a play by O. Mirabeau as propaganda, announced that it would not be expedient to forbid the publication as had been done in 1900.[97] The censorship was conducting a retreat, an orderly retreat, it hoped, as public interest in public affairs grew and changed from an interest in dangerous reading matter to street and school demonstrations.

One source which fed this growing opposition was socialism. The Moscow censorship expressed some perplexity about this new danger in 1903. It reported that its practice had been to forbid all works of extreme socialism especially in combination with revolutionary ideas. It had reserved its leniency for uncensored publications. Now it asked whether the committee should indeed forbid all presentations of socialism or only harmful and revolutionary statements of that doctrine. If the latter became the policy, continued the committee, then statements of German "socialism of the chair" such as Rodbertus' Foundation of Political Economy, permitted earlier by the Chief Board, might be permitted.[98] The Committee's perplexity was real. One censor, in 1901, argued that not all socialistic works need be forbidden but only those such as Marxism that argued the position that the existing social system must be destroyed. On these grounds, he decided that Zola's book Work might be permitted because Zola espoused Fourierism. The censor, who obviously felt the weakness of his position, also argued that prohibition of the five different editions of Zola's publication would destroy the publishing companies. He also argued that Zola's significance was less than that of Tolstoy and that prohibition would increase Zola's importance. The censor's dilemma was resolved by the decision of the publishers to exclude some material from the book.[99] The attitude of the censorship was clearly ambivalent.

This ambivalence was not the result of ignorance of Marxism but of the inimitable combination of complex social theory and revolutionary ideas that Marxism represented. In 1897 a convocation of ministers condemned Marx's ideas basically because its acceptance of majority rule constituted a revolutionary doctrine in Russia.[100] That same year the Chief Board decided to ban the provincial newspaper Samara Messenger (Samarskii Vestnik) because of its atheism and materialism in the spirit of Marxism.[101] A reprinting of Marx's Capital was forbidden in 1894 and in 1895 the Russian Marxist Materials for the Characterization of Our Economic Development was confiscated.[102] Marx's Poverty of Philosophy was destroyed in 1902 although an earlier, expurgated edition had appeared in Kiev.[103] According to one author, a new second edition of Marx's Capital, Volume I issued in 1899 only because of a 300 ruble bribe to censor Elagin.[104] But on the other hand the Chief Board rejected a censor's negative judgment about a work by the Marxist economist Tugan-Baranovskii on the grounds that the work would have a small circulation of 450; the same author's work on industrial crises was permitted with expurgations.[105] And although it forbid The Young Years of Marx by the Marxist economist Prokopovich because the price and size of the work indicated that a wide circulation was contemplated and also forbid another popular exposition of Marxist-like ideas,[106] it permitted Bernstein's Revisionist Social Problems in translation as a "weighty" critique of Marxism and an expression of the internal divisions within Marxism.[107] The censorship was not only aware of the growing importance of Marxism in Russia but also of the rift in socialism around the turn of the century.

The effort to make use of this knowledge of Marxism explains some of the ambivalence of the censorship to Marxism. After the closing of the Marxist journal New Word (Novoe Slovo) at the end of 1897, the government, as noted before, actually subsidized the new Marxist periodical The Beginning (Nachalo) in order to discover the "secret" aims of the Marxists. The aid lasted only a few months and in June, 1899 the Committee of Ministers advised Goremykin, the Minister of Interior, to forbid the journal.[108] Another important factor in the censorship's treatment of Marxist works was their accessibility, through size and style and price, to a large public.[109] Another factor was whether a particular work justified unions or the struggle of workers to organize instead of merely describing the process.[110] The direct application of socialist ideas to Russia as well as the depiction of the situation of Russian workers in "dark colors" was likely to lead to prohibition.[111] These clear principles were not always clear in practice but they guided the censorship in the examination of socialist works.

Foreign philosophical works and works of social thought posed a special problem for censors because these works in translation might reach a wider audience than the original. Nietzsche's Thus Spake Zarathustra was however permitted in 1900 after expurgation and that same year his Birth of Tragedy was permitted.[112] Exclusions were required before John Morley's work On Compromise was distributed. A discussion of Renan that quoted his views on Christ was expurgated before printing and a few years later, in 1903, Renan's studies in the history of religion were forbidden.[113] In this light, the complaint of the Chief Board in 1902 seems suspect; the Chief Board accused speculators of publishing poor translations of European philosophers. Specifically the Chief Board accused translators of Nietzsche of omitting examples of his wit and his antipathy towards socialism and democracy.[114] The Board's complaint was confused. It was clearly troubled by speculators seeking profit as well as the philosophical works themselves. Its criticism unaccountably confused the two categories.

The audience for some of these translated philosophical works, the common people, remained of great concern to the censorship. But a change in this concern was occurring. Now there was less fear that the material read by the common people be edifying and more concern about the sophisticated material they read. Thus, in 1902, the censorship noted that cheapness and small size were no longer the hallmarks of literature for the common people since they now bought books of a large size and high price.[115] In 1903 the Moscow committee noted that the works of Marx, Gorkii and Korolenko circulated widely among the common people. Despairing of prohibitive measures, the committee called for the government to publish more sophisticated works itself.[116] The character of a book prohibited by the Moscow censors in 1902 shows the new sophistication of the popular audience. The work was accused of discussing in a "foggy way" the principle of freedom of conscience. A popularization of evolutionary theory was forbidden in 1895.[117] A special circular that obliged censors to verify that works for the common people were "unconditionally harmless" provides some evidence of the new concern of the censorship.[118] The older style of popular work continued; many of Tolstoy's stories in this vein were either banned, expurgated, or banned from public libraries; and some of DeMaupassant's tales were now prohibited by the censorship in an inexpensive edition accessible to the common people although published only two years before in another edition.[119] As before some officials discouraged reading among the common people. One local official made the receipt of the subsidized Village Messenger (Sel'skii Vestnik) difficult for peasants. But now the editor complained and tried to enlarge his audience.[120] And now censors worried about the discussion of public affairs, for example, the condition of Russian workers or peasants, or scientific and philosophical ideas, in literature for the common people. No longer was their chief concern the maintenance of a high standard of morality in such works.[121]

The masses within the Empire were also being stirred by the increase of non-Russian publications. In the Baltic provinces, the number of Latvian and Estonian works increased; in 1895, 1,328 Latvian works were permitted by the censor compared to 2,545 in German and 919 in Russian.[122] By 1901, the comparable figures were 1561, 2672, and 1358; 612 Latvian works, 915 German, 489 Russian to which should be added 949 issues of Latvian periodicals, 1757 German and 869 Russian.[123] In Reval, in 1895, 195 Estonian works were published but in 1900 the figure had risen to 284.[124] Moreover some of this new non-Russian literature was radical in its tendencies, and either critical of religion or sympathetic to national aspirations.[125] For example, the censors tried, unsuccessfully, to restrain the Jewish periodical The Sunrise (Voskhod) from complaining of persecution of the Jews. They were successful in forbidding Korolenko's defense of Jews as well as Chicherin's essay on the Poles and the Jews.[126] Prohibitory measures had been the main weapon against the demands of the nationalities. But in the course of the 1905 Revolution, such measures had to be abandoned by the government. In November, 1905 the order of 1875 prohibiting Ukrainian publications was revoked and as a result periodicals in Ukrainian immediately increased in number.[127] By this time the old ways of the censorship were all being discarded.

An important change in literature during this period was the development of new schools of literature generally called "decadent" that broke away from the dominating tradition of realism. The censorship noted this increase in decadent literature;[128] works by Fedor Sologub, K. Bal'mont, and M. Gorkii were forbidden or expurgated by censors because of their immoral or cynical character.[129] The censorship continued to check popular works for immorality or the undesirable propagation of popular superstitions.[130] It also checked health manuals.[131] But well written efforts to expound or describe a "decadent" view of life were a new phenomenon for censors.[132] Defense of religious beliefs against secularism continued as did the defense of the clergy against criticisms.[133] Works in Russian history were still closely examined; Baron Korf's memoirs were expurgated before being printed in <u>Russian Antiquity</u> (<u>Russkaia Stavina</u>) in February, 1900.[134] Shil'der's biography of Paul I was forbidden in a French translation[135] and a sketch of Stenka Razin's 17th century rebellion was also forbidden in 1904. Even a description of the trial of the Decembrist rebels was considered a sensitive topic and the manuscript, at first forbidden, was brought to the Chief Board for decision on petition of the publisher.[136] Long standing practices continued to guide censors. But the times had changed.

In the Foreign Censorship the change was marked by the increase in the number of books and periodicals imported. In 1895, over 9.5 million books and issues of periodicals passed through the Foreign Censorship; by 1900 the total reached 19.8 million and by 1903, 29.5 million. In addition, the number of foreign periodicals that passed through the Postal Censorship rose from 490 in 1882 to 5000 in 1900.[137] If in 1896 the chairman of the Foreign Censorship was complaining of the long, 12-14 hour, work day of censors, then a few years later there was even more justification for complaint.[138] In 1897, foreign censors in St. Petersburg were examining a total of 83,213 sheets of periodicals and books, and by 1900, the total was close to 106,000 sheets a year.[139] Despite an increase in the number of examiners, the burden on foreign censors was still great, over 7000 sheets per year per reader in 1900 and 5000 per reader in 1902.[140] The percentage of new works that were either prohibited or expurgated varied, from just over 7% in 1895 and 1900, to a high of 11% in 1902, when the number of new titles examined actually fell, and in 1904.[141] In 1901 the Foreign Censorship noted that it had been forced to exclude from foreign journals and books remarks about Russia and in addition pornographic, socialist, pacifist, and revolutionary works.[142] German works predominated among imports in 1895 and apart from Yiddish works, Polish works were most likely to be rejected, and German works more often than French.[143] In 1903 German works still dominated among imported new works and were rejected more often than French, 15% to 13%, but Russian, Polish, and Armenian titles were rejected more often than either.[144]

An analysis of the subjects of rejected books in 1901 indicates that the largest category of rejected works were belles-lettres and criticism. Next were works in history and politics and then theology and philosophy. Among German, Hebrew and Scandinavian works, the largest category of prohibitions involved works in philosophy and theology. In the Romance languages and Greek, the largest group among rejected works was fiction.[145] Another analysis, of the period from January to August, 1901, indicates that political works were most often rejected; the largest category of rejected works was socialist or anarchist works while the next largest category included works disrespectful of Russian monarchs.[146] Among the more notable rejected works were volume 3 of Aulard's Etudes et lecons sur la revolution francaise, because of its hostility to religion, A. Maude's work on Tolstoy, for its anti-religious spirit and sympathy towards Tolstoy's philosophy, and Nietzsche's The Will to Power, for its criticism of Christianity.[147] These statistics show the increasing awareness by censors of the threat posed by western socialist and secularist ideas.

Growth affected the theatrical censorship which noted in 1902 that it had examined 3083 plays during the previous year as compared to 1418 in 1891, 2,281 in 1899, and 2408 in 1900.[148] Fewer than half of the plays it examined in 1899 and 1900 were permitted without change.[149] The rejection rate in the regular censorship remained much lower; in St. Petersburg, in 1900, less than 1% of the 7,816 manuscripts and 1,012 works in proof examined were rejected (67), while in Moscow, just over 2% or 63 works were rejected of the 3,088 manuscripts and proofs it examined.[150] Even in 1904, when the popular movement that produced the 1905 Revolution was making itself felt, the Moscow censors forbade only 175 or 3% of the 5,562 censored non-periodical works it examined.[151] In the provinces, the rate of rejection was about the same except in the Caucases where it was 4% in 1894, 5½% in 1901, and about 7% in 1903.[152] Caucasian nationalism is probably the explanation for the high rate. Certainly, the Kiev censorship in the years from 1896 to 1900 was combatting Ukrainian nationalism by rejecting at least 15% of the Ukrainian manuscripts it examined.[153] On the other hand, the rejection rate in Kiev for manuscripts in all languages ran at about 2% except during the first nine months of 1900 when it was 4%. In 1904, of the 136 manuscripts rejected by the Moscow censors, 20 dealt with the war while the remaining manuscripts were either descriptions of the desolate life of workers and peasants, patriotic works subject to misinterpretations, or obscene works.[154]

As in earlier periods, censored publications outnumbered uncensored both in the number of published titles and copies issued. In 1895, in St. Petersburg, censors examined 4,221 censored non periodical works to 2,185 uncensored.[155] In Moscow, in 1900, 3,088 censored works issued as compared to 793 uncensored while in 1904, the figures were 5008 censored to 768 uncensored.[156] The work of the censor remained formidable. In 1902 the government tried to ease his task by creating a position of temporary censor for uncensored newspapers, primarily because Russian publishers were now using new presses capable of printing as many as 30,000 copies an hour.[157] The permission of uncensored publications in the provinces increased the tasks of censors; by 1904 uncensored publications were appearing in Kazan, Yuriev, Kharkov as well as Odessa, Kiev, and Vilna.[158] The appointment of separate censors in seven provincial cities in 1903 facilitated the appearance of uncensored publications there.[159] The censorship was accommodating itself to the revolution in publications.

Although there is no specific decree in the sources, internal evidence indicates that by 1900, with the appointment of the new head of the Chief Board, Prince Shakhovskoi, control of the censorship was decentralized and greater authority was given to local censorship committees. The sources indicate that in 1898, the Chief Board dealt with 708 cases; in 1901 the Council held only 12 sessions. In the previous year, 1900, the Council also held only 12 sessions and took up 37 complaints about the censorship.[160] The size of the Council staff remained stable: 23 officials plus a chief and chancellery help in 1901, while the budget for 1900 for the entire censorship was 261,844 rubles.[161] Daily surveys of the press with excerpts were prepared by the Chief Board. In addition to surveillance of the press and receipt of complaints on the censorship, this was an important duty of the Chief Board.[162] The decrease in the activity of the Chief Board after 1900 is confirmed by data for 1901. In that year the Chief Board considered only 24 uncensored works on the request of the capital censorship committees and heard a number of complaints about the censorship.[163] One complaint, by the editor of the newspaper, the <u>Bessarabian</u> (Bessarabets), P. Khrushevan, was resolved by a compromise. Although Khrushevan, a rabid anti-Semite, was brought to court for violating the censor's prohibition, the censor's rejection of a few articles was revoked and the censor replaced.[164] In 1900, the Council considered 37 complaints, 26 of which were based on the censor's prohibition of an article; generally the Council supported the censors.[165] It is apparent that a new boldness had gripped publishers and writers. This boldness became part of a popular movement that forced the government to make partial concessions. Ultimately the government had to end the system that had governed the publication of books and periodicals since 1865.

The period up to 1905 therefore marks an important change in the attitude of publishers and writers towards the censorship. This change cannot be disassociated from the growth of the reading audience and the growing influence and power of the press. Up to 1900, the government tried to restrain this force. It restricted the transfer of a periodical; in 1897, it ruled that all anthologies, no matter what their size, would have to pass the prior censorship. In 1898, the Minister of Interior, Goremykin, issued a new and more stringent rule for uncensored works, which effectively increased the size requirement for exemption from censorship from 160 pages to 480 pages. The order however was never put into effect. Another restraint that was enforced and that led to the closing of a few publications was the government's decision to appoint only temporary editors.[166] But after 1900 the stringency disappeared. The statute of limitations on the effectiveness of warnings to periodicals was one sign of the change. Another procedural change allowed uncensored works to be published in provincial cities. The apparent increase in the independence of local censorship committees was another sign. The number of penalties inflicted on periodicals from 1900 to 1904, 83, was much lower than in the previous five years, 101.[167] But in the twentieth century these concessions were insufficient. By this time writers and publishers were demanding greater freedom. Now partial concessions which did not concede the principle of freedom of the press no longer satisfied writers. And indeed, in the face of the demonstrations and disturbances that led to the 1905 Revolution, the government was forced into greater concessions. Just as the government offered a constitution and a duma to Russians, it was forced to offer greater freedom and legality to the press and literature.

Chapter IX   Censorship in 1905 and After

   Government concessions prior to the 1905 Revolution did not satisfy writers and publishers. Nor did government manifestoes promising political concessions satisfy political leaders primarily because the promises of concessions were combined with increased repression. In an effort to ward off further unrest, in December, 1904, the government issued a manifesto promising governmental reforms, among them the elimination of excessive constraints on the press. This promise as well as the gesture represented by the designation of Prince Sviatopolk-Mirskii as Minister of Interior after Pleve's assassination in July, 1904 did not still the popular movement. In January, 1905 came Bloody Sunday which initiated a series of strikes and demonstrations that mark the 1905 Revolution. The Revolution led to the abandonment of the censorship. It also produced the October Manifesto of 1905 in which Nicholas II promised civil and political liberties for his subjects. Although the Revolution continued, the most lasting achievement of the Revolution had been accomplished by April 1906 when Russia received a constitution from Nicholas establishing a two house legislature.

   On the strength of Nicholas' promise, in his December, 1904 manifesto, to place the press under the rule of law, the Committee of Ministers took up the status of the press at meetings of December 28 and 31, 1904. At that meeting the petition of the Academy of Sciences, prepared in 1903 but held back by the head of the Academy, Grand Duke Constantine Constantinovich, was presented. The Committee agreed that the situation of the press was difficult and recognized the need to work out new laws commensurate with the significance of the press. Among the defects the Committee noted were the lack of consistency, the collegiate organization of the Chief Board, and the situation of the provincial periodical press. The Committee even agreed that the harshness of the press regime had contributed to the growth of a spirit of opposition within the periodical press. A new press regime, the Committee believed, should be administered by an office composed of the highest judicial and administrative personnel to assure a consistent and dispassionate evaluation of the press. But the Committee was reluctant to turn over press cases to the courts as would be the case in a system relying on law. The Committee wanted this new office to decide press issues on a legal basis but without the participation of the courts. To work out new press legislation, the Committee proposed the establishment of a special commission.[1]

   More immediate gestures were required to appease the public. Accordingly, the Committee took up the suggestion of S. Witte, former Minister of Finance and now chairman of the Committee of

Ministers to revoke the numerous special decrees that had been issued to supplement the 1865 Press Law. The Committee proposed to revoke the provision of the Temporary Censorship laws of 1862 that allowed a Minister of Interior to ban a censored periodical temporarily without previous warnings. This provision, as well as a decree allowing the Caucasian viceroy to ban local newspapers would be replaced by a rule that would permit stoppage only when censored periodicals misled censors. Another old provision, from 1863, revived in 1879, which allowed the Minister to deny a private periodical the right to print private advertisements, was also to be abolished. Another restriction, that prevented publishers from issuing anthologies to satisfy subscribers, would be modified; anthologies prepared by persons other than the editors of a banned periodical might be offered to subscribers. The 1868 decree allowing the Minister to ban retail sale of issues of a periodical, would be replaced; the new measure would allow sale in bookstores and libraries but permit the ban on street sale. This halfway measure was undoubtedly a concession to Pobedonostsev who defended the 1868 decree. Indeed, the concession was minor since the original decree, in 1868, had justified the ban by noting that street sale might serve as an occasion for disorders. Only the distortion of the original motive for the ban had led to the prohibition of sale in bookstores. Another decree that the Committee would revoke was the 1872 decree allowing the Committee of Ministers to ban and destroy a book or an issue of a periodical. The Committee decided that a special group composed of representatives of the Academy of Sciences should pass on the requests of the Minister to ban a book. The Minister could decide to use the courts in any case. The 1874 decree requiring the complete printing and destruction of the type of uncensored publications was also removed. The Committee was more hesitant about revoking the Temporary Press Rules of 1882. A commission would be created to consider modification of the Rules. Pending their conclusions, the Committee restricted the Rules: names of authors of articles would have to be delivered to the government only when the article led to criminal prosecution or when it involved important matters of state security; the provision allowing the Minister to subject a renewed periodical to preliminary censorship remained in effect pending the work of the new commission; the provision that allowed the banning of any periodical by a special convocation of ministers was modified and the minister might issue a temporary ban provided that he asked the Senate at the same time to ban the periodical. Details of the new procedures would be worked out by the ministers of interior and justice. The Committee also revoked the 1897 decree requiring the agreement of the minister to the transfer of ownership of periodicals. Finally, the Committee of Ministers put off decision on the secret decrees of 1875 and 1881 that banned publication of all works in Ukrainian except dictionaries, historical documents, and works of belles-lettres. On January 21, 1905 the Emperor agreed to all these proposals and ordered the establishment of the special commission.[2]

The new commission was constituted on January 23, 1905. The chairman was D. Kobeko, a member of the State Council and director of the Imperial Public Library. High officials as well as representatives of the Academy of Sciences and the public made up its membership. Included were Senator A. F. Koni, a liberal jurist, as well as the head of the Chief Board, N. A. Zverev. Also included were the historian and Academician V. O. Kluchevskii, Academician K. K. Arsen'ev, editor of the liberal Messenger of Europe as well as M. Stasiulevich, the publisher of the journal. Also members were the conservative publishers A. S. Suvorin of the New Times and Prince Mescherskii of The Citizen. The Commission first met on February 10, 1905; by May 24 it had held 25 meetings while a subcommittee held seven additional meetings. Although a project was almost prepared at that time, the Commission delayed its conclusions and met for five additional sessions in September and October. By that time Russia was in the midst of strikes and demonstrations that culminated in the October general strike. The Commission ended its work in November, 1905 with a formal expression of the Emperor's gratitude. But in fact the Emperor was dissatisfied with Kobeko's attitude towards the press. Soon after, Kobeko was retired from his duties as a member of the State Council. A conservative member of the Commission and editor of the conservative newspaper The Kievan (Kievlianin) and professor at St. Vladimir University, D. I. Pikhno, bitterly condemned Kobeko for making the Russian press an instigator of the revolution.[3] The accusation was misplaced. The Commission was influenced not only by the recommendations of the Committee of Ministers but also by the developing revolution.

The Commission interpreted the intent of the Committee of Ministers to be the establishment of greater freedom for the press. The project it prepared eliminated entirely prior censorship for all works, including spiritual works but excluding broadsides. This decision was made early in the Commission's deliberations; by March 14 it voted to end the prior censorship and use the courts for the trial of press cases. This decision was made despite the proposal of the ministry of interior to retain censorship for non-Russian languages and for provincial periodicals.[4] The Commission also proposed to eliminate all special censorships except the medical and finance ministry censorships on the grounds that prior censorship had not prevented the propagation of harmful ideas. The decision to end censorship for periodicals was unanimous. Also unanimous was the Commission's recommendation to end administrative penalties for periodicals; the grounds were that these penalties had produced irritation and extended the notion of harmful tendency arbitrarily without ending truly harmful tendencies. Articles 140 and 156 of the Code would be revoked because they had been used arbitrarily to prevent the press from dealing with important subjects. Instead the Commission proposed an article forbidding publication of defense information during a war or when war threatened. In the courts, where the Commission proposed to punish guilty works, the Commission thought the concept of a harmful tendency would be rejected because of its subjective and indefinable content.

The Commission proposed to maintain the existing regulations that required the presentation of printed works to the censors before distribution. In this period censors might have the opportunity to begin prosecution of criminal works. Publication without circulation was defined by the Commission as the preparation for a crime if the work was judged criminal, and not a crime in itself. The penalty would be destruction of the work but the author would not be punished. On the grounds that in the past the Minister had not judged the petitioner but instead the question whether it was desirable to limit or increase publications in a particular area, the Commission proposed the end of the requirement that the minister of interior consent to the publication of a periodical. This authority would be vested in a special commission much like that required for judges. The posting of a bond by periodicals was retained in the Commission's project. In addition, the Commission proposed the end of the Foreign Censorship because foreign works were read by few and so constituted no danger. The exception would be for works dealing with members of the Imperial House, foreign periodicals, works of belles-lettres, and works in the languages of the Empire including Russian. The licensing of presses and bookstores, which the Commission decided was an arbitrary procedure, would end except in rural areas where the local governor would hold this power of decision. Finally, the Commission voted to deprive the minister of interior of the authority to ban certain works from public reading rooms or from retail sale. The Commission thought that the minister's decisions, under a law of 1890, had been subjective.[5]

In the course of the Commission's deliberations, the Emperor issued the October Manifesto with its promise to grant freedom of speech. As a result Witte rushed to issue the new Temporary Press Laws of November 24, 1905. These rules, according to Witte were based on Kobeko's proposals and were considered by the State Council and the Council of Ministers. The Temporary Rules ended prior censorship and clerical censorship for periodicals published in cities. Without expressly saying so, the law preserved prior censorship for published works of less than ten sheets in octavo. The law also established the principle that a ban on a periodical could only be imposed by the courts. Moreover, the Rules abolished administrative penalties and the payment of a bond as well as article 140 which had allowed the Minister to exclude sensitive topics from periodicals. In addition, the Rules allowed publishers to present periodicals to censors simultaneously with issuance. Finally, local officials might reject petitions to publish a periodical only because of past criminal convictions of the petitioner or the immoral content of the proposed periodical. These proposals went beyond the Commission's project, especially in easing permission of new periodicals and ending the requirement of a monetary bond. Accordingly the Commission had to reconsider its project after November, 1905.[6]

On reconsideration, the Commission approved a proposal to reaffirm its earlier decision to abolish prior censorship for books; it also proposed that efforts be made to spread the new freedom to rural areas. If however the government decided to preserve the old system, it should be as a temporary measure. Further, the Commission favored the retention of the special censorship of judicial accounts, Orthodox service books, and news about the Imperial Court. The Commission also maintained its position on the censorship of foreign works and recommended that the Council of Ministers be empowered to forbid a foreign periodical or any other foreign work for two years. The Commission recommended that as soon as the government discovered some means of maintaining surveillance in rural areas, it allow the opening of presses and bookstores without special permission. Finally the Commission proposed to end the censorship of advertisements and military information.[7] In the light of these changes, the new project of the Commission was short. It established freedom of the press subject to stated limitations and the principle of court trial of press crimes. A minority favored jury courts. Four members of the Commission, among them the noted lawyer F. Koni, did not sign the project.[8]

One dissenter was the conservative V. M. Iuzefovich. He argued unsuccessfully for the retention of administrative penalties for periodicals. Despite the position of some members that a "harmful tendency" was difficult to define legally, he believed that this lack was a legal but not a real problem since no one could doubt the existence of a tendency in a periodical. Tendencies, he argued, might be communicated by satire, allegory or fables or by the tendentious selection of facts, or the one sided treatment of social and state questions. A tendency became harmful when it contained an animus against the state or a class. He argued vigorously that to allow harmful tendencies to appear was equivalent to allowing some incautious or ill-intentioned person to play with fire near inflammable materials. He for one believed that even if such a malevolent person had done nothing illegal, he should not be allowed to act freely.[9] In previous years, these arguments would have been compelling in an official body since they were redolent of traditional principles among officials. But in the midst of the 1905 Revolution, Iuzefovich's position was quixotic. Not even the censorship, let alone the system of administrative penalties, could be retained at this time.[10]

All through 1905 the censors had difficulty with the growing popular movement. Censorship circulars during the year are indicative. In January and again in June, 1905, St. Petersburg editors were advised to send material to General D. Trepov's office for censoring. In January, censors were advised to ban news of disorders and strikes or even articles about workers that might worsen relations between employers and workers. In May, discussion of the zemstvo congress or references to the various unions being established at the time were banned. In July came an advisory that only authorized news about the Russo-Japanese War might be permitted; also, that month, censors were told to prohibit news which might encourage class conflict, justify public action against the government, or encourage separatist tendencies in the Empire. Other forbidden issues were private property, the family, fundamental reorganization of the political system, and zemstvo congresses.[11] The censorship was active during the year and not without effect. Its treatment of the satirical periodical The Spectator (Zritel') shows how damaging the censorship could be. In August, 1905 the censors forbade material for the entire issue. On another day, they forbid twenty texts or sketches, the content of almost an entire issue. Ultimately the periodical was banned in October, 1905.[12]

But the censorship faced, in 1905, an aroused Russian public which was now unwilling to accept traditional controls without question. During 1905 petitions and manifestos of writers and journalists called for freedom of the press. Now these manifestoes and petitions were backed by strikes and demonstrations by typographical workers calling for an end to the censorship as well as other reforms. The Congress of Russian Journalists in April, 1905 called for freedom of the press and soon after the newly created union of Moscow writers accepted this demand as its own.[13] In the course of the general strike in October, 1905 the St. Petersburg Soviet ruled, on October 19, that only newspapers that ignored the official censorship could be published; newspapers that violated this new unofficial rule would be confiscated. The Chief Board in the face of the breakdown of order, responded by advising censors to maintain their surveillance and to use criminal legislation as the basis for their activities, informing local prosecutors of breaches of the law.[14] The Chief Board's acceptance of a de facto punitive censorship was of course made official with the new Temporary Press Rules of November, 1905. But from October 17 to December, 1905 about 22 Moscow firms issued their publications ignoring the official censorship but subject to the new revolutionary censorship which banned reactionary newspapers.[15] Proprietors of Moscow presses, about 130, agreed to the demand of the Moscow Soviet that they have no contact with the censorship.[16] Since the government, in the last months of 1905, found its authority challenged it could not retain the existing censorship even had it wished to do so.

By April, 1906, with Witte serving as Prime Minister, the government was in a better condition to impose its will. New rules for illustrated periodicals and non-periodicals were adopted by the Emperor on March 18 and April 26, 1906 after the Council of Ministers had recommended such changes and the State Council approved them. The latter law was confirmed the day before the Duma opened its session and a few days before Witte retired as Prime Minister. The new rules allowed books of five sheets or more (80 pages in *octavo*) to be issued simultaneously with presentation to the Committees on Press Affairs or the clerical censorship. Works of from one to five sheets had to be presented to the committees seven days before issuance and those of less than one sheet, at least two days before. Illustrated periodicals had to be presented to the press authorities at least one day before issuance. Periodicals were to be subject to fines, which were high especially for repeated offenses. But fines and other penalties, including imprisonment, might be imposed only by the courts although a periodical might be suspended simultaneously with presentation of the case to the prosecutor. Foreign books remained subject to preliminary censorship. Moreover a few express prohibitions were retained in the new rules: the printing of untrue information; the stimulation of hostility between classes; the misrepresentation of the status of credit institutions; and praise of criminal acts. Censorship committees were renamed committees on press affairs and the Chief Board was reorganized; separate committees under the ministry of interior were established for the various regions of the Empire. Finally, publishers of arrested periodicals were forbidden to issue a replacement until the court decided the case.[17]

These laws, open as they were to arbitrary interpretation, still were based on the principle of legal responsibility of the press before the courts. Further, since circulation of a newspaper coincided with the presentation of an issue to the press committee, it was possible for from 80% to 90% of an issue to reach the public despite confiscation. Since it took one and a half hours for a copy from a press run to reach the press committee and during that time, the run might be distributed, it was physically impossible to confiscate a whole run of newspapers.[18] But this freedom was circumscribed ty the government's power under the 1881 law which permitted the establishment of Exceptional Regimes and states of emergency in parts of the Empire. In the period after 1905 the government made frequent use of this authority. In fact, on one occasion in 1912, only 5 million of the 162 million inhabitants of the Empire lived under ordinary laws; the remaining inhabitants lived under some form of emergency regime. Further, the Prime Minister after June 1906, Peter Stolypin established a common procedure in the treatment of the press in provinces under exceptional regimes in June 1907.[19] These procedures restricted the writer's freedom. Witte, in his memoirs, notes that Stolypin, dissatisfied with the press rules drawn up by Witte, decided that the use of exceptional regimes was preferable to revision of the rules. Witte comments that as a result freedom of the press remained an "unfulfilled promise".[20]

One result of the change in rules for printed works was that the number of penalties inflicted on periodicals was greater after October, 1905 than before the revolution. From October, 1905 to March 31, 1906, 93 separate issues of periodicals were banned.[21] After Stolypin became Prime Minister, the repression increased. For the fourteen month period from October, 1905 to January, 1907, 361 books were confiscated and 433 issues of periodicals banned in St. Petersburg alone. In addition, 371 periodicals in Russia were forced to end publication and 607 editors and publishers either imprisoned or fined.[22] From 1905 to 1910, the number of penalties imposed on periodicals numbered 4,386 as compared to 82 from 1900 to 1904. Moreover, over one quarter of the penalties on periodicals closed the periodical. The high point of penalties came in 1907 when 175 editors or publishers were imprisoned, 413 periodicals banned, and 291 fines imposed. Three quarters of the bans were imposed by administrative authorities and not the courts.[23] The de facto abrogation of the press rules by the exceptional regimes was so palpable that in December, 1908, Mikhail Rodzianko, a right wing Octobrist, said that the "present laws on the press contradict the principles of the October Manifesto." The Octobrists, supported by the liberal Kadets, the Progressists, and the Polish Kolo, voted at the time to support a review of the press laws by the Duma.[24] The issue of censorship did not die with the press rules of 1905-1906.

These repressive measures were not successful in curbing the press to the government's satisfaction. The Russian Reports, fined 18 times from 1906 to 1910 and 39 more times from December, 1910 to August, 1911, continued to propagate its views.[25] A police official complained that government measures against Bolshevik periodicals had failed since fines and imprisonment did not destroy them.[26] The prosecutions against Pravda and other radical periodicals were numerous: from January, 1912 to September, 1913, 126 criminal prosecutions, or one for about every three issues were begun against 416 issues of Pravda; 130 were begun against the Menshevik newspaper Luch (Light); 46 prosecutions against the Socialist-Revolutionary Voice of Labor (Trudovoi Golos). But a closed periodical could quickly be reopened; officials could not deny any individual without a criminal record the right to publish a periodical. And Pravda by changing its name and editor, continued to appear and even was sent through the mail.[27] In fact, the number of Bolshevik publications remained large during the period. In 1906, 60 were being published; the following year 87, 43 in 1908 and 21 in 1909.[28] Certainly, after 1906 there was repression. But newspapers hired "responsible editors" for the express purpose of sitting in prison while the newspaper under a new responsible editor continued publication.[29] By means of deceit, but also by taking advantage of the government's occasional adherence to the law extracted from it during the 1905 Revolution, Russian printed works during this period experienced greater freedom of the press than at any time in history.

The government did not limit itself simply to repressive measures. Against the flood of free and sometimes revolutionary works, it turned to the idea of spreading its own propaganda.[30] In 1905, even before the October Manifesto, Minister of Interior Bulygin requested 100,000 rubles to subsidize the transfer of the St. Petersburg Reports to a reliable publisher. Subsequently the government tried to present its views through the Village Messenger (Sel'skii Vestnik) and other subsidized publications. Witte proposed to publish subsidized pamphlets under the Village Messenger and subsidized a periodical called The Russian State (Russkoe Gosudarstvo).[31] Stolypin's administration saw the newspaper Russia (Rossiia) founded as an approved government organ.[32] But now the government had to be heard in competition with the 3,111 periodicals being published in 1914 of which 1,220 dealt with public affairs and literature. By 1913, 856 newspapers were being published in the Empire in 2.7 million copies daily. And in 1914, the number of titles published in the Empire was 32,338 of which 25,521 were in Russian. The number of copies published in 1912, with 34,630 titles appearing, was 133 million.[33] Russian literature and the periodical press had its audience, and as a result, power.

It is understandable that conservative officials like the Minister of Interior N. A. Maklakov sought to return to some form of censorship. It is also understandable that right wing conservatives pushed for a return to the better days when radical opinions could not openly be expressed in print. Moderate and liberal groups prepared their own schemes. In 1913, Maklakov proposed a new press law, under consideration since 1908, that would have restored the preliminary censorship.[34] The project competed with one prepared by the right winger, V. M. Purishkevich, as well as projects of the Octobrists, Progressists and Kadets. The government's project was examined by a Duma Commission created earlier in February, 1912. Maklakov proposed a system that would have restored the procedure used before 1905 for uncensored periodicals; newspapers would have to present copies to the press committees three or four hours before issuance. While retaining the foreign and clerical censorship, the law would also establish government control of the publication of newspaper advertisements. Enforcement provisions included the imposition of legal responsibility on the printer and the seller of newspapers as well as the publisher and writer. Moreover monetary fines would have to be deposited by the periodical with a court as surety if the violation it was charged with entailed a fine above 3,000 rubles. This deposit would supplement the compulsory bond demanded of all periodicals. The amount of bond was higher than before 1905 as were the fines. With respect to editors, all would have to present a certificate from a Russian middle school, a clear hardship for provincial and non-Russian periodicals. Further, those accused of a press crime would temporarily lose the right to be an editor, an impediment to further publication of a periodical. Those convicted would lose the right to become an editor of any publication.[35] Miliukov, for the Kadets, and liberal journals attacked the project as did writers. Lenin, distrusting the Duma, feared that the project would become law and so encouraged the growth of an illegal press. But the project had not become law by the time World War I began in August, 1914.[36]

The war changed the situation as the civil censorship was entrusted to the police. War correspondents, including six Russians by 1915, each posting a bond of 25,000 rubles, were accredited to the army and tight control was maintained over military information. Moreover the government heavily subsidized pro-government newspapers and tried to acquire control of the commercial distribution of newspapers. It even began to buy control of The New Times (Novoe Vremia), the conservative newspaper that was in financial difficulties in 1916. But the purchase had not been completed by the time of the February, 1917 Revolution. On the other hand, by the end of 1915, new Bolshevik publications had appeared.[37] The overthrow of Nicholas in March, 1917 ended the imperial regime. The Provisional Government was preparing a new press law when it was in turn overthrown by the Bolsheviks. The long history of the Imperial censorship had ended.

Chapter X   Conclusion

Throughout its existence, the censorship constituted an important device for control of society by the government. The proof of its importance is the reluctance to abandon it until forced by the pressure of the 1905 Revolution. That the autocracy should retain the censorship is not surprising. It was an authoritarian state and followed the practices of other European authoritarian states. It believed that the role of the printed word was to advance the aims of the government and preserve social and religious standards; it did not accept the liberal postulate that the conflict of opinions could advance the welfare of society and indeed lead to the triumph of truth.[1]

The authoritarian ideal was perhaps best expressed in the satire of Koz'ma Prutkov, published in the satirical supplement to The Contemporary in 1863. The fictional author argued there the virtues of uniformity of thought; a government periodical, he said, could prevent error and combat malevolent rumors by establishing correct ideas.[2] In fact this ideal had been enforced rigorously by the censorship under Nicholas I: only by allusions and innuendo could writers deviate from this standard. On occasion, as in 1848, the government demanded a positive support by writers that would prevent them from showing their independence by silence. The reign of Alexander II brought a true although temporary innovation in the treatment of printed works. Just as some individual and social initiative was tolerated, so the printed word was granted some freedom. Golovnin could even express the liberal ideal of the "market place" of ideas in a meeting of the Council of Ministers. The impetus for this innovation, Alexander's desire to strengthen Russia militarily and economically after its defeat in the Crimean War, did not last. After the attempt on his life in 1866, Alexander and his ministers retreated from the moderate concessions made in the 1865 Press Law.

From 1866 until the 1905 Revolution, with the exception of the short interval during which Loris-Melikov expressed a desire to conciliate society by concessions to the printed word, the censorship followed a repressive policy. The degree of repression differed with different ministers. Valuev was satisfied to curb the independent writer while silencing the radicals. In despair, he abandoned the idea of achieving the elusive uniformity of thought that he would have preferred. Timashev and his successors, excluding Loris, sought and achieved more thorough control even over moderates. In part, they acted in allegiance to the conservative ideal of uniformity of thought. But the real impetus for their repressive policy was the abandonment by the autocracy of the reforming ideas that had enlisted the sympathy of many writers early in Alexander II's reign. The limits of permissible comments on the government and society narrowed with Timashev; further, Timashev ended the effort Valuev had made to establish a censorship regime based on law. He canonized arbitrariness as the method of the censorship. Expediency governed the censorship after Timashev. As the government's fears of radicalism grew a curious sort of ambiguity entered government policy in the censorship. While repression continued, the more moderate critics of governmental policy became more palatable to the government simply in contrast to more outspoken opponents. Arbitrariness and expediency did not always mean repression for writers. But it did make the relationship between censors and writers political rather than legal. Only with the demise of general censorship for most printed works in 1905-1906 did governmental policy towards the printed word acquire a legal basis. And as indicated, even after 1905, the government preferred to bypass the law and the courts.

Uniformity of thought remained an ideal of the government up to the 1905 Revolution. Pobedonostsev argued this position by indirection: he railed against the destructive activity of the self-appointed critics of government and society in the press.[3] The conservative Moscow Reports and the reformed radical L. Tikhomirov put their demand for uniformity of thought in a more positive way. They proposed, early in the 1890s, that writers and journalists be organized into a guild which would police itself, ousting the unworthy and disciplining the errant. This union of writers and journalists would maintain a monopoly of the printed word. This brilliant and prophetic suggestion was criticized by K. K. Arsen'ev, a principled liberal.[4] Elenev, the censorship official, also believed in this ideal of uniformity of thought. Such was the import of his suggestion that only the reeducation of society could force literature to be moral and patriotic. But his doubt that such a task would be undertaken by the autocracy led him to propose additional repressive measures to restrict the evil consequences of the corruption that had entered Russian society.

Indeed, the history of the censorship recounted here indicates that the government settled for less than uniformity. It settled for a system that limited the harmful consequences of a critical attitude, of diversity and variety of opinion. Pobedonostsev attributed the critical attitude towards government and society to the Fall of Man which began the reign of falsehood. Elenev and other officials referred to the presence of Jews and capitalist speculators who purveyed criticism of the government in order to win a popular following. The persistence of statements like that of Elenev indicates that right up to the 1905 Revolution, some important censorship officials refused to accept the critical attitude towards the government as representative of public opinion. Despite the growing audience for the printed word, censorship officials talked as if the critical attitude represented a minor current among a few writers that falsely presented itself as the voice of the public. This disparaging attitude went hand in hand with real concern for the impact of criticism on the population. Despite their show of confidence, they took precautions against these dangers from writers.

To avert the evil of criticism, the censorship sought the cooperation of writers. Despite the record given in this work, it would appear that this cooperation was given at least in a negative way. Most writers tried to stay within the bounds set by the government. But unfortunately for them, the government refused to accept the behavior of writers as complaisant. The kind of cooperation that would have satisfied the government would have ended the independence of writers. The model for the government was the behavior of Katkov or Prince Mescherskii, and even these paragons were sometimes too independent for the censorship. For the government, the achievement of cooperation remained a lesser virtue as compared to uniformity of thought. This remained the ideal for the censorship and the independence of even cooperative writers remained a potential threat to the government.

In the process of creating safeguards against the independent printed word, the censorship gave much attention to the "direction" or tendency of a printed work. As used by the censorship, this word took on a variety of meanings; originally the word was used to refer to the point of view of the work. With modifications, the word came to refer also to the unintentional position of a work, the intended or unintended attitude of the author, and ultimately the impression produced by the work on the reader. This last meaning involved the censorship in a delicate task of weighing the words in relationship to the political and social situation at the time. The ambiguity of the meaning of "tendency" was of course an invitation to arbitrariness. When the censors pretended to precision, they used the word "tendency" as if it were a characteristic of the work they were examining. When they did not have to conceal their arbitrariness, they concerned themselves with the author's intentions, conscious or not, or they acknowledged that political and social circumstances dictated their decision. In all cases the censors could move easily from evaluating the author's intentions or the implicit logic of a work to the impression the work produced, intentional or not. They chose freely the most incriminating or the least incriminating evaluation of "direction" or "tendency" as suited their needs. The dissembling of the censors was perhaps no greater than the dissembling of writers. Censors and writers both became skillful in the art of dissimulation.

Arbitrariness and expediency were often accompanied by suppression of a work. But they could also lead the censors to be lenient in their treatment of printed works. Censors did not want to appear before writers and society as oppressors; moreover, some censors considered themselves to be silent partners with writers and journalists in the task of enlightening the Russian public. For these reasons, the censors imposed limits on their own activity. They hesitated before they closed a periodical or even issued a warning. They weighed the repercussions of their actions against the possible dangers that might be incurred if the "dangerous tendency" persisted. They also considered the sizable financial investment represented, in particular, by a periodical. Only when the dangers appeared too significant or when some important official took particular offense did the censorship use its most severe measures: the closing of a periodical or the confiscation of a book. But if the dangers were not too apparent and powerful officials not aroused, then the censorship was often willing to cooperate with writers to eliminate the dangerous article or phrases and so avoid the open conflict.

Other motives besides the avoidance of conflict led to mitigation of the harshest features of the censorship. Censors hesitated to ban the works of noted foreign and Russian authors. Even when a well known foreign author was banned, censors recognized that at most they were merely limiting the audience for his works. Travel to western Europe was permitted and Russians returning from abroad brought in foreign works.[5] Accordingly a ban on a foreign author, especially a well known author, would be imposed only if the possible danger seemed great enough to justify the irritation it would cause educated readers. The same kind of expediency governed decisions to ban works of noted Russian authors.

Another consideration that restricted censors was, at times, the desire to keep track of dangerous ideas and dangerous people by permitting them to express their ideas in a muted way. This was the idea expressed by censor F. Tolstoy in the 1860's. Although the minister at the time objected, the idea persisted as witnessed by the censorship's tolerance of the Marxist periodical The Beginning (Nachalo) in 1899. Of course, the tolerance of radical opinions might end at any moment, as it did for the Marxist periodical. But temporarily at least the censors allowed the appearance of a "legitimate" radicalism. By the same token, a "legitimate" liberal point of view was also tolerated. What made these points of view acceptable depended on the attitude of the minister and the Chief Board. But in turn the very existence of a point of view over a period of time made the censors hesitate to strike it down. Notes of the Fatherland and The Deed (Delo) became part of the status-quo and as such, the censorship hesitated before it cracked down on them.

A muted journalism and a circumspect literature were

allowed by the censorship to express gentle criticism of the
government and society. Russian writers became expert at the use
of elliptical language, at innuendo and allusion, at the art of
not saying explicitly what they meant and not meaning exactly what
they said. This Aesopian language, which included the art of
knowing when to say nothing, permitted Russian writers to get
their books and articles into print. It permitted them to express
a quiet, but nevertheless consistent, critical attitude towards
the government and society. It permitted a legal liberal even
radical opposition.

But to emphasize the skill of writers as the explanation for
the appearance of a critical attitude in printed works would
distort the truth about the censorship in Russia. Censors were
neither blind nor fools; as university graduates they were often
as well equipped as other members of educated society to read
"between the lines." Clearly the limitations the censors imposed
on themselves, their willingness to cooperate with writers in
softening the harsh phrase or eliminating the culpable sentence
explains the existence of this legal criticism. The censorship,
despite its sometimes harsh words about writers, did not consider
itself to be at war with writers; or perhaps, borrowing a
contemporary phrase, the warfare between censors and writers was
a "cold war" in which ultimate weapons, confiscation or stoppage,
were sparingly used, as sparingly as the openly radical or harsh
criticism of the government and society. Censors and writers
were enemies but enemies did not destroy each other; they merely
fought each other, carefully observing rules for limited warfare.
The autocracy did not see itself as the oppressor of an unruly
people; instead it saw itself as the tutor to a sometimes mis-
guided people. Liberal and even radical writers may have believed
much the same about the government.

Thus we can explain the anomalies in the history of the
censorship. The critical attitude towards the government and
society manifested itself in printed works, in muted form, with
the acquiescence of the censorship. The censorship was repressive; already repressive policies became more repressive.
Timashev's regime was more repressive than Valuev's and the
regime of Tolstoy and Feoktistov was even more repressive. But
the critical attitude appeared in printed works, in more muted
form in more repressive times than in more lenient periods.
Writers were not destroyed physically nor were they imprisoned
very often. The government would even hesitate to act harshly
against influential or well established critics simply because
mere existence over a period of time conferred a sort of legiti-
macy on a publication. Moreover, the measure of the harshness of
the censorship is not only the list of prohibited works and
articles but often the list of works that passed the vigilant
censor and appeared in print and led to correspondence in the
censorship office.

It could justly be argued that the true measure of the repressiveness of the censorship should be different. It should be based not on what was printed or even what was not printed, the fewer than 5% of the manuscripts that it rejected. It should instead be based on what writers would have written had there been no censorship, had they been able to write as they did after 1905-1906. Then, indeed, the number of penalties imposed on periodicals and books was great. But in fact, it is not argued here that the censorship was not repressive and that it permitted writers the same freedom they would have had if no repressive censorship existed. All that is contended here is that the repressiveness of the censorship was limited; that these limitations were self-imposed; that the repression varied from minister to minister and from time to time, depending on the political situation, the fears and anxieties of ministers and the willingness of writers to risk losses or penalties. The Tsarist government was authoritarian. It sought uniformity of thought. But it imposed limits on its power; it hesitated to force uniformity on society; it retained some respect for tradition, position, wealth, public reaction, and even its enemies. It sought to preserve institutions rather than change them.

Statistics on Foreign Censorship

Year	Vols. imported	New works examined	New permitted	New expurgated	New forbidden
1861		5,120[1]			
1866	3,709,661[2]	5,608			
1867		5,323	5,026	172	125[3]
1868		4,039	3,714	194	131[4]
1869		3,576	3,301	151	124[5]
1870		3,276	2,951	194	131[6]
1871		5,806	5,116	279	41[7]
1872		6,321			646 forbidden[8]
1873		6,615			576 forbidden[9]
1874		9,391	8,752	353	286[10]
1875	7,886,045	9,412	8,839	325	238[11]
1876		10,343	9,690	391	262[12]
1877		10,408			873 forbidden[13]
1878		10,457[14]	7,415	1744	1298[15]
1879		12,615	11,571	657	387[16]
1880		14,712	13,633	763	316[17]
1881		10,867[18]			
1891		14,757[19]			
1892	7,034,456	15,138	13,534	657	947[20]
1893	9,061,919	12,336	11,321	353	662[21]
1894	10,678,784	12,215	11,299	329	587[22]
1895	9,546,638	12,543		384	609[23]

Statistics on Foreign Censorship

Year	Vols. imported	New works examined	New permitted	New expurgated	New forbidden
1900	19,802,937	12,496	11,616	274	606[24]
1901	22,719,690	12,905	11,591	478	836[25]
1902	25,544,722	10,882	9,667	390	825[26]
1903	29,525,673	14,013	12,230	538	1245[27]
1904	29,562,643[28]	14,317	12,613	761	943[29]

Footnotes to Statistics on Foreign Censorship

1. F.776,1896,op.21,d.2,pp.218-19.

2. F.776,1876,d.105,pp.53b-57b.

3. F.776,d.660,1867,p.222.

4. F.776,op.4,1870,d.5,pp.90-93.

5. F.776,op.4,1870,d.5,pp.90b-92b.

6. F.776,1871,d.154,p.321a and b,330,339. Another figure of 290 forbidden is given in F.776,op.4,d.5,1870,pp.90b-92b.

7. F.776,1871,d.154,pp.321b-330,339. For another figure of 690 forbidden and expurgated see F.776,1871,d.154,pp.321a and b,330,339.

8. F.776,1874,d.2a,p.194b.

9. F.776,1880,d.195,pp.210-12.

10. F.776,1876,d.105,pp.53b-57b.

11. F.776,1876,d.105,pp.53b-57b.

12. F.776,1877,d.1,pp.168-175b.

13. F.776,1880,d.195,pp.200-202b.

14. F.776,1880,d.195,pp.200-202b,210-212.

15. F.776,1879,d.88,p.6b.
16. F.776,1880,d.195,pp.200-202b,210-212.
17. F.776,1881,d.3,pp.234-36b.
18. F.776,1896,op.21,d.2,pp.218-19.
19. F.776,1896,op.21,d.2,pp.218-19.
20. F.776,1895,d.1444,pp.264-69b.
21. F.776,1895,d.1444,pp.272-77b.
22. F.776,1895,d.1444,pp.280-85b.
23. F.776,1896,op.21,d.2,pp.218-23b.
24. F.776,1901,d.1,pp.251b-52,175-77b.
25. F.776,1902,d.1,pp.29b-33b.
26. F.776,1903,d.1,pp.311-319b.
27. F.776,1904,op.22,d.1,pp.399-402.
28. Figures of volumes imported include periodicals. Approximately one half of these imported works from 1892 came through the postal censorship and so were censored by officials other than the foreign censors.
29. F.776,1905,d.1,pp.391-96b.

Footnotes Chapter I

1. C. Ruud, "The Russian Empire's New Censorship Law of 1865," Canadian Slavic Studies Summer No. 2 (1969), p. 236.

2. Ibid., p. 236; (S.M.Seredonin) Istoricheskii obzor deiatel' nosti komiteta ministrov 5 vols. (SPB:1902), III, Part 2, pp. 196-197. The Emperor expanded his concession on January 23, 1858 to include other political questions.

3. Ruud, "The Russian Empire's. . .," Canadian Slavic Studies No. 2 (1969, p. 237; Iu. Gerasimova, "Krizis pravitel'- stvennoi politiki v gody revoliutsionnoi situatsii i Aleksandr II," in V. A. D'iakov, Ia. I. Linkov et al, (ed.), Revoliutsionnaia situatsiia v Rossii v 1859-1861 gg. (Moscow: 1962), p. 97.

4. F. 109, op. 213, d.25, Fifth Eks. 1857, p. 1. For Alexander's attitude towards emancipation, see D. Field, The End of Serfdom (Cambridge, Mass.: 1976), pp. 93-95.

5. Gerasimova, "Krizis.....," In D'iakov, Linkov et al (ed.), Revoliutsionnaia..., p. 96. See also Iu. I. Gerasimova, Iz istorii russkoi pechati v period revoliutsionnoi situatsii kontsa 1850-kh --nachala 1860-kh gg. (Moscow: 1974), p. 18.

6. Gerasimova, "Krizis...," in D'iakov, Linkov et al (ed.), Revoliutsionnaia..., p. 97.

7. Ibid., p. 99; F. 728, op. 1, d. 2612, p. 2. Gerasimova may have erred in her footnote.

8. F. 109, op. 1, First Eks., 1858, d. 406. See for activity of this committee, A. V. Nikitenko, Dnevnik Ed. by L. Brodskii, V. V. Gladkov et al., 3 vols. (Moscow: 1955-56), II, pp. 68-70, 76-78, 81-82, 84, 87, 96, 100 and M. K. Lemke Ocherki po istorii russkoi tsenzury i zhurnalistiki XIX stoletiia (SPB: 1904), pp. 330-68.

9. F. 728, op. 1, d. 2612; Gerasimova, "Krizis...," in D'iakov, Linkov et al. (ed.), Revoliutsiionnaia...., pp. 99-100; Gerasimova, Iz istorii....., p. 81.

10. F. 772, 1860, d. 5177, op. 1, pp. 37b-38a.

11. V. Ia. Laverychev, "Russkie kapitalisty i periodicheskaia pechat' vtoroi poloviny XIX v." Istoriia SSSR No. 1 (1972), pp. 26-30. The number of periodicals published rose from 165 in 1858 to 199 in 1859 and 230 in 1860; Gerasimova,

11. (continued) Iz istorii....., p. 49.

12. B. I. Esin, Kratkii ocherk razvitiia gazetnogo dela v Rossii XVIII-XIX vekov (Moscow: 1967), pp. 38-41.

13. E. M. Feoktistov, Vospominaniia E. M. Feoktistova. Za kulisami politiki i literatury, 1848-1896 (Leningrad: 1929), pp. 121-22. See also A. F. Koni Na zhiznennom puti 2 vols. (SPB: 1912), II, p. 238. Koni says that ideal of political freedom, i.e. an end of constraints on thought and esteem to the person, characterized the state of mind of Russian society at this time.

14. F. 109, First Eks., d. 57, pp. 85-90. See also Gerasimova, Iz istorii..., p. 85 for the Third Section's comment that literature supported socialism and materialism.

15. Ibid., p. 97; Feoktistov, pp. 129-33, 161.

16. F. 851 Golovnina, op. 1, d. 5, pp. 43, 44a and b, 49b, 50, 52-53. In 1862 Katkov, Leont'ev, Pavlov, Kraevskii, Usov and Starchevskii, all publishers or editors, received this right to uncensored foreign works. See Materialy...1869, Part V, pp. 44-45. Feoktistov reports that Golovnin asked him to compose a list of needy scholars and editors because Golovnin had secured money from the Tsar to help them. See Feoktistov, pp. 133-35. See also Ruud, "The Russian Empire's...," Canadian Slavic Studies No. 2 (1969), pp. 239-40; (Seredonin) Istoricheskii obzor....kom...min..., III, Part 2, pp. 199-202; D. Balmuth, "The Origins of the Russian Press Reform of 1865, "Slavonic and East European Review no. 109 (Jan., 1969), pp. 369-88. The policy of giving favors and subsidies began before Golovnin became minister. Gerasimova, Iz istorii...., pp. 89, 133.

17. F. 772, op. 1, 1862, d. 5976, pp. 137b-39.

18. F. 109, op. 1, d. 1780, 1862, pp. 1a-14a.

19. F. 772, op. 1, 1862, d. 5976, pp. 140a-43b. This memorandum is almost the same as a memorandum in the MSS room of the Saltykov-Shchedrin Library, F. 833 Tsey (Tsee), No. 54, 1865 (This date is in error). The library manuscript seems to have been a first draft of Tsey's recommendations to Golovnin. Golovnin sent the manuscript on to a secretary on May 17, 1862.

20. See Tsey's memorandum in F. 833 Tsey, No. 54, 1865, p. 2 in MSS room of the Saltykov-Shchedrin Library.

21. F. 772, op. 1, 1862, d. 5976, pp. 1a-5a, 10a, 20a and also d. 5905, p. 27, 28a. See also Balmuth, "The Origins....," Slavonic and East European Review (Jan., 1969); Ruud, "The Russian Empire's....," Canadian Slavic Studies no. 2 (1969) C. Ruud, "A. V. Golovnin and Liberal Russian Censorship, Jan.-June, 1862," Slavonic and East European Review No. 119 (Apr., 1972).

22. P. Valuev, Dnevnik P. A. Valueva Ed. by P. A. Zaionchkovskii 2 vols. (Moscow: 1961), I, pp. 166-67, 175; Gerasimova Iz istorii...., pp. 134-37, 162. The temporary closing of the two periodicals was delayed until publication of the Temporary Censorship Rules.

23. F. 851 Golovnina, op. 1, d. 8, pp. 9b-16a.

24. Istoricheskiia svedeniia o tsenzure (SPB: 1862), Supp. V(E) pp. 35-36.

25. Izvlechenie iz otcheta ministerstva vnutrennikh del za 1861, 1862 i 1863g. (SPB: 1865), p. 115; Gerasimova, Iz istorii..., p. 102. In 1861 Valuev won approval to add a supplement to the ministry's journal dealing with agriculture and aimed at the peasantry as an audience. The government also published communiques on peasant affairs.

26. Valuev, Dnevnik..., I, pp. 28-32, 35-38, 137, II, pp. 496-97; also N. G. Sladkevich, "Oppositsionnoe dvizhenie dvorianstva v gody revoliutsionnoi situatsii," in D'iakov, Linkov et al (ed.), Revoliutsionnaia..., pp. 76-77. For D. Miliutin's views, reformist but demanding firm unity, see D. A. Miliutin, Dnevnik D. A. Miliutina 1873-1882 Ed. by P. A. Zaionchkovskii, 4 vols. (Moscow: 1947-50) I, p. 32.

27. Istoricheskiia svedeniia o tsenzure, Supp. V(E), pp. 29-30. Valuev wrote to Golovnin 67 times in 1862 about censorship matters. See M. I. L'vova, "Kak podogotovlialos zakritie 'Sovremennika' v 1862 g., "Istoricheskie Zapiski XLVI (1954), p. 316.

28. Istoricheskiia svedeniia..., Supp. V(E), pp. 31-32.

29. Ibid., Supp. V(E), pp. 42-45; see also Supp. V(B), p. 20.

30. Ibid., Supp. V, p. 16.

31. Ibid., Supp. V, pp. 18-19.

32. Ibid., Supp. V (B), pp. 21-22.

33. Ibid., Supp. V (E), pp. 30-31.

34. Ibid., Supp. V (D), pp. 28-29.

35. Ibid., Supp. V (E), pp. 37-38.

36. F. 777, op. 1, 1862, d. 5905, pp. 29a-30a.

37. Istoricheskiia svedeniia..., Supp. V(E), pp. 32-34.

38. See Ibid., Supp. V (B), pp. 19-20 and Supp. V (D), pp. 25, 27 and Supp. V, pp. 65-66.

39. Ibid., Supp. V, p. 66; Gerasimova, Iz istorii..., p. 181.

40. Istoricheskiia svedeniia..., Supp. V (D), pp. 27-28.

41. Ibid., Supp. V, pp. 17-18.

42. Ibid., Supp. V (E), pp. 38-40.

43. Materialy...1869, Part V, pp. 82-84. Here can be found a ministry report on periodicals in 1862 which argued the usefulness of literature. See P. I. Kapnist, Sochineniia grafa P. I. Kapnista 2 vols. in 1 (Moscow: 1901), I, p. CXI, II, pp. 428-509.

44. Istoricheskiia svedeniia..., Supp. V (E), pp. 46-64. Tolstoy was under surveillance by the Third Section in 1862. See "Delo III otd. S.E.I.V. Kantseliarii 1862 gg.," Vsemirnyi Vestnik No. 6 (June, 1906), Supp. p. 1-32, No. 7 (July, 1906), Supp. pp. 33-74; Gerasimova, Iz istorii..., p. 180. Tolstoy's estate was searched in July, 1862 on the suspicion that proclamations had been printed on a secret press there.

45. Istoricheskiia svedeniia..., Supp. V (E), pp. 34-35.

46. Ibid., Supp. V (D), pp. 24-25.

47. Feoktistov, pp. 133-35.

48. Istoricheskiia svedeniia..., Supp. V (V), pp. 21-22.

49. Ibid., Supp. V (D), pp. 26-27. The French edition was permitted as part of Hugo's collected works with the exclusion of places approving revolution. However the censor did acknowledge that his decision was based on the author's notoriety and fear that prohibition would increase interest in the work. See I. Aizenshtok, "Frantsuzskie pisateli v

49. (continued) otsenkakh tsarskoi tsenzury." <u>Literaturnoe Nasledstvo</u> Vol. 33-34 (1939), pp. 788-90. In the case cited in the text, the censor was reprimanded by the Emperor himself and the Russian translation, as a separate volume, was forbidden. Heine's works were permitted in 18 volumes about this time because of his fame. See A. Fedorov, "Genrikh Geine v tsarskoi tsenzure," <u>Literaturnoe Nasledstvo</u> Vol. 22-24 (1935), pp. 662-72.

50. <u>Istoricheskiia svedeniia...</u>, Supp. V (E), pp. 40-42. Golovnin and Tsey made comments on Shcheglov's article which probably served as a guide to refutations. See F. 833 Tsey, No. 107, pp. 9b-13a.

51. <u>Istoricheskiia svedeniia...</u>, Supp. V (G), pp. 22-24. See also <u>Materialy... 1869</u>, Part V, pp. 5-7 for Valuev's special instructions of May 19, 1862 supplementing the Temporary Censorship Rules of May 12, 1862.

52. F. 833 Tsey, No. 103, pp. 2a, 25, 36, 44, 46, 47, 64 and F. 833, No. 72. See also <u>Sbornik stat'ei nedozvolennikh tsenzuroiu v 1862g</u>. 2 vols. (SPB: 1862).

53. M. K. Lemke, <u>Epokha tsenzurnikh reform</u> (SPB: 1904), pp. 253-58.

54. <u>Vsepoddaneishii doklad ministra narodnago prosveshcheniia po proektu ustava o knigopechatanii chitannyi v sovet ministrov 10 Ianvaria 1863 goda</u> (n.p.n.d).

55. Valuev, <u>Dnevnik...</u>, I, pp. 199, 201, 203; Lemke, <u>Epokha...</u>, pp. 260-63; (Seredonin) <u>Istoricheskii obzor ...kom...min..</u>, IV, Part 2, pp. 202-203. Valuev refers to a change of mind by Golovnin at the end of December. Perhaps Golovnin hesitated to rid himself of the censorship. Valuev, in this connection, also mentions a disucssion in the Council in which Golovnin was attacked for wanting to maintain some link with the censorship. See Valuev, <u>Dnevnik...</u>, I, p. 198. Tsey suggested transfer of the censorship after presenting a few arguments for its retention. See F. 833 Tsey, No. 48 "Vsepodd. doklad o resul'tatakh raboty kommiss. dlia peresmotra, izmen. i dopol. po delam pechati" in MSS room of the Saltykov-Shchedrin Library.

56. F. 851 Golovnina, op. 1, d. 5, pp. 53a-59b, 63a-80a, 377a-377b. See Nikitenko, <u>Dnevnik</u> II, p. 109 for the accusation that Golovnin attacked the Obolenskii project for political reasons. Thus, if the project were approved, Golovnin could show liberals that he opposed it. If the project were not approved, he could show his foresight.

Footnotes   Chapter II

1. Zhurnaly vysochaishe uchrezhdennoi kommissii dlia razsmotreniia proekta ustavo o knigopechatanii (SPB: 1863) pp. 5-6.

2. Sbornik rasporiazhenii po delam pechati s 1863 po 1-e sentiabria 1865 goda (SPB: 1865), pp. 3-5. In June, 1863, Valuev established a Council on Press Affairs as an advisory body. It was composed of the St. Petersburg and Moscow chairmen and the director of the executive police. See Materialy...1869, Part V, pp. 9-12.

3. The Obolenskii Commission expressed the view in 1862 that there was no way legally to define a "harmful direction" and so decided not to conceal this inadequacy. For use of the concept of "direction" or tendency in the French censorship law of 1819, see I. Collins, The Government and the Newspaper Press in France 1814-1881 (London: 1959), p. 37.

4. Sbornik. ras....1863-1865, pp. 5-6, 11-13. See also F. 777, 1863, op. 2, d. 2, p. 30.

5. Sbornik ras....1863-1865, pp. 28-29.

6. Ibid., p. 38.

7. Ibid., pp. 17-18, 30-31, also 28-29.

8. Ibid., pp. 41-42.

9. Ibid., p. 25.

10. F. 777, 1863, op. 2, d. 2, p. 25.

11. Sbornik ras....1863-1865, pp. 11-13.

12. F. 777, 1863, op. 2, d. 2, pp. 22-23.

13. Sbornik ras....1863-1865, pp. 31-32.

14. F. 777, 1863, op. 2, d. 2, p. 20.

15. Sbornik ras....1863-1865, pp. 9-11; Materialy....1869, Part V, pp. 7, 174.

16. Sbornik ras....1863-1865, pp. 8-9.

17. Ibid., pp. 19-20.

18. Materialy....1869, Part V, p. 140.

19. Sbornik ras...1863-1865, pp. 13-14.

20. Ibid., pp. 27-28.

21. Ibid., pp. 21-22.

22. Ibid., pp. 42-48; Materialy....1869, Part II, pp. 193-96 note

23. Sbornik ras....1863-65, p. 52.

24. Ibid., p. 26; F. 109, 1861, First Eks, d. 12, Part 2, pp. 6-7.

25. F. 109, 1861, First Eks., d. 12, Part 2, pp. 9-22, 30-31.

26. Sbornik ras...1863-1865, pp. 11-13.

27. Materialy....1869, Part V, pp. 178-179.

28. Sbornik ras....1863-1865, p. 33.

29. Ibid., p. 33.

30. F. 777, 1863, op. 2, d. 2, p. 10.

31. Sbornik ras...1863-1865, p. 34.

32. Ibid., pp. 38-39.

33. Ibid., pp. 37-38.

34. Ibid., p. 41. Here Valuev agreed to permit some "healthy" criticism of French utopian socialists. On the other hand, see Sbornik ras....1863-1865, p. 15 where Valuev complained that the Moscow Reports sometimes printed incorrect information which upset people without reason and gave grounds for complaints about the government.

35. Sbornik ras...1863-1865, pp. 18-19.

36. Ibid., p. 51.

37. Ibid., pp. 50-55, 48.

38. Ibid., pp. 6-7.

39. Ibid., p. 20.

40. Ibid., pp. 23-25.

41. Ibid., pp. 32-33; Materialy....1869, Part V, pp. 197-98.

42. F. 777, 1863, op. 2, d. 2, p. 16.

43. Sbornik ras....1863-65, pp. 48-50.

44. Materialy....1869, Part V, pp. 178-79.

45. Ibid., Part V, p. 12. Valuev received this right in June, 1863. He was allowed to deny this privilege, first granted in 1862, for two to eight months.

46. Istoricheskiia svedeniia...., pp. 122-23, 125; "Predstavlenie" of Minister of Interior, Nov. 17, 1864, pp. 1-2 in Proekt ustava o knigopechatanii (SPB: 1863); L'vova, "Kak podgotovlialos....," Istoricheskie Zapiski XLVI (1954), p. 302.

47. "Mnenie raznykh lits o preobrazovanii tsenzury. Fevral'1862 g" pp. 11-95 in Proekty i zapiski o tsenzure (n.p.,n.d); K. N. Zhuravlev,"K voprosu ob avtore zapiski redaktsii zhurnala 'Sovremennika' o preobrazovanii tsenzury," Istoricheskie Zapiski XXXVII (1951), pp. 215-216. A collection of censors' opinions and some additional briefs by editors and publishers were also prepared at the time.

48. "Zapiska predsedatelia komiteta dlia peresmotra tsensurnago ustava d.t.s. Bert i chlena sego komiteta st. sov. Iankevicha," in Proekty i zapiski o tsenzure; Valuev, Dnevnik...., I, p. 130.

49. "Zapiski o tsenzure st. sov. Fridberga, 1862) pp. 4-27 and "Zapiski o tsenzure kol. ass. Fuksa, 1862", pp. 5-58 in Proekty i zapiski o tsenzure.

50. K. S. Veselovskii, "Vospominaniia K. S. Veselovskago. Vremia prezidentstva gr. D. N. Bludova v Akad. Nauk 1855-1864" Russkaia Starina CVIII (Dec., 1901), pp. 516-18; Materialy.....1869, Part I, pp. 38-39; (Seredonin) Istoricheskii obzor...kom...min..., III, Part 2, pp. 199-202.

51. Veselovskii, "Vospominaniia....," Russkaia Starina (Dec., 1901), pp. 517-518; Lemke, Epokha...., pp. 166-69, 197.

52. Proekt ustava o knigopechatanii (SPB: 1862), Part I, pp. 167-71.

53. Ibid., Part I, Introduction, pp. III-X, 1-31, 34-45, 69-98; Collins, The Government......, pp. 116-17.

54. Proekt ustava o knigopechatanii (SPB: 1862) Part II, Division VI, pp. 2-92.

55. V. Binshtok, "Materialy po istorii russkoi tsenzury (60-kh godov)," Russkaia Starina LXXXIX (Mar., 1897), pp. 590-94. The author incorrectly states that the material refers to the project of the ministry of interior.

56. Ibid., p. 594.

57. Lemke, Epokha...., pp. 253-58. Nikitenko thought that Golovnin wanted to play the role of a liberal and avoid responsibility for the project. See A. Nikitenko, Moia povest' o samom sebe i o tom 'chemu sviditel' v zhizni byl' Zapiski i dnevnik. 1804-1877, Ed. by M. K. Lemke 2nd ed., 2 vols. (SPB: 1904), II, pp. 107, 109, 117.

58. Valuev, Dnevnik...., I, pp. 199, 201, 203; (Seredonin) Istoricheskii obzor...kom...min.., IV, Part 2, pp. 202-203; Vsepoddanneishii doklad ministra narodnago prosveshcheniia.. 10 Ianvaria 1863 god....

59. Materialy... 1869, Part I, pp. 39-40.

60. Zhurnaly vysochaishe uchrezhdennoi kommissii..., pp. 5-6.

61. Proekt ustava o knigopechatanii (SPB: 1863), Division I, pp. 1-20; Division II, paragraphs 87-92, pp. 20-21.

62. "Otzyv" of Minister of Education, Dec. 7, 1863 and "Predstavlenie" of Minister of Interior, Nov. 17, 1864 in Ibid., Part III, pp. 31, 43-50.

63. "Otzyv" of head of Second Section, Baron Korf, Feb. 7, 1864 and "Predstavlenie" of Minister of Interior, Nov. 17, 1864 in Ibid., Part III, pp. 8-14, 55-118.

64. "Otzyv" of Minister of Justice, Mar., 13, 1864 and "Predstavlenie" of Minister of Interior, Nov. 17, 1864; "Otzyv" of head of Second Section, Count Panin, Sept. 19, 1864 and "Predstavlenie" of Minister of Interior, Nov. 17, 1864 in Ibid., pp. 15-21, 24-27, 118-29, 135-47.

65. Materialy... 1869, Part I, pp. 384-409 (Journal of Department of Laws, 16, 20, 21 and 23 January, 1865); Valuev, Dnevnik...., II, pp. 14, 17, 18, 443-44.

66. Valuev, Dnevnik...., II, pp. 23-24; Materialy... 1869, Part I, pp. 460-88 (Journal of State Council).

67. <u>Materialy....1869</u>, Part I, pp. 489-512.

68. <u>Ibid.</u>, Part I, pp. 512-27 (Journal of Department of Laws 10, 13 March, 1865).

69. <u>Ibid.</u>, Part I, pp. 545-48 (Excerpt from Journal of State Council 24 March 1865); Valuev, <u>Dnevnik....</u>, II, pp. 26, 29, 445; K. K. Arsen'ev, <u>Zakonodatel'stvo o pechati</u> (SPB: 1903), pp. 15-17; <u>Gosudarstvennyi Sovet 1801-1901</u> (SPB: 1901) p. 117. See also Ruud, "The Russian Empire's....," <u>Canadian Slavic Studies</u> No. 2 (1969), pp. 241-44; Balmuth, "The Origins....," <u>Slavonic and East European Review</u> (Jan., 1969).

70. Quoted from Nikitenko's <u>Diary</u> in Ruud, "The Russian Empire's ....," <u>Canadian Slavic Studies</u> No. 2 (1969), pp. 243-44.

71. Valuev, <u>Dnevnik......</u>, II, p. 446. Zaionchkovskii, in these notes, quotes Valuev's memorandum "O polozhenii del pechati."

Footnotes   Chapter III

1. F. 776, d. 72, pp. 212-13b, 218-220; F. 776, op. 3, 1865, d. 4, pp. 5-14, 16-23; Materialy....1869, Part V, pp. 38-40, Part II, pp. 177-78.

2. Materialy....1869, Part II, p. 134.

3. Materialy....1869, Part IV, pp. 46-60 and Part II, pp. 263-268 quoting the Northern Post in 1865 and 1867.

4. Materialy....1869, Part II, pp. 68-76 (Opinion in Moskva case).

5. V. V. Garmiza, "Predlozheniia i proekty P. A. Valueva po voprosom vnutrennei politiki 1862-1866 gg." Istoricheskii Arkhiv, No. 1 (Jan.-Feb., 1958), pp. 150-51; M. V. Teplinskii, Otechestvennye Zapiski 1868-1884 (Iuzhno-Sakhalinsk: 1966), pp. 42-43. I. V. Orzhekhovskii, Administratsiia i pechat'mezhdu dvumia revoliutsionnymi situatsiiami 1866-1878 gg. (Gorkii: 1973), p. 55. In November 1867 Valuev instructed the Chief Board that his aim was to eliminate from printed works all that might shake the authority of the government and to permit all that did not weaken the integrity of the Empire. In February, 1868, Valuev was even less optimistic about the power of the government subsidized or sponsored press. Now he hoped only to keep the anti-government press within limits. Garmiza dates Valuev's memorandum in April, 1866. Zaionchkovskii dates it to the end of October, 1866. See Valuev, Dnevnik..., I p. 42. In 1866 Valuev wrote with respect to the censorship: "force will not produce good consequences and cannot end bad." See Ibid., II, p. 127.

6. P. Gurevich, "K kharakteristike reaktsii shestdesiatikh godov," O Minuvshem, (SPB: 1909), pp. 100-109; Orzhekhovskii, pp. 23, 26.

7. SPR 1865-68, p. 27.

8. F. 777, 1866, op. 2, d. 11, p. 67a and b; Orzhekhovskii, pp. 24-25.

9. SPR 1865-68, pp. 165-69; Materialy....1869, Part II, pp. 240-42. This is probably the circular Valuev referred to in his diary which Zaionchkovskii did not find in the archives. See Valuev, Dnevnik..., II, p. 129.

10. F. 776, d. 5, op. 4, 1870, p. 65; Materialy....1869, Part I, pp. 646-49. The Murav'ev Commission also precipitated an extended consideration of books for elementary schools and the common people. See Materialy....1869, Part II, pp. 209-11, 216-22; Orzhekhovskii, pp. 28-29.

11. F. 776, d. 17, 1866, pp. 11-12b; F. 776, d. 662, 1867, pp. 58-59. Thus a case involving the anthology Light (Luch) began in 1866 and with the case still undecided in 1874, the Committee of Ministers ordered the book, confiscated since 1866, destroyed. See L. M. Dobrovolskii, Zapreshchennaia kniga v Rossii 1825-1904 (Moscow: 1962), p. 58.

12. Materialy...1869, Part II, pp. 73-74. (in a Senate opinion in the Moskva case).

13. Ibid., Part III, p. 335, Part I, pp. 587-642. Of 21 cases from 1866 to 1868, the minister of justice refused to prosecute 8. See Orzhekhovskii, pp. 35, 43-44. This December 12, 1866 law also allowed arrest of a publication as soon as prosecution was initiated. The original law allowed arrest only on sentence by the court or by the Chief Board on the initiative of prosecutor. It may be that Valuev, by this law was giving the courts an opportunity to prove their usefulness to the government.

14. Materialy...1869, Part IV, pp. 122-23, Part I, pp. 587-642.

15. (K. K. Arsen'ev), "Iz vospominanii K. K. Arsen'eva," Golos Minuvshago, No. 2 (1915), pp. 121-23; SPR 1865-1868, pp. 151-52; Materialy....1869, Part III, pp. 65-118 (Case of Suvorin). Of 13 cases from 1866 to 1868, three of the accused were vindicated completely. See Orzhekhovskii, p. 44.

16. M. K. Lemke, "K sorokaletiiu 'velikoi reformy'" Mir Bozhii (Apr., 1905), pp. 21-26; V. Rozenberg and V. Iakushkin, Russkaia pechat' i tsenzura v proshlom i nastoiashchem (Moscow: 1905), pp. 136-38, 139-40. Another periodical, Moskva, was closed by the State Council.

17. F. 776, d. 662, 1867, pp. 216-19.

18. F. 776, d. 17, 1866, pp. 4a and b, 9-10b; F. 776, d. 662, 1867, p. 212b. In December, 1866, all warnings issued up to January, 1867 were expunged. Materialy...1869, Part II, p. 1.

19. F. 776, op. 4, 1870, d. 5, p. 30; F. 776, d. 17, 1866, p. 4a and b. In Germany, in 1868, 2,992 newspapers were being published, of which 942 dealt with politics. Materialy.... 1869, Part IV, p. 508 from Vestnik Evropy, No. 1, 1869.

20. F. 776, d. 662, 1867, pp. 137-138b. There are different figures in another folio: The Voice 16,390 and St. Petersburg Reports 16,600. See F. 776, d. 17, 1866, pp. 4a and b.

21. F. 776, d. 662, 1867, pp. 148, 150-52.

22. F. 776, d. 17, 1866, pp. 9-10b.

23. F. 776, d. 5, op. 4, 1870, pp. 46b-47b.

24. SPR 1865-1868, p. 32.

25. F. 776, d. 17, 1866, p. 28b. Only the editors of Moscow Reports and Russian Invalid retained the privilege.

26. SPR 1865-1868, pp. 77-78; V. Evgen'ev, "D. I. Pisarev i okhraniteli" Golos Minuvshago, No. 1-4 (1919), pp. 138-40; Materialy....1869, Part II, p. 122.

27. SPR 1865-1868, p. 78; A. A. Plotkin, Pisarev i literaturno-obshchestvennoi dvizhenie shestidesiatikh godov (Leningrad, Moscow: 1945), p. 291; V. Bogucharskii Iz proshlogo russkogo obshchestva (SPB: 1904), p. 370; Materialy....1869, Part II, pp. 122-23.

28. V. Evgen'ev, "I. A. Goncharov kak chlena soveta glavnogo upravleniia po delam pechati" Golos Minuvshago, No. 11 (1916), pp. 137-42. The relative freedom granted by the new press law is indicated by the following: Shelgunov's article had been originally rejected by the censors as an "apotheosis of communism." As soon as the journal was freed of the preliminary censorship, the publisher printed it. See F. F. Kuznetsov, "Zhurnal Russkoe Slovo i narodnichestvo" in A. V. Zapadov (ed.), Iz istorii russkoi zhurnalistiki (Moscow: 1959), p. 98.

29. Evgen'ev, "I. A. Goncharov....," Golos Minuvshago, No. 11 (1916), pp. 137-42; SPR 1865-1868, pp. 79-80; Materialy.... 1869, Part II, pp. 124-25.

30. Evgen'ev, " I. A. Goncharov....," Golos Minuvshago, No. 11 (1916), pp. 148-49. The second volume of the anthology, after a long and inconclusive prosecution, was forbidden by the Committee of Ministers in October, 1874. Dobrovol'skii, Zapreshchennaia kniga...., pp. 57-58.

31. K. Voenskii, "Goncharov-tsenzor. Neizdannoe materialy dlia ego biografii" Russkii Vestnik, Vol. 305, No. 10 (1906) pp. 579-83; Evgen'ev, "D. I. Pisarev..." Golos Minuvshago, No. 1-4 (1919), pp. 138-40.

32. SPR 1865-1868, pp. 74-75; Materialy....1869, Part II, pp. 118-19.

33. Evgen'ev, "I. A. Goncharov....," Golos Minuvshago, No. 11 (1916), p. 131; SPR 1865-1868, pp. 76-77; Rozenberg and Iakushkin, pp. 247-48; Materialy....1869, Part II, pp. 121-22.

34. V. Evgen'ev-Maksimov, Ocherki po istorii sotsialisticheskoi zhurnalistiki (Moscow-Leningrad: 1927), pp. 119-20.

35. A. D. Alekseev, Letopis' zhizni i tvorchestva I. A. Goncharova (Moscow-Leningrad: 1960), p. 156; Orzhekhovskii, p. 45.

36. Arsen'ev, "Iz vospominanii.." Golos Minuvshago, No. 2 (1915), pp. 121-23; SPR 1865-1868, pp. 150-51.

37. Materialy....1869, Part III, pp. 155, 186.

38. Ibid., Part II, pp. 119-20; SPR 1865-1868, pp. 75-76.

39. SPR 1865-1868, pp. 153-54; Materialy....1869, Part III, pp. 12-64.

40. SPR 1865-1868, p. 84; Materialy....1869, Part II, pp. 129-30.

41. SPR 1865-1868, pp. 86-87; Materialy....1869, Part II, p. 132.

42. SPR 1865-1868, pp. 95, 96; Materialy....1869, Part II, pp. 142, 143.

43. F. 776, d. 662, 1867, pp. 116-18, 171b-173.

44. Rozenberg and Iakushkin, pp. 230-31.

45. Voenskii, Russkii Vestnik No. 10 (1906), pp. 585-601; Evgen'ev, "I. A. Goncharov....," Golos Minuvshago No. 11 (1916), pp. 128-31.

46. SPR 1865-1868, p. 88; Bogucharskii, Iz proshlogo..., pp. 377-78; Materialy....1869, Part II, p. 134; Laverichev, Istoriia SSSR No. 1 (1972), p. 31.

47. SPR 1865-1868, p. 90; Bogucharskii, Iz proshlogo...., pp. 377-378; Materialy... 1869, Part II, p. 136.

48. SPR 1865-1868, pp. 91-92; Materialy... 1869, Part II, p. 138; Bogucharskii, Iz proshlogo...., pp. 377-78. The warning did not mention the agreement of the Council, the usual form for such warnings. Bogucharskii says the suspension was for three months. Orzhekhovskii says four months and that Alexander approved the warning. Orzhekhovskii, p. 60.

49. SPR 1865-1868, pp. 93-94; Bogucharskii, Iz proshlogo...., pp. 377-78; Materialy... 1869, Part II, pp. 140-41.

50. SPR 1865-1868, pp. 96-98; Bogucharskii, Iz proshlogo...., pp. 378-79; Materialy... 1869, Part II, pp. 143-45.

51. Ibid., Part II, pp. 3-5; Orzhekhovskii, pp. 61-62.

52. SPR 1865-1868, pp. 99-100; Bogucharskii, Iz proshlogo...., pp. 378-79; Materialy... 1869, Part II, pp. 146-48.

53. SPR 1865-1868, p. 101; Bogucharskii, Iz proshlogo...., pp. 378-79; Materialy... 1869, Part II, p. 150.

54. K. K. Arsen'ev, Zakonodatel'stvo o pechati (SPB: 1903), p. 26; F. 776, op. 4, 1870, d. 5, pp. 37b-38; Bogucharskii, Iz proshlogo...., pp. 378-83; Materialy... 1869, Part II, pp. 153-54, 7-103; Laverichev, Istoriia SSSR No. 1 (1972), p. 33. The State Council also decided that henceforth the Senate should simply decide whether the Minister's reason for requesting a ban was sufficient and not consider whether another kind of punishment was preferable. After the suspension, Aksakov decided to end the publication. See Orzhekhovskii, pp. 63-64.

55. F. 776, d. 662, 1867, pp. 179-80b.

56. Materialy.....1869, Part II, pp. 99-103.

57. Arsen'ev suggests that the principal crime of Moskva and the Moskovskie Vedemosti was their lack of respect for the tradition of circumlocution and caution. See Materialy... 1869, Part IV, pp. 70-73 from Vestnik Evropy, No. 4 and 6, 1869. Also in Arsen'ev, Zakonodatel'stvo...., pp. 32-35. Note a comment of a Council member in the 1870s that the radicals had to "muffle" their theories and as a result these theories lost their attractiveness to readers. See Teplinskii, pp. 92-93. In 1885, the censorship, while condemning a periodical, noted that the publisher did not

consider it necessary to express himself by allusions or allegories and stated his ideas with "striking frankness." See P. A. Zaionshkovskii, Rossiiskoe samoderzhavie v k.ontse XIX stoletiia (Moscow: 1970), p. 294.

58. SPR 1865-1868, p. 81. The Council considered the case but five members of seven opposed the warning. Valuev decided on a warning. See Materialy... 1869, Part II, p. 126. For the influence of Moskovskie Vedemosti, see Feoktistov, pp. 64-65. Valuev and the Tsar thought it an act of courage for Valuev to challenge Katkov. See Valuev, Dnevnik..., II, pp. 112, 436. Orzhekhovskii, p. 47.

59. SPR 1865-1868, pp. 82-83; Materialy... 1869, Part II, p. 128.

60. SPR 1865-1868, pp. 82-83; Materialy... 1869, Part II, pp. 128-29.

61. Bogucharskii, Iz proshlogo....., pp. 372-375; Valuev, Dnevnik...., II, pp. 124, 443, 466. This special protection offered in 1866 repeated a similar decision by the Committee of Ministers in January, 1865, confirmed by the Emperor. Then Valuev was asked to show all possible leniency to Moskovskie Vedemosti. Apparently Katkov was not satisfied with this concession. According to Valuev he wished to become his own censor. Valuev, Dnevnik, I, pp. 359-60.

62. SPR 1865-1868, pp. 104-105; Orzhekhovskii, pp. 47-52.

63. F. 776, d. 662, 1867, pp. 125b-27, 86b-87; F. 109, 1861, 1st. Eks., d. 12, Part II, pp. 14-31.

64. Alekseev, Letopis'...., pp. 148-49, 152-53; F. 776, d. 17, 1866, pp. 10b, 11, 14b; SPR 1865-1868, pp. 79, 86, 87, 88-90, 93, 94-95, 98-99, 100-101, 110-111, 153, 157-58.

65. SPR 1865-1868, pp. 114-16; Materialy... 1869, Part II, pp. 235-36.

66. F. 777, op. 3, 1865, d. 6, pp. 8-13b, 14-16; Materialy.... 1869, Part II, pp. 435-43.

67. SPR 1865-1868, pp. 119-21; Materialy... 1869, Part II, p. 247.

68. F. 777, op. 3, 1865, d. 6, pp. 34, 39; Materialy... 1869, Part II, p. 238. In March, 1866, the Baltic press was allowed to refute Katkov's contention that the Baltic Germans were separatists. In November, 1867, Valuev

advised the Council that it must expurgate all that stimulated hostility among the various parts of the Empire. Orzhekhovskii, p. 55.

69. Evgen'ev, "I. A. Goncharov....," Golos Minuvshago No. 12 (1916), pp. 141-46.

70. Voenskii, Russkii Vestnik No. 10 (1906), pp. 579-83; Evgen'ev, "D. I. Pisarev...." Golos Minuvshago No. 1-4 (1919), pp. 138-40.

71. Evgen'ev, "I. A. Goncharov....," Golos Minuvshago No. 11 (1916), pp. 137-42, 142-48.

72. Ibid., pp. 152-55. Goncharov recommended that the ministry of education be advised regularly of books that might be harmful to children.

73. Ibid., No. 12 (1916), pp. 171-73.

74. Evgen'ev, "D. I. Pisarev....," Golos Minuvshago No. 1-4 (1919), pp. 142-44; V. Evgen'ev-Maksimov, I. A. Goncharov (Moscow-Leningrad: 1925), pp. 107-12.

75. In 1866, Goncharov was prepared to permit a translation of Beranger's poems against the will of the censor on the grounds that the work, a sixth edition, had done its harm already. But the Council and the Minister supported the censor. Aizenshtok, "Frantsuzskie pisateli...," Literaturnoe Nasledstvo, Vol. 33-34 (1939), pp. 799-800.

76. Evgen'ev, "D. I. Pisarev....," Golos Minuvshago No. 1-4 (1919), pp. 144-48.

77. Ibid., p. 148; SPR 1865-1868, p. 159.

78. Evgen'ev, "D. I. Pisarev....." Golos Minuvshago No. 1-4 (1919), pp. 148-53; Materialy... 1869, Part III, pp. 526-32.

79. Evgen'ev, " D. I. Pisarev....," Golos Minuvshago No. 1-4 (1919), pp. 148-53.

80. Evgen'ev, "I. A. Goncharov....," Golos Minuvshago No. 12 (1916), pp. 158-59.

81. Ibid., pp. 146-48; F. 776, d. 17, 1866, pp. 11-12b. The work was prosecuted.

82. Materialy... 1869, Part II, pp. 209-12, 216.

83. B. V. Bank, *Izuchenie chitatelei v Rossii* (XIX v.) (Moscow: 1969), pp. 12, 14-15; A. Sinel, *The Classroom and the Chancellery* (Cambridge, Mass.: 1973), pp. 61-62.

84. *Materialy...1869*, Part II, pp. 212-22, Part V, pp. 181-90.

85. F. 776, d. 17, 1866, p. 22 a and b; Orzhekhovskii, pp. 15-16.

86. F. 776, d. 662, 1867, p. 222; F. 776, op. 4, 1870, d. 5, pp. 90-93.

87. F. 777, 1866, op. 2, d. 11, pp. 68-69b.

88. F. 776, d. 17, 1866, pp. 22a and b. Another archival source lists 3.7m. volumes as imported in 1866. F. 776, 1876, d. 105, p. 53a-57b. Orzhekhovskii p. 16 gives the figure of 1.8m. publications in 6.1m. volumes and issues of periodicals.

89. F. 776, d. 17, 1866, pp. 5-7b. The Council held 52 sessions (at least twice weekly) in 1865, 84 in 1866, and 75 in 1867. Orzhekhovskii, p. 55.

90. F. 776, d. 662, 1867, pp. 213b, 214a and b.

91. F. 776, op. 3, d. 17, 1866, pp. 2a and b. This figure was over 40,000 rubles more than the cost of the censorship in 1863. In *Materialy...1869*, Part I, pp. 586-87, the cost is given as 219,500 for the year.

92. F. 776, d. 662, 1867, pp. 210b-211.

93. F. 776, d. 17, 1866, p. 24.

94. F. 776, d. 5, op. 4, 1870, pp. 76b-77.

95. F. 776, d. 662, 1867, pp. 244b-45. St. Petersburg had 14 bookstores and 98 libraries; Moscow had 90 bookstores and 15 libraries; the Empire had 338 bookstores and 304 libraries.

96. *Materialy...1869*, Part II, pp. 164-66.

97. F. 776, d. 17, 1866, p. 4b.

98. F. 777, op. 2, 1867, d. 31, pp. 8-9.

99. F. 776, op. 2, 1867, d. 31, pp. 7-8.

100. F. 776, d. 662, 1867, p. 33b.

101. F. 777, op. 2, 1867, d. 31, pp. 6a and b. In F. 776, d. 17, 1866, pp. 9-10b the figures of 8 articles from The Voice and 5 from the St. Petersburg Reports are given.

102. N. I. Sokolov, "Delo" in V. G. Berezina, N. P. Emel'ianov et al (ed), Ocherki po istorii russkoi zhurnalistiki i kritiki (Leningrad: 1965), II, p. 314.

103. F. 776, d. 17, 1866, p. 20.

104. F. 776, d. 662, 1867, p. 221. In 1867, the Emperor agreed to allow the performance of Schiller's "The Robbers" in Russian and Beaumarchais' "Marriage of Figaro", previously performed in Russian and then forbidden. "William Tell" was permitted with the exclusion of Act 5. Materialy... 1869, Part II, pp. 1-2.

105. Cited in Orzhekhovskii, p. 55, In 1867, Kudiakov's Ancient Russia appeared after the censorship decided that the author's interpretation of Russian history showed the Grand Princely power in an unfavorable light. The Committee decided that so long as the book did not become a school text, it could be tolerated since the facts it related were not invented and the period treated was pre-Petrine Russia. The book was the sole publication of the radical "Society of the Ruble". See I. E. Barenboim, "Tipograf M. A. Kukol'-Iasnopol'skii i demokraticheskoe knizhnoe delo 60-kh godov XIXv." in Problemy ruskopisnoi i pechatnoi knigi (Moscow: 1976), pp. 281-83.

106. Valuev, Dnevnik, I, p. 42.

107. Orzhekhovskii, p. 56.

Footnotes   Chapter IV

1. Valuev, <u>Dnevnik</u>...., I, pp. 42-44.

2. Feoktistov, pp. 108-109, Orzhekhovskii, pp. 56, 65-66; Valuev, <u>Dnevnik</u>, II, pp. 252, 254, 258. The views of the Third Section, headed by Timashev's friend, Count Shuvalov, coincided with those of Timashev. Shuvalov, in his account for 1869, said the patriotic and conservative critics of government policy were more harmful than the open opponents of the government who could easily be penalized. In the school of conservative and patriotic critics, Shuvalov included Kraevskii's <u>Golos</u> and Katkov's <u>Moskovskie Vedomosti</u> and <u>Russkii Vestnik</u>.

3. Garmiza, Predlozheniia....," <u>Istoricheskii Arkhiv</u> (No. 1 (Jan.-Feb., 1958), pp. 150-51. Garmiza gives the date April 26, 1866 but Zaionchkovskii dates the memorandum as October, 1866. Valuev, <u>Dnevnik</u>...., I, p. 42.

4. Gurevich, "K kharakteristike....," <u>O Minuvshem</u>, pp. 102-103. Orzhekhovskii corrects Gurevich who attributed this memorandum to Murav'ev. Orzhekhovskii, pp. 26-27.

5. Gurevich, "K kharakteristike....," <u>O Minuvshem</u>, pp. 100-105; "Predstavlenie" of Minister of Interior, April 15, 1869 in <u>Materialy....1869</u>, Part I, pp. 648-49; Orzhekhovskii, p. 28. The Committee proposed also to restrict the authority of the judiciary over administrators. The proposal was so extreme that Gagarin and two ministers protested. See R. Wortman, <u>The Development of a Russian Legal Consciousness</u> (Chicago: 1976), p. 272.

6. <u>Materialy... 1869</u>, Part I, pp. 706-707 (Remarks of 2nd Section October 18, Nov. 11, 1866); Part III, p. 335, Part IV, pp. 122-23. Clearly, the mandatory character of the indictment violated the spirit of the judicial reform. See Wortman, pp. 273-74. It would appear that by this measure Valuev was giving the courts a chance to show their usefulness to the government.

7. Remarks of Minister of Justice, July 16, 1868 in <u>Materialy.. 1869</u>, Part I, pp. 710-21.

8. <u>Materialy... 1869</u>, Part I, pp. 649-85.

9. "Predstavlenie" of Minister of Interior, April 15, 1869 in <u>Materialy... 1869</u>, Part I, pp. 685-704.

10. Remarks of Minister of Justice, April 27, 1869 in <u>Materialy ... 1869</u>, Part I, pp. 721-28.

11. Remarks of head of Second Section, July 4, 1869 in <u>Materialy ... 1869</u>, Part I, pp. 728-33.

12. Journal of Council of Chief Board, October 10 and 17, 1869 in <u>Materialy... 1869</u>, Part I, pp. 735-41.

13. Valuev, <u>Dnevnik....</u>, II, pp. 272-73. In August, 1869 Timashev showed his dissatisfaction with the courts when he argued in a memorandum to the Emperor that the courts protected periodicals which advocated a limited monarchy. Orzhekhovskii, p. 65.

14. F. 776, op. 4, d. 5, 1870, p. 65; F. 776, 1869/71, op. 28, d. 1, p. 1. On November 20, 1869, Timashev denounced Katkov's <u>Moscow Reports</u> in the Council of Ministers for acting as if it were beyond the power of the administration. Valuev, <u>Dnevnik....</u>, II, pp. 503-504.

15. F. 776, 1869/71, op. 28, d. 1, pp. 1-2; <u>Zhurnal osoboi kommissii vysochaishe uchrezhdennoi 2-go noiabria 1869 g. dlia peresmotra deistvuiushchikh postanovlenii o tsenzure i pechati</u> (SPB: 1870) Nos. 1 and 2, p. 2, 7.

16. <u>Materialy... 1869</u>, Part III, pp. 1273-76 (undated).

17. <u>Zhurnal... 1869</u>, pp. 58-60; F. 776, d. 197, pp. 70-73.

18. <u>Zhurnal... 1869</u>, pp. 69-71.

19. <u>Ibid.</u>, pp. 75-82.

20. <u>Ibid.</u>, p. 125. Some recommended six days. See F. 776, 1869/71, d. 1, p. 364b.

21. <u>Zhurnal... 1869...</u>, pp. 291-302.

22. <u>Ibid.</u>, pp. 332-37; F. 776, 1869/71, d. 1, pp. 472ff.

23. <u>Zhurnal... 1869...</u>, pp. 423-24.

24. <u>Ibid.</u>, pp. 386-87.

25. F. 776, op. 28, d. 9, pp. 2a and b.

26. F. 776, 1869/71, d. 1, p. 350b.

27. F. 776, d. 197, p. 95b.

28. F. 776, op. 28, d. 9, p. 3b.

29. F. 776, 1869/71, op. 28, d. 2, pp. 108-109.

30. F. 776, 1869/71, d. 1, p. 348.

31. F. 776, 1869/71, d. 1, p. 412. The Code is in F. 776, d. 76, pp. 250-53 and in F. 776, 1869/71, d. 1, pp. 350-410, 438-98.

32. F. 776, d. 197, p. 85. The members of the group were P. A. Shuvalov, D. A. Tolstoy, C. Pahlen, Urusov and the vice-minister of interior, M. K. Shidlovskii. Orzhekhovskii, p. 70.

33. F. 776, d. 72, p. 169. The quoted words replaced a sentence crossed out in the original, which attributed the fate of the Commission's project to the changes in the press regulations. Valuev's archive notes that special political conditions led the government to put aside the idea of publishing a law emphasizing judicial responsibility. See Orzhekhovskii, p. 70.

34. F. 776, d. 72, pp. 2-11; Orzhekhovskii, p. 72.

35. Valuev, Dnevnik...., II, pp. 279-80; Orzhekhovskii, pp. 72-74.

36. F. 776, d. 72, p. 12.

37. F. 776, d. 72, pp. 13-21b; Materialy... 1905, pp. 30-33.

38. F. 776, d. 72, pp. 92-93 (undated note)

39. F. 776, d. 72, pp. 40-42.

40. F. 776, d. 1, 1877, pp. 334-36.

41. F. 776, 1880, d. 195, pp. 135, 143 a and b.

42. F. 777, 1871, d. 100 pp. 39b-40; see also F. 776, d. 154, 1871, p. 197.

43. F. 776, op. 4, 1870, d. 5, p. 36. In 1871, Timashev refused to prosecute Notes of the Fatherland despite the request of the head of the Chief Board, Shidlovskii. Timashev accepted a proposal to exclude the offending article. Teplinskii, pp. 81-82.

44. F. 776, 1871, d. 150 Part III, p. 38.

45. F. 776, 1871, d. 150 Part III, pp. 47b-50.

46. Evgen'ev, "D. I. Pisarev....," *Golos Minuvshago* No. 1-4 (1919), pp. 144-48; *SPR 1865-1868*, p. 159.

47. Evgen'ev, "D. I. Pisarev....," *Golos Minuvshago* No. 1-4 (1919), pp. 148-53; *Materialy... 1869*, Part III, pp. 526-32.

48. *Materialy... 1869*, Part III, pp. 259-333; *Zakony o pechati, Sobranie deistvuiushchikh zakonodatel'nykh postanovlenii o pechati* (SPB: 1873), pp. 200-201. Pavlenkov was arrested on September 3, 1868 for a speech he gave at Pisarev's funeral and for collecting money for a memorial. On May 14, 1869 the Senate gave its decision. But Pavlenkov was exiled to Viatka. See Nikitenko, *Dnevnik*, III, p. 441.

49. *Materialy... 1869*, Part IV, p. 349. Pavlenkov published the guilty articles in Moscow after changing their titles. Nikitenko, *Dnevnik*, III, p. 441.

50. *Materialy... 1869*, Part V, p. 13 note.

51. *Materialy... 1869*, Part III, p. 541-59.

52. Dobrovol'skii, *Zapreshchennaia kniga....*, pp. 57-59.

53. *Materialy... 1869*, Part III, pp. 5-12.

54. *Materialy... 1869*, Part III, pp. 499-505; L. Polianskii, "Arkhivnyi fond glavnogo upravleniia po delam pechati," *Literaturnoe Nasledstvo* Vol. 22-24, (1935), p. 630.

55. *Materialy... 1869*, Part III, pp. 925-74. Valuev himself had collaborated in the journal *Vest'* but was no longer minister when this case came to court in 1868.

56. *Ibid.*, Part III, pp. 806-95.

57. *SPR 1865-1868*, pp. 150-60, Orzhekhovskii says that in 13 trials from 1866-68, the defendants won in three cases; that the censorship initiated 21 cases but that the prosecutor would not agree to prosecute 8 of the cases. Orzhekhovskii, pp. 43, 44.

58. *Materialy... 1869*, Part III, pp. 439-92; Barenboim, "Tipograf....," *Problemy rukopisnoi i pechatnoi knigi*, pp. 283-84. The Russian edition was prepared by P. Shchapov.

59. *Materialy... 1869*, Part III, pp. 508-19.

60. Ibid., Part III, pp. 519-25.

61. Ibid., Part III, pp. 334-90.

62. Ibid., Part III, pp. 532-37; Aizenshtok, "Frantsuzskie pisateli...," Literaturnoe Nasledstvo Vol. 33-34 (1939), pp. 789-90; Polianskii, "Arkhivnyi fond....," Literaturnoe Nasledstvo Vol. 22-24 (1935), p. 628; Dobrovol'skii, Zapreshchennaia kniga...., pp. 69-70. Volume 2 was destroyed in 1870 on the order of Alexander.

63. Materialy... 1869, Part III, pp. 189-258.

64. Ibid., Part III, pp. 65-125; Dobrovol'skii, Zapreshchennaia kniga...., pp. 54-56; E. Ambler, Russian Journalism and Politics 1861-1881. The Career of Aleksei S. Suvorin (Detroit: 1972), pp. 68-69.

65. In 1869, nine senators argued that the courts had in fact upheld the press laws. The senators even proposed a definition of a "harmful tendency" that might entail the use of administrative measures but wanted other press cases tried in the courts. The Chief Board demurred. See Wortman, pp. 274-75. The case involved Aksakov's Moskva.

66. Materialy... 1869, Part IV, pp. 64-128 from Vestnik Evropy No. 4 and 6, 1869.

67. Wortman perhaps best expresses the attitude of more traditional officials towards the courts; "For the Russian autocracy to accept an independent judiciary required it to betray its essence and cease to be the Russian autocracy." See Wortman, p. 285.

Footnotes   Chapter V

1. F. 776, op. 4, d. 5, 1870, pp. 66a and b; Orzhekhovskii, pp. 67-68.

2. B. I. Esin, <u>Russkaia zhurnalistika 70-80 godov XIX veka</u> (Moscow: 1963), pp. 180-184. In 1868, Valuev said a government press was appropriate to countries where there were political parties or an excess of talented writers. Neither of these conditions existed in Russia, he said. See Orzhekhovskii, pp. 68-69.

3. <u>SPR 1865-1868</u>, p. 37; <u>Materialy....1905</u>, pp. 29, 106-108; <u>Materialy....1869</u>, Part I, pp. 643-46, Part V, pp. 114-15; Arsen'ev, <u>Zakonodatel'stvo....</u>, pp. 26-27.

4. <u>Materialy....1869</u>, Part IV, pp. 92-93; (Mikhnevich) <u>Piat'-nadtsatiletie gazety Golos 1863-1877</u> (SPB: 1878), p. I. From 1870 the prohibition of retail sale affected sale at bookstores also. See Rozenberg and Iakushkin, pp. 130-31.

5. Rozenberg and Iakushkin, pp. 144-46.

6. F. 776, op. 11, d. 72, p. 2-31, 46a and b, 248a and b; <u>Materialy....1905</u>, pp. 30-33.

7. F. 776, op. 11, d. 72, p. 42.

8. <u>Materialy....1905</u>, pp. 36-37; F. 776, d. 72, pp. 126-33; F. 776, 1874, d. 2a, p. 140b. The occasion for this order was supplied by N. V. Shelgunov's <u>About the Education of Man</u>, an uncensored work which the publisher had printed in only 15 copies. Orzhekhovskii, p. 76.

9. Kraevskii, publisher of <u>Notes of the Fatherland</u>, used this method in 1867. See V. E. Evgen'ev-Maksimov, "Iz tsenzurnoi istorii, 'Otechestvennye Zapiski' (1868-1884)" <u>Russkoe Bogatstvo</u> No. 1-3 (1918), pp. 114-17. In 1879, in connection with a proposal to arrest an issue of the same periodical, the St. Petersburg chairman requested permission of the Chief Board to exclude culpable material from the journal to avoid confiscation. The Chairman indicated that this was the practice and that the procedure was known to the Chief Board. The request was granted. Evgen'ev-Maksimov, <u>Ocherki ....</u>, pp. 200, 202-204.

10. F. 776, d. 72, pp. 51-52. The works were volumes I and II of Lassalle's works and Blanc's <u>History of the February Revolution of 1848</u>, Vol. I.

11. F. 772, d. 72, pp. 92-93. Note is undated but internal evidence would suggest November, 1873 as the date.

12. M. K. Lemke, "Rasporiazheniia komiteta ministrov ob unichtozhenii proizvedenii pechati za 1872-1904 gody" <u>Vestnik Prava</u> (April, 1905), pp. 124-33; M. K. Lemke, "Neobkhodimyia dopolneniia" <u>Vestnik Prava</u> (Oct., 1905), p. 229.

13. F. 776, d. 1, 1877, p. 350.

14. <u>Materialy....1905</u>, pp. 33-36; F. 776, d. 72, p. 196; Lemke, "K sorokaletiiu..." <u>Mir Bozhii</u> (April, 1905), pp. 17-19; M. K. Lemke, "V mire usmotreniia (st. 140 i 156 ust. o tsen. i pech.)" <u>Vestnik Prava</u> (Sept., 1905), pp. 125, 129, 133-134, 135, 141-43, 151-52, 155-56; F. 777, op. 3, d. 95, pp. 6, 10; F. 777, op. 3. d. 95, p. 11; F. 777, op. 2, d. 8, 1879, pp. 44, 63-64.

15. Lemke, "V mire..." <u>Vestnik Prava</u> (Sept., 1905), pp. 110-11, 116; F. 777, op. 3, d. 95, pp. 3-4b. See also <u>Samoderzhavie i pechat' v Rossii</u> (SPB: 1906), pp. 43-52 and <u>Materialy dlia kharakteristiki polozheniia russkoi pechati</u> (Geneva: 1898), I, p. 99.

16. F. 776, d. 72, pp. 186-96 (Copy of Timashev's letter to the Committee of Ministers, Nov. 10, 1875).

17. Arsen'ev, <u>Zakonodatel'stvo...</u>, p. 243; Rozenberg and Iakushkin, pp. 132-33. In 1863 the government had ruled that it had the power to prohibit private advertisements in censored periodicals. Now it could withdraw that privilege from uncensored periodicals.

18. F. 777, 1870, d. 28, pp. 11b-12.

19. F. 776, d. 1, 1877, pp. 334-36.

20. F. 776, 1880, d. 195, pp. 135, 143a and b.

21. F. 777, 1871, d. 100, pp. 39b-40; see also F. 776, d. 154, 1871, p. 197b.

22. F. 776, op. 4, 1870, d. 5, p. 36.

23. F. 776, 1871, d. 150, Part III, p. 38.

24. F. 776, 1871, d. 150, Part III, pp. 47b-50.

25. Teplinskii, pp. 81-82.

26. F. 776, op. 4, 1870, d. 5, p. 31.

27. F. 776, 1880, d. 195, pp. 231b-32.

28. F. 776, op. 2, 1870, d. 5, pp. 100-105b.

29. F. 776, d. 1, 1877, p. 379b; F. 776, d. 3, 1881, pp. 140-41; F. 776, d. 95, 1880, pp. 128-33.

30. Bogucharskii, Iz proshlogo...., pp. 384-85.

31. Rozenberg and Iakushkin, p. 14.

32. F. 776, d. 195, 1880, pp. 244-45; Orzhekhovskii, p. 85.

33. F. 776, 1880, d. 195, pp. 248-52b. Thirty one periodicals received a total of 109 warnings in this period. Orzhekhovskii, p. 85.

34. F. 776, 1871, d. 150, Part III, pp. 34-36b.

35. F. 776, 1874, d. 2a, pp. 129, 140b.

36. F. 776, 1880, d. 195, pp. 99-102.

37. Evgen'ev-Maksimov, "Iz tsenzurnoi...," Russkoe Bogatstvo No. 1-3 (1918), pp. 134-36.

38. See for example Timashev on Katkov in Valuev, Dnevnik... , II, p. 503 and Nikitenko, Dnevnik, III, p. 161. The Third Section, in its account for 1869, saw Katkov's patriotism as a mask that allowed him to stimulate disorder. Orzhekhovskii, pp. 58-59.

39. A. F. Berezhnoi, Tsarskaia tsenzura i bor'ba bol'shevikov za svobodu pechati (1895-1914) (Leningrad: 1967), p. 52; Gerasimova, Iz istorii..., p. 89-90. In 1862 Kraevskii received a subsidy of 6,000 rubles from the ministry of interior for agreeing to "subject himself to the influence of the Third Section."

40. F. 777, 1870, d. 28, p. 17.

41. K. Chukovskii, "F. M. Tolstoi i ego pis'ma k Nekrasovu," Literaturnoe Nasledstvo Vol. 51-52 (1949), pp. 608-609.

42. F. 776, d. 72, pp. 97b, 103-105.

43. See F. 777, 1871, d. 100, p. 4; F. 777, 1871, d. 100, pp. 49-50.

44. (N. M. Lisovskii), "Materialy dlia kharakteristiki polozheniia russkoi pechati" Vsemirnyi Vestnik No. 8 (1908), p. 50; (Mikhnevich), Piat'nadtsatiletie....., pp. LI-LII.

45. Rozenberg and Iakushkin, pp. 231-32. See also F. 776, d. 1, 1877, pp. 325a and b; F. 776, d. 1, 1877, p. 323.

46. F. 776, 1880, d. 195, pp. 248-252b.

47. F. 776, d. 1, 1877, pp. 336-37.

48. (Lisovskii), "Materialy....," Vsemirnyi Vestnik No. 8 (1908) p. 50.

49. F. 777, 1870, d. 28, pp. 5-7; F. 776, 1880, pp. 128-33b.

50. Teplinskii, pp. 21-23, 24-25.

51. Teplinskii, pp. 42-50.

52. B. I. Esin, "Skvoz' prepony tsenzury" Kniga Vol. XIV (1967), p. 239.

53. F. 777, 1870, d. 28, p. 7b.

54. F. 777, 1874, d. 2a, p. 151b.

55. F. 776, d. 1, 1877, p. 149.

56. F. 776, d. 3, 1881, p. 142.

57. F. 777, 1871, d. 100, pp. 38-39.

58. F. 777, 1871, d. 100, p. 19b. See also Teplinskii, pp. 25-26 for 1867 opinion.

59. F. 777, 1870, d. 28, p. 9.

60. N. I. Sokolov, "Delo" in Berezina, Emel'ianov et al (ed.), Ocherki..., II, pp. 318-19.

61. A letter of the St. Petersburg chairman to the head of the Chief Board notes without comment the complaint of a publisher that censors were bribed to pass articles for The Deed. The Third Section finally extracted from the publisher a promise of silence. Teplinskii, p. 374. In 1888, The Deed closed on the basis of the rule that periodicals had to appear at least once within six months to retain the right to publish. The government, after arresting the

61. (continued) editor in 1884, made difficulties that hindered the sale of the journal. After I. S. Durnovo became publisher, the journal limped on until 1888. B. I. Esin, I. V. Myl'tsyn, "K kharakteristike zhurnala 'Delo'. Pis'mo N. F. Bazhina D. N. Maminu-Sibiriaku" in B. I. Esin (ed.), Iz istorii russkoi zhurnalistiki (Moscow: 1973), pp. 238-42.

62. Teplinskii, pp. 76-77, 87-88, 44-50; A. M. Garkavi, N. A. Nekrasov v bor'be s tsarskoi tsenzuroi (Kaliningrad: 1966), pp. 84, 87-89, 81-84.

63. Ibid., p. 250, Teplinskii, pp. 70-72, 82-84, 94-96. In 1874 Lazarevskii stubbornly defended the journal to the astonishment of Timashev. See for examples of excluded articles F. 776, d. 88, 1879, pp. 23a and b and F. 776, 1880 d. 195, p. 134b.

64. Evgen'ev-Maksimov, "Iz tsenzurnoi...," Russkoe Bogatstvo No. 1-3 (1918), pp. 140-43.

65. F. 777, 1870, d. 28, pp. 21a and b.

66. F. 777, 1871, d. 100, pp. 13a and b. But see Lebedev's critical remarks about Nekrasov's poems in Garkavi, pp. 121-23.

67. F. 776, 1871, d. 150, Part III, pp. 18b-19, 23-24, 43a and b; F. 776, d. 154, 1871, pp. 197-198; F. 777, 1871, d. 100, p. 40.

68. Teplinskii, pp. 114-18, 124-26.

69. Evgen'ev-Maksimov, "Iz tsenzurnoi...," Russkoe Bogatstvo No. 1-3 (1918), p. 130.

70. Evgen'ev-Maksimov, Ocherki...., pp. 188-89; Teplinskii, pp. 98-101.

71. Teplinskii, pp. 42-46. Teplinskii suggests that Valuev's policy explains his agreement to the transfer of Notes of the Fatherland to Nekrasov. According to the contract, after a first warning, Kraevskii could veto an article in which case the final decision would be made by an arbitrator. After a second warning, Nekrasov would give up the editorship of the journal. Garkavi, pp. 73-77.

72. Teplinskii, pp. 75-76.

73. Ibid., pp. 46-50, B. Papkovskii and S. Makashin, "Nekrasov i literaturnaia politika samoderzhavia," Literaturnoe Nasledstvo, Vol. 49-50 (1946), pp. 433-34; Garkavi, pp.81-84.

74. Teplinskii, pp. 71-72.

75. Ibid., pp. 98-101.

76. Quoted from K. K. Arsen'ev's article in Materialy...1869, Part IV, pp. 73-74.

77. Laverichev, Istoriia SSSR No. 1 (1972), pp. 31, 37.

78. (Mikhnevich) Piat'nadtsatiletie....., p. LI.

79. Evgen'ev-Maksimov, Ocherki..., pp. 119-20.

80. Note the comment of M. Sobolevskii that the Russian Reports (Russkie Vedemosti), by muting its tone and writing calmly was able to present its opposition views to the public. See V. Rozenberg (ed.), Russkiia Vedemosti 1863-1913. Sbornik stat'ei (Moscow: 1913), p. 282.

81. Note a negative report on a French edition of Hugo's Les Miserables in 1862. The censor argued that the author's notoriety in Europe saved the book from prohibition. He also argued that in the case of famous authors, prohibited works always reached the public and with a special cachet conferred by prohibition. Accordingly he recommended exclusion of only a few places, a decision approved by the Minister. See Aizenshtok, "Frantsuzskie pisateli..." Literaturnoe Nasledstvo Vol. 33-34 (1939), pp. 788-89. See also the comment by the head of the Chief Board, V. Grigor'ev that everything can be said in print with "propriety" and that police measures were used only for daily publications which could not be dealt with otherwise. Orzhekhovskii, p. 91.

82. Lemke, "K sorokaletiiu..." Mir Bozhii (Apr., 1905), pp. 22-23. See first warnings to Nedelia in Materialy...1869, Part II, pp. 148-49, 155-56, 157-59.

83. F. 777, 1870, d. 28, pp. 20b-21; F. 776, op. 4, 1870, d. 5, p. 39b; N. I. Sokolov, Russkaia literatura i narodnichestvo (Leningrad: 1968), pp. 46-47.

84. Rozenberg and Iakushkin, pp. 238-39.

85. F. 777, 1871, d. 100, pp. 55b-56.

86. F. 776, 1874, d. 2a, p. 151b; F. 776, d. 88, 1879, p. 20b.

87. Esin, Russkaia zhurnalistika..., pp. 67-68.

88. Berezhnoi, Tsarskaia..., p. 52; B. P. Baluev, Politichesk-
    aia reaktsiia 80-kh godov i russkaia zhurnalistika (Moscow:
    1971), pp. 202-209. See G. S. Lapshina, "Gazeta Nedelia v
    1868-69 gg. i tsenzura," Vestnik Moskovskogo Universiteta,
    Zhurnalistika No. 1 (1968), pp. 46-56.

89. F. 777, 1871, d. 100, pp. 20-21b; F. 777, 1870, d. 28, pp.
    21b-22.

90. F. 777, 1871, d. 100, pp. 20-21b; F. 776, 1871, d. 150
    Part III, p. 41; Rozenberg and Iakushkin, pp. 231-32;
    Teplinskii, p. 84.

91. F. 776, d. 195, 1880, p. 134b, 245b-46; M. K. Lemke (ed.),
    M. M. Stasiulevich i ego sovremenniki v ikh perepiske
    5 vols. (SPB: 1911-15), II, pp. 144-45, 518; (Seredonin),
    Istoricheskii obzor...kom. min., Vol. 3, Part 2, p. 207.

92. F. 776, 1876, d. 105, p. 46; Lemke (ed.), Stasiulevich...,
    II, pp. 184-204.

93. Count D. Tolstoy, the Minister of Education, prevented the
    faculty of St. Petersburg University from honoring the
    publisher Stasiulevich in 1876. Only in 1898 did the
    publisher receive the honor intended for him over twenty
    years before. Lemke (ed.) Stasiulevich..., II, p. 263.
    The Third Section named the journal a member of a group
    including The Voice and Notes of the Fatherland which
    expounded the advantages of elected representatives,
    criticized Biblical tales, bewailed the sad state of the
    state economy, propagated Slavic nationalism while critici-
    zing non-Russian nationalities and developed hatred towards
    the government. See Orzhekhovskii, pp. 65-66.

94. Berezhnoi, Tsarskaia..., p. 58; Rozenberg (ed.), Russkiia
    Ved...., p. 69.

95. F. 776, 1881, d. 3, pp. 126-33; for examples of warnings,
    see F. 776, 1874, d. 2a, p. 88b. For loss of right to
    retail sale, see F. 776, 1879, d. 88, p. 40.

96. F. 776, 1871, d. 154, p. 162; Rozenberg (ed.), Russkiia Ved.
    ..., p. 28.

97. For the constitutionalism of the staff, see Rozenberg (ed.),
    Russkiia Ved...., pp. 14-15; for techniques, see p. 282.
    For the high prestige of the newspaper among writers, see
    M. N. Gurenkov, "A. Tolstoi---voennyi korrespondent 'Russ-
    kikh Vedomostei' (1914-1917 gg.)" Voprosy istorii russkoi
    zhurnalistiki (Uch. zap. Leningr. Univ., No. 218, Ser. Fil.

97. (continued) Nauk, Vyp. 33) (1957), p. 181; V. Korolenko, "Chertochka iz avtobiografii" in Rozenberg (ed.), <u>Russkiia Ved...</u>, p. 310. In 1895 the Minister of Justice observed that the <u>Russian Reports</u> and the <u>Messenger of Europe</u> were "decent" and "honored" periodicals. See <u>Ibid</u>., pp. 273-74.

98. L. A. Vezirova and A. D. Eikhengol'ts, <u>Khrestomatiia po istorii russkoi knigi, 1564-1917</u> (Moscow: 1965), pp. 211-12 from <u>Materialy....1869</u>, Part I, pp. 646-47.

99. F. 776, 1871, d. 154, p. 203b; F. 777, 1870, d. 28, pp. 84, 85b; F. 776, 1871, d. 154, p. 196b.

100. M. I. Privalova and V. I. Ganshin, "Satiricheskaia zhurnalistika," in Berezina, Emel'ianov et al (ed.), <u>Ocherki....</u>, II, p. 436.

101. F. 776, 1871, d. 154, p. 219b.

102. I. Iampolskii, <u>Satiricheskaia zhurnalistika 1860-kh godov</u> (Moscow: 1964) pp. 429, 430, 431, 437-42, 599. A Third Section report of 1870 related the information that the publisher was trying to organize a section of the Workers' International in Russia.

103. Privalova and Ganshin, "Satiricheskaia..." in Berezina, Emel'ianov et al (ed.), <u>Ocherki....</u>, II, pp. 431-432, 437. From 1875 to 1890, 170 literary works and sketches were forbidden from the satirical periodical <u>The Dragonfly</u> (Strekoza) which began publication at the end of 1875.

104. F. 776, 1876, d. 105, p. 45, 47b.

105. F. 776, 1879, d. 88, pp. 44b-50b.

106. F. 776, 1880, d. 195, pp. 94a and b; F. 776, 1881, d. 3, pp. 120-22.

107. F. 776, 1880, d. 195, p. 78; F. 776, 1881, d. 3, p. 74; F. 776, 1879, d. 88, pp. 60-63.

108. F. 776, op. 4, 1870, d. 5, pp. 69-70b.

109. F. 776, 1880, d. 195, p. 79.

110. Berezhnoi, <u>Tsarskaia...</u>, p. 50; A. V. Muratov and M. I. Ul'man, "Tipologicheskaia kharakteristika zhurnal'noi periodiki 1870-1890-kh godov," in Berezina, Emel'ianov et al (ed.), <u>Ocherki...</u>, II, pp. 261-63.

111. F. 776, 1880, d. 195, pp. 157b, 166; F. 776, 1879, d. 88, p. 52b; F. 776, 1871, d. 154, p. 156b; *Materialy...1869*, Part II, pp. 150-52.

112. *Materialy....1905*, pp. 3-6.

113. F. 776, 1874, op. 11, d. 3, p. 169b.

114. F. 776, 1877, d. 1, p. 286b.

115. F. 776, 1880, d. 195, pp. 138b-39b; F. 777, 1871, d. 100, p. 39. See also F. 776, 1877, d. 1, p. 87b; F. 776, 1871, d. 154, p. 155; F. 776, 1880, d. 195, pp. 138b-39.

116. F. 776, 1880, d. 195, pp. 95b-96; F. 776, 1881, d. 3, p. 124b for another case.

117. F. 776, 1871, d. 150, Part III, pp. 36a and b.

118. F. 776, 1880, d. 195, p. 212. The remark was underlined in blue pencil and marked in the margin, whether for exclusion or as an exclamation, is unknown. The reference was to foreign periodicals like the *Jewish Chronicle*.

119. F. 776, 1880, d. 195, pp. 97-98b.

120. F. 776, 1880, d. 195, pp. 135b-36, 140b-42.

121. F. 776, 1871, d. 154, pp. 157a and b; see also F. 776, 1874, d. 2a, pp. 153b-55.

122. F. 776, 1871, d. 154, p. 229b; see also F. 776, op. 4, d. 5, pp. 82-86; F. 776, 1870, op. 4, d. 5, pp. 86b-87 for an uncensored work.

123. F. 776, 1877, d. 1, pp. 118-19.

124. Lemke (ed.), *Stasiulevich....*, II, pp. 184-204.

125. F. 776, 1879, d. 88, p. 25. A panegyric to Nekrasov for joining the Emperor in the task of ending prejudice against the peasant was forbidden in 1878. See Bel'chikov and Pereselenkov, "N. A. Nekrasov...," *Krasnyi Arkhiv* Vol. I (1922), p. 361.

126. F. 776, 1880, d. 195, pp. 140a and b.

127. F. 776, 1880, d. 195, pp. 136b-37.

128. Teplinskii, pp. 97-98, 102-103.

129. F. 776, 1880, d. 195, pp. 257b-58.

130. F. 776, 1881, d. 3, p. 147b.

131. F. 776, 1880, d. 195, pp. 256b-57; F. 776, d. 88, 1879, p. 51; Orzhekhovskii, p. 91.

132. Rozenberg and Iakushkin, pp. 136-37, 146, 156.

133. Note exclusion from <u>Messenger of Europe</u> (No. 1, 1879) of an internal survey by Polonskii. In it he suggested vaguely that Russia's stagnation could not be overcome except with the cooperation of society. He argued that such cooperation would strengthen social authority. He also reaffirmed trust in the government which would be the source of peaceful reform. See Lemke (ed.), <u>Stasiulevich...</u>, I, pp. 464-82.

134. F. 777, 1876, op. 3, d. 29, pp. 26-27.

135. G. K. Gradovskii, <u>Itogi 1862-1907</u> (Kiev: 1908), pp. 40-41, 47-49, 292-97.

136. F. 776, 1880, d. 195, pp. 74-75. See also F. 776, 1874, d. 2a, pp. 112, 114b; F. 776, 1871, d. 154, p. 229b.

137. F. 776, 1879, d. 88, p. 25b; F. 776, 1874, d. 2a, pp. 114b, 115; F. 776, 1881, d. 3, p. 123.

138. F. 776, 1874, d. 2a, pp. 106-107; Dobrovol'skii, <u>Zapreshchennaia kniga....</u>, pp. 107-108.

139. F. 776, 1877, d. 1, p. 87.

140. F. 776, 1877, d. 1, pp. 126, 354.

141. F. 776, 1880, d. 195, pp. 138a and b.

142. F. 776, 1874, d. 2a, p. 115b.

143. F. 776, 1871, d. 154, pp. 155a and b.

144. F. 776, 1871, d. 154, p. 155.

145. F. 776, 1877, d. 1, p. 87; F. 776, 1879, d. 88, p. 25b.

146. F. 776, 1879, d. 88, p. 54.

147. Berezhnoi, *Tsarskaia....*, p. 51.

148. *Ibid.*, p. 53.

149. F. 776, 1880, d. 195, p. 97b.

150. F. 776, d. 88, 1879, p. 53b.

151. F. 776, op. 11, d. 1, 1877, p. 38.

152. F. 776, 1880, d. 195, p. 136b.

153. F. 776, 1880, d. 195, pp. 138a and b; F. 776, 1877, d. 1, p. 87b.

154. F. 776, 1874, d. 2a, p. 107b. See also F. 776, 1879, d. 88 p. 54.

155. F. 776, 1881, d. 3, p. 124.

156. F. 776, 1880, d. 195, p. 98b.

157. F. 776, 1880, d. 195, p. 97b.

158. F. 776, 1877, d. 1, p. 153b; F. 776, 1879, d. 88, p. 26b. See also F. 776, 1874, d. 2a, p. 156.

159. F. 776, 1870, op. 4, d. 5, pp. 83b-84; F. 776, 1871, d. 150, Part III, p. 65; Dobrovol'skii, *Zapreshchennaia kniga....*, pp. 65-66.

160. F. 776, 1871, d. 150 Part III, p. 63b; F. 776, 1871, d. 154 p. 234.

161. F. 776, 1876, d. 105, p. 39. See also F. 776, 1879, d. 88, p. 53b.

162. F. 776, 1874, d. 2a, p. 109b.

163. See also F. 776, 1881, d. 3, p. 124.

164. F. 776, 1874, d. 2a, pp. 109b, 111, 114. See also F. 776, 1880, d. 195, p. 98.

165. F. 776, 1877, d. 1, pp. 85b-87.

166. F. 776, 1879, d. 88, p. 25b.

167. F. 776, 1871, d. 150 Part III, pp. 44a and b, 45.

168. F. 776, 1879, d. 88, p. 52b.

169. F. 777, 1870, d. 28, pp. 60, 84b-85; F. 776, 1876, d. 105, pp. 45-46; F. 776, 1874, d. 2a, p. 93b; F. 776, op. 4, d. 5, 1870, p. 44; F. 776, 1874, d. 2a, pp. 97-98b. See also Bel'chikov and Pereselenkov, "N. A. Nekrasov...," Krasnyi Arkhiv Vol. I (1922), p. 361.

170. F. 776, 1876, d. 105, pp. 53b-57b.

171. F. 776, 1871, d. 154, pp. 32a and b, 330, 339.

172. F. 776, 1876, d. 105, pp. 53b-57b.

173. F. 776, 1881, d. 3, pp. 234-36b.

174. F. 776, 1877, d. 1, pp. 168-74b. Orzhekhovskii cites official statements that in 1872 the foreign censors forbid one out of twenty works and expurgated one of nineteen. Orzhekhovskii, p. 16.

175. Katalog razsmotrenikh inostrannoiu tsenzuroiu sochinenii zapreshchennikh i dozvolennikh s iskliucheniiami s 1-go iulia 1871 g. po 1 ianvaria 1897 g (SPB: 1898).

176. F. 776, 1880, d. 195, pp. 210-12. In 1867 there were ten censors in the St. Petersburg post office who censored the 480 (in 1865) permitted foreign periodicals. (S. A. Adrianov) Ministerstvo vnutrennikh del. Istoricheskii ocherk (SPB: 1901), II, p. 113.

177. F. 776, op. 4, 1870, d. 5, p. 9; F. 776, 1880, d. 195, pp. 224b-28. With additions the budget in 1879 was 269,209 rubles. Orzhekhovskii gives figures of 259,900 rubles in 1870 and 266,300 in 1873. Orzhekhovskii, pp. 10, 79.

178. F. 776, op. 4, 1870, d. 5, pp. 8, 9; F. 776, d. 195, 1880, pp. 223-24b.

179. F. 776, op. 4, 1870, d. 5, pp. 21, 22; F. 776, 1876, d. 105, pp. 15a and b; F. 776, 1880, d. 195, p. 229.

180. Teplinskii, pp. 88-89.

181. Berezhnoi, Tsarskaia..., pp. 201-202 note.

182. See e. g. F. 776, 1871, op. 11, d. 154 Part III, pp. 16-17; F. 776, 1880, d. 195, p. 229, F. 776, 1876, d. 105, p. 15b.

183. F. 776, 1871, d. 150 Part III, p. 77. A daily survey as part of the Chief Board's duties from 1882 to 1892 is mentioned in F. 776, 1894, op. 20, d. 1441, p. 6b. Orzhekhovskii mentions daily surveys of periodicals for the Emperor dating from 1860. Orzhekhovskii, p. 11.

184. F. 776, 1877, d. 1, pp. 309b-11.

185. F. 776, 1877, d. 1, pp. 296-98, 298-301.

186. F. 776, 1877, d. 1, pp. 97a and b.

187. F. 776, op. 4, d. 5, 1870, pp. 76b-77.

188. F. 776, 1876, d. 105, pp. 74b-75.

189. In 1870, in St. Petersburg, 93 manuscripts were prohibited out of 1665 manuscripts and 241 proofs. F. 777, 1870, d. 28, pp. 85a and b. In 1879, 49 works were forbidden of 2184 manuscripts and 648 proofs. F. 776, 1880, d. 195, pp. 135b-36, 142a and b. In 1880, in St. Petersburg, 32 works were forbidden of 2246 manuscripts and 578 proofs. F. 776, 1881, d. 3, pp. 143b-44.

190. F. 776, 1880, d. 195, pp. 297b-98

	1869	1873	1878
Permitted unconditionally	47	100	111
Permitted with exclusions	37	90	112
Forbidden	12	18	34

191. For rewards, see F. 776, 1880, d. 195, pp. 224b-25b. For penalties, see F. 776, op. 4, 1870, d. 5, pp. 45b-47b.

192. F. 776, 1880, d. 195, p. 224b; W. Pintner, "Social Characteristics of the Early 19th century Russian Bureaucracy" *Slavic Review* (Sept., 1970), p. 431.

Footnotes Chapter VI

1. Teplinskii, pp. 102-103.

2. P. A. Zaionchkovskii, Krizis samoderzhaviia na rubezhe 1870-1880 godov (Moscow: 1964), pp. 59, 66. This must be the meeting that D. Miliutin refers to in his diary of April 17, 1878, a meeting of the Ministers of Interior, Justice and State Domains. At this meeting various measures against revolutionaries were discussed. See Miliutin, Dnevnik..., III, p. 33, 47-48, 83, 87 for other meetings dealing with the revolutionaries.

3. Zaionchkovskii, Krizis..., p. 75.

4. Miliutin, Dnevnik..., III, pp. 129, 134.

5. Zaionchkovskii, Krizis..., pp. 85-86.

6. Ibid., p. 90.

7. N. Emel'ianov, "Iz istorii russkikh ofitsiozov 1879-1880g," Voprosy zhurnalistiki:mezhvuzovskii sbornik statei, V. 2, Bk. 2 (Leningrad: 1960), pp. 72-74, 75; Zaionchkovskii, Krizis...., pp. 172-73.

8. Zaionchkovskii, Krizis..., pp. 172-173.

9. Emel'ianov, "Iz istorii..." Voprosy zhurnalistiki: mezhvuzovskii sbornik statei, V. 2, Bk. 2 (Leningrad: 1960) pp. 76-80.

10. Miliutin, Dnevnik..., III, pp. 215, 216, I, pp. 60-61.

11. Zaionchkovskii, Krizis..., pp. 148-149.

12. Ibid., pp. 204, 206.

13. Ibid., p. 211; Prince N. V. Golitsyn, "Konstitutsiia grafa Loris-Melikova: materialy dlia eia istorii," Byloe No. 4-5 (1918), p. 160.

14. Gradovskii, with some irony, says that Valuev prided himself on his liberal attitude towards the press and literature. Gradovskii, pp. 6-10.

15. Lemke (ed.), Stasiulevich..., II, p. 29 (Letter of V. D. Spasovich August 1/13, 1880.)

16. Zaionchkovskii, Krizis..., p. 226.

17. Ibid., p. 224.

18. Ibid., pp. 235-37.

19. Letter of Kavelin, July 4, 1880 in Lemke (ed.), Stasiulevich...., II, p. 152 note; Zaionchkovskii, Krizis...., pp. 261-62. Zaionchkovskii notes that four warnings were given in 1880 and two periodicals were banned. In the first two months of 1881, there were no penalties imposed on periodicals.

20. Gradovskii, pp. 68-73; see also Evgen'ev-Maksimov, Ocherki. ...., pp. 204-205; Teplinskii, pp. 110-11.

21. Zaionchkovskii, Krizis..., p. 226.

22. Ibid., p. 262.

23. Ibid., p. 237.

24. Ibid., pp. 262-64; Lemke (ed.), Stasiulevich...., I, pp. 544-49; Lemke, "K sorokaletiiu....," Mir Bozhii (April, 1905), p. 19; Materialy dlia kharakteristiki......, I, pp. 38-41; Arsen'ev, Zakonodatel'stvo...., pp. 102-14; B. P. Baluev, Politicheskaia reaktsiia 80-kh godov XIX veka i russkaia zhurnalistika (Moscow: 1971), p. 201.

25. Zaionchkovskii, Krizis...., pp. 264-65 (Letter of Dec. 8, 1880). Valuev gathered material from periodicals that displayed the press as actively critical of government policies. F. Valueva No. 559, No. 25, pp. 62-65 in Pushkinskii Dom.

26. Zaionchkovskii, Krizis...., pp. 265-66.

27. Ibid., pp. 266-67.

28. Ibid., pp. 267-68.

29. Ibid., pp. 268-69.

30. Ibid., pp. 283-95.

31. Golitsyn, "Konstitutsiia....," Byloe No. 4-5 (1918), p. 160.

32. Lemke, "K sorokaletiiu....," Mir Bozhii (Apr., 1905), p. 19 Materialy dlia kharakteristiki...., I, pp. 38-41; Arsen'ev, Zakonodatel'stvo...., pp. 102-114.

Footnotes   Chapter VII

1. Zionchkovskii, Rossiiskoe...., p. 308.

2. Baluev, p. 21. Alexander called Kraevskii a "swine" and in his marginal notations showed his hatred for the press. See Teplinskii, pp. 118-19.

3. Baluev, p. 22.

4. Ibid., p. 23; Zaionchkovskii, Krizis..., pp. 317-20. Zaionchkovskii notes other proposals for representation of the country in other memoranda in March, 1881 by A. A. Bobrinskii and P. P. Shuvalov, pp. 320-22.

5. Baluev, pp. 25-26; Zaionchkovskii, Krizis...., p. 314.

6. Ibid., p. 314.

7. Ibid., pp. 314-15; Baluev, pp. 28-30. Baluev argues convincingly that the closing of the St. Petersburg Reports came for the reasons given above and not for the reasons stated in (Lisovskii) "Materialy....," Vsemirnyi Vestnik No. 7 (1908), pp. 37-38. Loris-Melikov, according to Baluev, took these actions on the basis of emergency powers, without warnings or the customary procedure. The sources do not mention any extraordinary grant of powers. Loris' action was simply based on an Imperial decision.

8. Baluev, p. 30, Zaionchkovskii, Krizis..., p. 315. Gradovskii says that Abaza told the editor of Order that an even harsher penalty was considered for the newspaper at first. See Gradovskii, p. 79.

9. Baluev, pp. 30-31. The words in Russian were Otsom-muchenikov instead of otsom-muchenikom.

10. Baluev, pp. 31-32. Loris also restricted press comments on arrests and political cases in general as well as references to revolutionaries abroad.

11. Zaionchkovskii, Krizis...., p. 328; Miliutin, Dnevnik...., I, pp. 61-65.

12. Zaionchkovskii, Krizis...., pp. 352-57; Baluev, p. 33.

13. Zaionchkovskii, Krizis...., pp. 363-67; Miliutin, Dnevnik... I, pp. 61-65.

14. Zaionchkovskii, Krizis...., pp. 367-74; Miliutin, Dnevnik..., I, pp. 61-65.

15. Ibid., pp. 61-65; Zaionchkovskii, Krizis..., pp. 374-76.

16. Baluev, p. 33.

17. Teplinskii, pp. 112-13.

18. Zaionchkovskii, Krizis...., p. 342.

19. Feoktistov, pp. V-VI in introduction by Presniakov, 220-222. For Pobedonostsev's comments on the press see I. Aizenshtok (ed.), "Pis'ma K. P. Pobedonostseva k E. M. Feoktistovu 1883-1896" Literaturnoe Nasledstvo Vol. 22-24 (1935), pp. 529-31.

20. Zaionchkovskii, Krizis...., pp. 341-42. Zaionchkovskii, citing State Secretary Perets, indicates that Loris chose Ignat'ev.

21. Baluev, pp. 34, 35.

22. Ibid., p. 39.

23. Zaionchkovskii, Krizis...., pp. 410-11; Baluev, p. 37.

24. Zaionchkovskii, Krizis...., pp. 412-13; (Seredonin) Istoricheskii obzor....kom...min..., Vol. 4, pp. 444-45.

25. Zaionchkovskii, Rossiiskoe...., pp. 263-64; Lemke, "K sorokaletiiu....," Mir Bozhii (Apr., 1905), pp. 19-20; Materialy....1905, pp. 38-39, 108-109; Baluev, pp. 41-43.

26. Arsen'ev, Zakonodatel'stvo...., p. 132.

27. Lemke, "V mire....," Vestnik Prava (Sept., 1905), pp. 98-103, 142-143.

28. Ibid., pp. 133-34, 141.

29. Ibid., pp. 135-36.

30. Ibid., pp. 129-31; see also Samoderzhavie i pechat' v Rossii (SPB: 1906), pp. 52-72.

31. Zaionchkovskii, Rossiiskoe...., pp. 269-70.

32. Ibid., pp. 297-98; Baluev, p. 80; Feoktistov, pp. 213-14.

33. F. 776, 1894, op. 20, d. 1441, pp. 10-11b. Avseenko, publisher of the <u>St. Petersburg Reports</u>, received a government subsidy in 1883; Aizenshtok (ed.), "Pis'ma...." <u>Literaturnoe Nasledstvo</u> Vol. 22-24 (1935), pp. 515-16. Prince Meshcherskii, a friend of Alexander III, was heavily supported by the government, receiving 108,000 rubles in 1882, 90,000 in 1883, and 30,000 in 1884; Baluev, p. 80. The difference in figures for subsidies is probably the result of the use of separate accounts. See also (Adrianov) Min...Vnut...Del..., I, p. 219.

34. Zaionchkovskii, <u>Rossiiskoe....</u>, p. 307.

35. <u>Ibid.</u>, pp. 273-74. See Feoktistov, pp. 239-40.

36. Baluev, pp. 102-104, 125-27; Ambler, pp. 176 ff.

37. Rozenberg (ed.), <u>Russkiia Ved....</u>, pp. 60-61.

38. F. 776, d. 442, 1882, pp. 134-37b.

39. F. 776, 1885, op. 20. d. 734, pp. 177-82b.

40. F. 776, 1887, op. 20, d. 856, pp. 217-18, 148b-49.

41. F. 776, 1890, d. 1095, pp. 229-34; F. 776, d. 1043, 1889, p. 151.

42. F. 776, 1894, op. 20, d. 1441, pp. 12-14; Zaionchkovskii, <u>Rossiiskoe...</u>, p. 281.

43. F. 776, op. 3, d. 95, pp. 24a and b.

44. F. 776, 1894, op. 20, d. 1441, pp. 14-15.

45. F. 776, 1894, op. 20, d. 1441, pp. 15b-16.

46. F. 776, 1894, op. 20, d. 1441, pp. 30-36b.

47. The government report in 1894 refers to the "lenient" policy of the late 1870s. See F. 776, 1894, op. 20, d. 1441, pp. 12-14.

48. F. 776, 1894, op. 20, d. 1441, pp. 12-14; Zaionchkovskii, <u>Rossiiskoe...</u>, p. 281.

49. Rozenberg and Iakushkin, p. 134. On January 1, 1892, the number of periodicals being published was 736. F. 776, 1894, op. 20, d. 1441, pp. 12-14.

50. Rozenberg and Iakushkin, p. 34.

51. Zaionchkovskii, Rossiiskoe..., pp. 280-81, 294 citing figures from Rozenberg and Iakushkin. The most important means of taming the press during the first years of Alexander III's reign, from 1880 to 1884, was a warning. From 1885 to 1894, prohibition of retail sale was the penalty inflicted most frequently. See Lemke, "K sorokaletiiu..." Mir Bozhii (Apr., 1905), pp. 24-25.

52. Baluev, pp. 51-52.

53. Rozenberg and Iakushkin, pp. 136-38; Zaionchkovskii, Rossiiskoe... , pp. 280-81.

54. F. 777, op. 3, d. 95   pp. 215, 218. Whether this prohibition meant that lower rates could not be offered is unknown.

55. (Lisovskii), "Materialy...," Vsemirnyi Vestnik No. 8 (1908) pp. 38-39; F. 776, 1894, op. 20, d. 1441, pp. 30-36b.

56. Rozenberg and Iakushkin, p. 139; The Petersburg Leaves (Listok) was forbidden retail sale from 1871 to 1876.

57. Rozenberg and Iakushkin, pp. 141-42. This last penalty was imposed on 25 publications in 31 cases. Of these occasions, 12 came from 1885 to 1894, and 15 from 1895 to 1904.

58. (Lisovskii) "Materialy...," Vsemirnyi Vestnik No. 8 (1908), pp. 38-39.

59. Arsen'ev notes that in 1899, a provincial censored newspaper was banned for violating a prohibitory circular. He points out that these circulars were binding only on uncensored periodicals and that officially editors of censored publications would not be informed of these circulars. See Arsen'ev, Zakonodatel'stvo..., p. 183. On October 29, 1881, official provincial newspapers were freed of preliminary censorship. Responsibility for the publications was vested in the local officials. See Z. Mseriants, Zakony o pechati: nastoial'naia spravochnaia kniga 8th ed. (Moscow: 1899, p. 23.

60. Feoktistov, p. 284; Baluev, p. 80; F. 776, 1887, op. 20, d. 896, p. 220; F. 776, 1886, op. 20, d. 825, pp. 237b-38b; F. 776, 1883, op. 20, d. 548, pp. 127-28.

61. Rozenberg and Iakushkin, pp. 138-39.

62. V. P. Meshcherskii, Moi vospominaniia (SPB: 1912) Part III (1881-1894), pp. 40-43, 211-16; Baluev, p. 164; Feoktistov, pp. 246-48.

63. F. 776, 1887, op. 20, d. 896, pp. 87a and b, 148b.

64. F. 776, 1887, op. 20, d. 896, p. 156b note. See F. 776, 1885, op. 20, d. 734, p. 110; F. 776, 1886, op. 20, d. 825, pp. 97a and b; Zaionchkovskii, Rossiiskoe...., p. 295; (Lisovskii) "Materialy... ," Vsemirnyi Vestnik No. 8 (1908), pp. 44-45.

65. F. 776, 1882, d. 442, p. 138; (Lisovskii), "Materialy...," Vsemirnyi Vestnik No. 8 (1908), pp. 43-44.

66. Arsen'ev, Zakonodatel'stvo... , pp. 137-40; Feoktistov, p. 240; Zaionchkovskii, Rossiiskoe... , pp. 284-86; Baluev, p. 44.

67. F. 777, 1881, d. 26, pp. 221-22; F. 776, 1882, d. 442, p. 139; Baluev, p. 77.

68. Evgen'ev-Maksimov, Ocherki... , p. 209.

69. Esin, Russkaia zhurnalistika..., pp. 26-27; Teplinskii, pp. 114-18.

70. Esin, Russkaia zhurnalistika..., pp. 26-27.

71. Bogucharskii, Iz proshlogo..., pp. 386-87; Teplinskii, pp. 120-21; 124-26; Feoktistov, pp. 241-42; Zaionchkovskii, Rossiiskoe..., pp. 289-92; Aizenshtok (ed.), "Pis'ma....," Literaturnoe Nasledstvo, Vol. 22-24 (1935), pp. 511-12.

72. Arsen'ev, Zakonodatel'stvo... , pp. 137-40; Zaionchkovskii, Rossiiskoe... , pp. 286-87; Baluev, p. 44. See F. 776, 1882, d. 442, p. 139 for citation of "notable" issues of periodicals in 1881.

73. F. 776, 1882, d. 442, p. 110b; F. 776, 1884, op. 20, d. 645, pp. 124, 125b, 96; V. L. Giliarovskii, Sochineniia 4 vols. (Moscow: 1967), III, pp. 70-72; Zaionchkovskii, Rossiiskoe... pp. 282-83.

74. F. 776, 1881, d. 3, p. 107b; Baluev, pp. 36-37; Giliarovskii, III, pp. 73-76.

75. F. 776, 1884, op. 20, d. 645, p. 124b.

76. (Lisovskii,) "Materialy... ," Vsemirnyi Vestnik No. 7 (1908), p. 41; Zaionchkovskii, Rossiiskoe...., pp. 283-84.

77. F. 776, 1890, op. 20, d. 1095, p. 94; (Lisovskii), "Materialy... ," Vsemirnyi Vestnik No. 7 (1908), pp. 45-46; F. 776, 1882, d. 442, pp. 109a and b; Zaionchkovskii, Rossiiskoe... , p. 296; Aizenshtok (ed.), "Pis'ma...." Literaturnoe Nasledstvo Vol. 22-24 (1935), pp. 504, 510, 511; Laverichev, Istoriia SSSR No. 1 (1972), pp. 43-44. In 1889, Alexander III commented on a report that it would be desirable to finish off the newspaper.

78. F. 776, 1882, d. 442, p. 139; F. 776, 1884, op. 20, d. 645, pp. 145b-46; F. 776, 1883, op. 20, d. 548, pp. 127a and b.

79. Baluev, p. 184. See also Esin, Russkaia zhurnalistika... , pp. 125, 126.

80. B. I. Esin, "Zakrytie 'Otechestvennye Zapiski' i sud'ba ego sotrudnikov posle 1884 goda" in A. V. Zapadov (ed.), Iz istorii russkoi zhurnalistiki vtoroi poloviny XIX v. (Moscow: 1964), pp. 47-48; B. I. Esin, "K kharakteristike zhurnala 'Russkaia Mysl'" in A. V. Zapadov (ed.), Iz istorii russkoi zhurnalistiki (Moscow: 1959), pp. 239-40. Notes of the Fatherland was allowed to offer subscribers a choice of journals as substitutes and the largest group of subscribers chose Russian Thought.

81. F. 776, 1882, d. 442, pp. 90-91; F. 776, 1883, op. 20, d. 548, pp. 96b-97b; F. 776, 1885, op. 20, d. 734, p. 77b; F. 776, 1887, op. 20, d. 896, p. 155b; F. 776, 1890, d. 1095, p. 94b.

82. Zaionchkovskii, Rossiiskoe... , p. 262. He suggests that Katkov's ideas provided the theoretical support for this attempt to control the expression of thought.

83. Ibid., p. 298.

84. L. G. Mamulova, "Zemskii vopros v russkoi periodicheskoi pechat' epokhi kontrreform," Vestnik Moskovskogo Universiteta. Seriia IX. Istoriia No. 2 (1966), pp. 57-68; See Arsen'ev's criticism of Pazukhin's project in Messenger of Europe reprinted in K. K. Arsen'ev, Za chetvert' veka. 1871-1894, (Petrograd: 1915), pp. 156-69.

85. Baluev's argument that aside from the Marxist press, journalism confined itself to trivialities, eroticism, and "miserable reformism" appears to be too strong a statement of Zaionchkovskii's generalization. For discussion of

85. (continued) Baluev's work, see review by D. Balmuth in *Kritika*, IX, No. 3 (Spring, 1973), pp. 133-48.

86. See F. 777, op. 3, d. 95, pp. 43, 48, 52, 53, 65, 71, 83, 96, 153, 163, 169, 182, 184, 185, 187, 196, 200, 203, 211; F. 776, 1890, op. 20, d. 1095, p. 242.

87. F. 777, op. 3, d. 95, pp. 23, 39, 47, 68, 69, 70, 76, 77, 157, 159; F. 776, 1882, d. 442, pp. 141-43.

88. F. 777, op. 3, d. 95, pp. 28, 55, 57, 59, 89, 99, 195.

89. F. 776, 1889, d. 1043, pp. 153-54b. The list included 39 articles of which only a few had been excluded from periodicals. With respect to most of these articles, the Moscow Committee simply accepted them for reference or characterization of the periodical.

90. F. 776, 1894, op. 20, d. 1441, p. 20b.

91. F. 776, 1883, op. 20, d. 548, p. 130; see also F. 777, 1881, d. 26, pp. 68-74; F. 776, 1889, d. 1043, p. 99b.

92. F. 776, 1883, op. 20, d. 548, pp. 150-55, 98. See also F. 776, 1892, d. 1233, p. 147; F. 776, 1883, op. 20, d. 548, p. 132. (prohibition of a manuscript recommending land grants to peasants); Zaionchkovskii, *Rossiiskoe...*, pp. 270-71. Censors however permitted, after preliminary arrest, a work of G. Uspenskii which the censor said presented the peasant as threatened with catastrophe.

93. Zaionchkovskii, *Rossiiskoe...*, pp. 271-72; F. 777, op. 3, d. 95, p. 226.

94. F. 776, op. 20, d. 1043, p. 9b; F. 776, 1886, op. 20, d. 825, pp. 3-4b; F. 776, 1883, op. 20, d. 548, pp. 94-99b; F. 776, 1882, op. 20, d. 442, pp. 42-43.

95. F. 777, 1881, op. 3, d. 26, pp. 140, 308; F. 777, op. 3, d. 95, pp. 63, 85, 156.

96. F. 777, 1881, op. 3, d. 26, p. 340, F. 776, 1884, op. 20, d. 645, pp. 7a and b; F. 776, 1883, op. 20, d. 545, pp. 33-34.

97. F. 776, 1886, op. 20, d. 825, p. 245.

98. F. 776, 1894, op. 20, d. 1441, p. 22.

99. F. 777, 1881, d. 26, p. 300; F. 776, 1892, d. 1233, p. 47, 240; F. 776, 1882, d. 442, pp. 141-43.

100. F. 776, 1891, op. 20, d. 1161, p. 212b; F. 776, 1883, op. 20, d. 548, pp. 5a and b; F. 776, 1894, op. 20, d. 1441, pp. 19b-20.

101. F. 776, 1882, d. 442, p. 75.

102. Rozenberg and Iakushkin, p. 178; F. 776, 1892, d. 1233, p. 235b; F. 776, 1889, d. 1043, p. 250b; Baluev, p. 82. Feoktistov criticized Ignat'ev for permitting a Yiddish language press despite the fears of the Council of the Chief Board that it lacked knowledgeable censors to keep that press under surveillance. Feoktistov, p. 20.

103. F. 776, 1884, op. 20, d. 645, pp. 167b-77.

104. F. 776, 1891, op. 20, d. 1161, pp. 17b-21.

105. F. 776, 1894, op. 20, d. 1441, pp. 18-19b. The report noted that such works began with the proposition that man must be considered an animal.

106. F. 776, 1892, d. 1233, p. 146; Dobrovol'skii, *Zapreschennaia kniga....*, p. 182.

107. F. 776, 1889, d. 1043, p. 99; F. 776, 1888, op. 20, d. 262, p. 68b. Alexander III personally banned the printing of V. Solov'ev's philosophical works as shocking and disparaging for Russians. But Solov'ev's article about imitations was printed in *Messenger of Europe* in 1891. See Zaionchkovskii, *Rossiiskoe....*, p. 300; Aizenshtok (ed.), "Pis'ma..." *Literaturnoe Nasledstvo* Vol. 22-24 (1935), p. 545.

108. F. 776, 1890, op. 20, d. 1095, p. 45; F. 776, 1884, op. 20, d. 645, p. 147b.

109. F. 776, 1890, op. 20, d. 1095, pp. 239a and b.

110. F. 776, 1883, op. 20, d. 548, pp. 154-55.

111. F. 777, op. 3, d. 95, p. 170.

112. Baluev, pp. 274, 281, 282-85, 285-87, 294-97.

113. *Ibid.*, pp. 299-300.

114. Note V. Rozenberg's complaint in 1905 that many events in Russia which occur in public can only appear in the form of memoirs. Quoted by Baluev, p. 268. See Arsen'ev, *Za chetvert'....*, pp. 124-30, 359-63, 552-54 for examples

114. (continued) of Arsen'ev's discussions of public topics.

115. F. 776, 1889, d. 1043, p. 98b; F. 776, 1892, d. 1233, p. 240; F. 776, 1893, d. 1297, p. 98.

116. F. 776, d. 442, 1882, p. 140b-41; F. 777, op. 3, d. 95, pp. 108, 173, 232.

117. F. 776, 1892, d. 1233, pp. 47b, 108b; Aizenshtok (ed.), "Pis'ma...," Literaturnoe Nasledstvo Vol. 22-24 (1935), pp. 540-42, 547.

118. N. L., "Aleksandr III o L've Tolstom," Krasnyi Arkhiv Vol. I (1922), p. 417; Feoktistov, pp. 242-44; Aizenshtok (ed.), "Pis'ma..." Literaturnoe Nasledstvo Vol. 22-24 (1935), pp. 524-27; Zaionchkovskii, Rossiiskoe..., p. 300.

119. A. Anninskii, "Tsenzura i L. N. Tolstoi," Krasnyi Arkhiv Vol. I (1922), pp. 413-14.

120. Aizenshtok (ed.), "Pis'ma...," Literaturnoe Nasledstvo Vol. 22-24 (1935), pp. 534,-537, Dobrovol'skii, Zapreshchennaia kniga..., pp. 174-175.

121. F. 776, 1892, d. 1233, p. 146b; F. 776, 1890, op. 20, d. 1095, pp. 239-40; F. 777, op. 3, d. 95, p. 194; F. 776, 1882, d. 442, p. 90; F. 776, 1885, op. 20, d. 734, pp. 75a and b.

122. F. 776, 1885, op. 20, d. 734, p. 186; F. 776, 1894, op. 20, d. 1441, p. 21. Tolstoy's article "Religion and Morals" was forbidden for the Northern Messenger (Severnyi Vestnik) in 1894 for presenting religion as a source of morality without distinguishing Christianity from paganism. But the article appeared soon after under another name. See Anninskii, "Tsenzura...," Krasnyi Arkhiv Vol. I (1922), pp. 415-16.

123. F. 776, 1884, op. 20, d. 645, pp. 97b, 123.

124. F. 776, 1883, op. 20, d. 548, pp. 154-55; Aizenshtok, "Frantsuzskie pisateli....," Literaturnoe Nasledstvo Vol. 33-34 (1939), pp. 783-84.

125. F. 776, 1883, op. 20, d. 548, pp. 134a and b; F. 776, 1890, op. 20, d. 1095, pp. 79-80b. See also F. 776, 1893, d. 1297, p. 283b.

126. F. 776, 1891, op. 20, d. 1161, pp. 211b-12; F. 776, 1890, op. 20, d. 1095, pp. 239a and b; F. 776, 1885, op. 20, d. 734, p. 185b; Zaionchkovskii, Rossiiskoe...., p. 299;

126. (continued) Aizenshtok, "Frantsuzskie pisateli...,"
   Literaturnoe Nasledstvo Vol. 33-34 (1939), p. 784.

127. F. 776, 1892, d. 1233, pp. 235b-36; F. 776, 1890, op. 20, d. 1095, p. 235.

128. F. 776, 1891, op. 20, d. 1161, p. 83; F. 776, 1892, d. 1233, p. 110b.

129. F. 776, 1894, op. 20, d. 1441, pp. 25b-26b, 27b-28.

130. F. 776, 1895, d. 1444, pp. 264-69b.

131. F. 776, 1895, d. 1444, p. 272-77b.

132. F. 776, 1895, d. 1444, pp. 264-69b. German titles numbered 7186 and French 2539 of the 15,138 titles examined in 1892.

133. F. 776, 1895, d. 1444, p. 272-77b.

134. Volume II of Marx's Capital was permitted because it would be understood only by specialists. In 1894, Feoktistov proposed to forbid a new Russian edition. But in 1897, Volume III appeared because the censor considered it incomprehensible. Aizenshtok (ed.), "Pis'ma... ," Literaturnoe Nasledstvo Vol. 22-24 (1935), p. 531.

135. F. 776, 1894, op. 20, d. 1441, pp. 14-15.

136. F. 776, 1894, op. 20, d. 1441, pp. 15b-16b. In Moscow 265 uncensored works appeared in 1882 and 397 in 1891.

137. F. 776, 1885, op. 20, d. 734, p. 184b. The figures were 2309 censored works in 6,874,630 copies; and 1652 uncensored works in 1,843,475 copies.

138. F. 776, d. 1043, 1889, p. 253b-54.

139. See Balmuth, Kritika (Spring, 1973), p. 142; B. I. Esin, Russkaia dorevoliutsionnaia gazeta 1702-1917 gg (Moscow: 1971), pp. 65-66.

140. F. 776, 1885, op. 20, d. 734, pp. 172a and b.

141. F. 776, 1887, op. 20, d. 896, pp. 211a and b.

142. F. 776, 1891, op. 20, d. 1161, pp. 200a and b.

143. F. 776, 1893, d. 1297, p. 272.

144. F. 776, d. 442, 1882, pp. 140a and b. Of 2,239 manuscripts and 652 proofs examined, 44 were rejected.

145. F. 776, 1883, op. 20, d. 548, pp. 128b-29. Of 2,993 manuscripts and proofs, 76 were rejected.

146. F. 776, 1885, op. 20, d. 734, pp. 183-84. Of 2,663 manuscripts and 719 proofs, 66 were rejected.

147. F. 776, d. 1043, 1889, pp. 252-53. Of 3,209 manuscripts and 841 proofs, 91 were rejected.

148. F. 776, 1891, op. 20, d. 1161, pp. 208b-209b. Of 3,694 manuscripts and 828 proofs, 94 were rejected.

149. F. 776, 1886, op. 20, d. 825, pp. 57b-60. Of 253 manuscripts in the Caucases in 1885, 10 were rejected. F. 776, 1891, op. 20, d. 1161, pp. 183-84. Of 2007 manuscripts in Warsaw in 1890, 66 were rejected.

150. F. 776, 1894, op. 20, d. 1441, pp. 21b-22b. Zaionchkovskii gives a total for the three committees of 65,237 manuscripts and 1561 prohibitions. His error is explained by a correction in the archives in which the original figures for Warsaw manuscripts was corrected from 18,987 manuscripts to 17,987. Zaionchkovskii, Rossiiskoe...., pp. 300-301.

151. F. 776, 1892, d. 1233, pp. 240b-41.

152. Esin, Russkaia zhurnalistika... , pp. 134-48.

153. F. 776, 1887, op. 20, d. 896, pp. 157-58b. The increase from 1882 to 1891 in St. Petersburg was 88% in censored works and 26% in uncensored works. Non-periodical works published in the provinces increased 16% in this period mostly after 1886. In Moscow, the increase for censored works was 128% and for uncensored works 71%. See F. 776, 1894, op. 20, d. 1441, pp. 14-15.

154. F. 776, 1894, op. 20, d. 1441, pp. 30-36b.

155. F. 776, 1892, d. 1233, p. 162 (Grodno).

156. Zaionchkovskii, Rossiiskoe... , pp. 301, 303-304.

157. F. 776, 1894, op. 20, d. 1441, pp. 14-15.

158. Censored non-periodicals in 1882 numbered 5,158 while in 1891 the figure was 8,535.

159. Rozenberg (ed.), *Russkiia Ved...*, pp. 20-23.
160. Lemke (ed.), *Stasiulevich...*, II, p. 162.

Footnotes   Chapter 8

1. A. Sidorov, "Iz vospominanii tsenzora," <u>Golos Minuvshago</u> No. 3 (1923), pp. 129-32; Arsen'ev, <u>Zakonodatel'stvo.....</u>, pp. 149-53; Aizenshtok (ed.), "Pis'ma....," <u>Literaturnoe Nasledstvo</u> Vol. 22-24 (1935), p. 559. Witte had another candidate to replace Feoktistov, E. L. Kochetov of the <u>Moscow Reports.</u>

2. F. Elenev, <u>O zloupotrebleniiakh literatury i o deistviiakh tsenzurnago vedomstva s kontsa piatidesiatikh godov po nastoiashchee vremia</u> (Geneva: 1898), p. 52. V. Evgen'ev-Maksimov, "Pis'ma k Nekrasovu," <u>Literaturnoe Nasledstvo</u> Vol. 51-52 (1949), p. 240.

3. <u>Elenev,</u> pp. 20-21.

4. <u>Ibid.</u>, p. 24.

5. <u>Ibid.</u>, p. 32.

6. <u>Ibid.</u>, p. 16.

7. <u>Ibid.</u>, pp. 26-27.

8. <u>Ibid.</u>, p. 45.

9. <u>Ibid.</u>, p. 33.

10. <u>Ibid.</u>, p. 23.

11. <u>Ibid.</u>, p. 25.

12. <u>Ibid.</u>, p. 31. A special committee in the ministry of interior acknowledged in 1869 that political interests, society's state of mind and its changes led the censorship to adapt its treatment of printed works to the time. See <u>Materialy...1869</u>, Part II, pp. 289-90.

13. Elenev, p. 48.

14. <u>Ibid.</u>, pp. 50-52.

15. <u>Ibid.</u>, pp. 56-61. By 1900, the number of separate periodicals examined by the postal censors was over 5000. (Adrianov) <u>Min. vnutrenn. del...</u>, II, p. 119.

16. Arsen'ev, <u>Zakonodatel'stvo....,</u> pp. 154-166.

17. Materialy...1905, pp. 5-18; Samoderzhavie i pechat' v Rossii (Berlin: 1898), pp. XVI-XIX; Gradovskii, pp. 299-300, 310-13; Berezhnoi, Tsarskaia..., pp. 66-70; Arsen'ev, Zakonodatel'stvo..., p. 152; Aizenshtok (ed.), "Pis'ma...," Literaturnoe Nasledstvo, Vol. 22-24 (1935), pp. 554-555; Polianskii, "Arkhivnyi fond...," Literaturnoe Nasledstvo Vol. 22-24 (1935), p. 605. Berezhnoi says 114 writers subscribed to this petition.

18. Materialy...1905, p. 43 (Apr. 29, 1898); Arsen'ev, Zakonodatel'stvo..., p. 184; Berezhnoi, Tsarskaia..., p. 70.

19. Ibid., pp. 116, 117-18.

20. Ibid., p. 111.

21. Materialy...1905, pp. 1-8 (Feb. 24, 1903).

22. S. S. Dmitriev, Khrestomatiia po istorii SSSR 2nd ed. (Moscow: 1952), Vol. III 1857-94, p. 682 citing M. N. Kufaev, Istoriia russkoi knigi v XIX veka (Leningrad: 1927), pp. 173, 217-18, 220.

23. F. 776, 1896, op. 21, d. 2, p. 195. Censored works thus averaged 4,968 copies and uncensored works, 1,118 copies.

24. F. 776, 1901, d. 1, p. 249.

25. F. 776, 1896, op. 21, d. 2, pp. 184-89b.

26. F. 776, 1901, d. 1, pp. 253b-56b, 271-75. The government restricted the right to sell periodicals. In 1902 in Moscow there were 227 stations and in 1903, in Kharkov, only two stations. B. I. Esin, "Russkaia legal'naia pressa kontsa XIX-nachala XX veka in B. I. Esin, Iz istorii..., (Moscow: 1973), p. 11.

27. F. 776, 1896, op. 21, d. 2, pp. 92-94b.

28. F. 776, 1902, op. 22, d. 1a, pp. 101-104b.

29. F. 776, 1905, d. 1, pp. 144-47.

30. M. S. Cherepakhov and E. M. Fingerit (ed.), Russkaia periodicheskaia pechat' 1895-Okt. 1917 g. Spravochnik (Moscow: 1957), pp. 7-10.

31. F. 776, 1901, d. 1, pp. 245b-48.

32. F. 776, 1902, d. 1, p. 25b; Esin, "Russkaia legal'naia...," in Esin, <u>Iz istorii...</u> (Moscow: 1973), p. 7. In 1894, of 785 periodicals published in the Empire, 342 appeared in the capitals and 443 in the provinces. Esin notes that the ratio of periodicals to inhabitants was 1:167,000 in Russia and 1:8000 in Germany in 1903.

33. Berezhnoi, <u>Tsarskaia...</u>, p. 50.

34. <u>Materialy dlia kharakteristiki...</u>, I, pp. 10-11.

35. <u>Ibid.</u>, p. 7 note. See Rozenberg and Iakushkin, pp. 88-89, 90-91, 100-103 for comments on the situation of the provincial press.

36. F. 776, 1903, d. 1, p. 112b.

37. Aizenshtok (ed.), "Pis'ma... ," <u>Literaturnoe Nasledstvo</u> Vol. 22-24 (1935), p. 556.

38. F. 776, 1905, d. 1, pp. 216b-19b.

39. F. 776, 1902, d. 1, p. 25b.

40. F. 776, 1902, kn. 1, pp. 92-93b.

41. B. Rigberg, "Tsarist Censorship Performance, 1894-1905," <u>Jahrbucher fur Geschichte osteuropas</u> Vol. 17, Bk. 1 (Mar., 1969), pp. 74-75; Berezhnoi, <u>Tsarskaia...</u>, p. 122.

42. Diuneo in collection <u>V zashchitu slov</u> 4th ed. (SPB: 1906), p. 56.

43. E. Chirikov in <u>Ibid.</u>, pp. 144-45.

44. E. V. Sviatkovskii in <u>Ibid.</u>, pp. 240-47.

45. <u>Materialy dlia kharakteristiki...</u>, I, pp. 11-12.

46. Arsen'ev, <u>Zakonodatel'stvo...</u>, p. 188.

47. F. 776, 1902, d. 1, pp. 12b-13. See complaint of Viatka newspaper in Berezhnoi, <u>Tsarskaia...</u>, p. 46.

48. Rozenberg and Iakushkin, p. 172.

49. M. K. Lemke, "Istoriia 'belogo' nomera," <u>Obrazovanie</u> No. 9 (1906), pp. 123-35.

50. N. S. Travushkin, "Izdatel'stvo 'Donskaia Rech'" <u>Kniga</u> Vol.

50. (continued) 22 (1972), p. 114.

51. F. 776, 1905, d. 1, pp. 269-84.

52. See for similar complaints of censors: in Nizhnii Novgorod, F. 776, 1904, op. 22, d. 1, pp. 7b-8; in Kazan, p. 22b; Rostov on Don, pp. 11-21b; Kharkov, pp. 270-72; and in Kiev, pp. 444-48b.

53. F. 776, 1902, op. 22, d. 1a, pp. 288a and b. For another sample of the provincial censorship, see list of unpermitted editorials from the Kursk Gazette: an editorial on the Dreyfus case which noted that the French government had stubbornly refused to review the case; an editorial that insisted that the government's efforts to improve the life of the peasants would fail because of the ignorance of the peasants and their lack of legal rights; an editorial that said the press must be free; an editorial critical of Prince Meshcherskii; an editorial criticizing corporal punishment; and a number of articles reprinting news from capital periodicals. See I. P. Belokonskii in V zashchitu slov, pp. 224-34. For additional indications of the arbitrariness of provincial censors see Rozenberg and Iakushkin, pp. 100-103 footnote, 105, 106-107. Sometimes local officials created a more genial atmosphere for the local press and censors. See N. G. Mardar'ev, "Nechto iz proshlogo. Iz vospominanii byvshego tsenzora 1886-1904," Golos Minuvshago No. 5-6 (1916), pp. 379-80, 390-91.

54. Arsen'ev, Zakonodatel'stvo...., pp. 185-88. Other amnesties had occurred in 1866, 1872, and 1877. See also Rozenberg and Iakushkin, pp. 136-37; Lemke, "K sorokaletiiu...," Mir Bozhii (Apr., 1905), p. 21; Materialy....1905, pp. 40-41.

55. Rozenberg and Iakushkin, pp. 136-46.

56. Materialy....1905, pp. 1-15.

57. Arsen'ev, Zakonodatel'stvo...., pp. 171, 179, 225-26.

58. Rigberg, "Tsarist Censorship...." Jahrbucher fur Geschichte osteuropas (Mar., 1969), p. 73; Arsen'ev, Zakonodatel'stvo... pp. 154, 166, 170.

59. Lemke, "V mire....," Vestnik Prava (Sept., 1905), pp. 98-103.

60. F. 776, 1902, d. 1, pp. 15b-18b. The official list contains 27 circulars for 1902 while Lemke lists 38 for the year. See also B. Rigberg, "The Tsarist Press Law 1894-1905," Jahrbucher fur Geschichte osteuropas, Vol. 13 (Sept., 1965),

60. (continued) pp. 338-40 for references to other circulars.

61. Lemke, "V mire....," **Vestnik Prava** (Sept., 1905), pp. 113-15; Lemke, "Neobkhodimyia....," **Vestnik Prava** (Oct., 1905), p. 230.

62. Rozenberg and Iakushkin, pp. 194-226; **Materialy dlia kharakteristiki....**, I, p. 93.

63. F. 776, 1903, d. 1, pp. 22, 150.

64. Rozenberg and Iakushkin, pp. 194-226; F. 776, 1902, d. 1, pp. 60a and b. Here the censorship took note of 15 articles in the periodical in 1901.

65. Rozenberg and Iakushkin, pp. 194-226.

66. F. 776, 1903, d. 1, p. 227.

67. F. 776, 1904, op. 22, d. 1, pp. 149-50.

68. F. 776, 1903, d. 1, pp. 226b-27.

69. F. 776, 1904, op. 22, d. 1, pp. 148-49.

70. F. 776, 1903, d. 1, p. 161. The words "and Jewish" as well as a few names of individuals were inserted in the report and described as opponents of the editor. F. 776, 1901, d. 1 pp. 123b, 248b. The newspaper was penalized in 1899 and 1900. Rozenberg and Iakushkin, pp. 194-226.

71. F. 776, 1903, d. 1, pp. 223-24.

72. (Rozenberg, ed.), **Russkiia Ved....**, p. 42.

73. **Ibid.**, pp. 35-36.

74. **Ibid.**, p. 35.

75. **Ibid.**, p. 305; Rozenberg and Iakushkin, pp. 194-226.

76. F. 776, 1902, op. 22, d. 1a, p. 109.

77. F. 776, 1904, op. 22, d. 1, pp. 144-46.

78. In 1902 a censor said of **Messenger of Europe** that its calm, academic, and frequently dull tone kept the journal from trouble. A. V. Savenkov, "Vestnik Evropy," in Berezina, Emel'ianov et al., ed., "Ocherki....,"II, pp. 371-72. See also Rigberg, "Tsarist Censorship...," **Jahrbucher fur**

78. (continued) Geschichte osteuropas (Mar., 1969), p. 62. Rigberg notes the ability of Messenger of Europe to convey its liberal position.

79. F. 776, 1903, d. 1, pp. 224b-26.

80. F. 776, 1904, op. 22, d. 1, pp. 146-47. The newspaper was forbidden retail sale in 1901 and 1903. Rozenberg and Iakushkin, pp. 194-226.

81. F. 776, 1903, d. 1, pp. 162b-64b; F. 776, 1904, op. 22, d. 1 pp. 152-55.

82. V. M. Doroshevich, Polveka dlia knigi (Moscow: 1916), p. 422.

83. M. D. Sytin, Zhizn' dlia knig (Moscow: 1960), pp. 116-26; Doroshevich, Polveka...., p. 407; Esin, Kratkii ocherk.... p. 52; Giliarovskii, Sochineniia...., III, pp. 199-202.

84. F. 776, 1905, d. 1, p. 177b.

85. F. 776, 1905, d. 1, p. 180.

86. F. 776, 1895, d. 1444, p. 84b.

87. F. 776, 1895, d. 1444, p. 85.

88. F. 776, 1896, op. 21, d. 2, p. 198b.

89. Teplinskii, p. 386; Dobrovol'skii, Zapreshchennaia kniga..., pp. 197-98; F. 776, 1895, d. 1444, pp. 84b, 59b.

90. F. 776, 1903, op. 22, d. 1, p. 132, 133.

91. F. 776, 1903, op. 22, d. 1, p. 131b.

92. Evgen'ev-Maksimov, Ocherki...., pp. 242-45.

93. F. 776, 1901, d. 1, p. 242b. It is not known whether this decision created a permanent official spokesman.

94. F. 776, 1905, d. 1, p. 158b.

95. F. 776, 1905, d. 1, pp. 174, 310.

96. F. 776, 1905, d. 1, p. 156b.

97. Aizenshtok, "Frantsuzskie pisateli...," Literaturnoe Nasledstvo Vol. 33-34 (1939), pp. 828-29.

98. F. 776, 1903, op. 22, d. 1, pp. 352b-53.

99. Aizenshtok, "Frantsuzskie pisateli...," *Literaturnoe Nasledstvo* Vol. 33-34 (1939), pp. 837-42.

100. Evgen'ev-Maksimov, *Ocherki...*, p. 240-41.

101. Polianskii, "Arkhivnyi....," *Literaturnoe Nasledstvo* Vol. 22-24 (1935), p. 617.

102. N. G. Malykhin, "Izdatel'skaia deiatel'nosti P. P. Soikina," *Kniga* Vol. 14 (1967), pp. 170-71; Dobrovol'skii, *Zapreshchennaia kniga...*, pp. 200-202; Polianskii, "Arkhivnyi....," *Literaturnoe Nasledstvo* Vol. 22-24, (1935) p. 615.

103. Ibid., pp. 611-12; Dobrovol'skii, *Zapreshchennaia kniga...*, p. 230.

104. S. B. Liublinskii, "Knigoizdatel'stvo O. N. Popovoi," *Kniga* Vol. 13 (1966) p. 125; see Polianskii, "Arkhivnyi....," *Literaturnoe Nasledstvo* Vol. 22-24 (1935), p. 612 for treatment of Engels' work.

105. F. 776, 1901, d. 1, pp. 237a and b.

106. F. 776, 1903, op. 22, d. 1, pp. 128b, 129a and b.

107. F. 776, 1903, op. 22, d. 1, p. 331b. The censors also permitted Bernstein's *Problems of Socialism* and *The Tasks of Social Democracy*.

108. Evgen'ev-Maksimov, *Ocherki...*, pp. 226-28, 241, 242-64; Dobrovol'skii, *Zapreshchennaia kniga...*, pp. 218-20.

109. A history of the working class in England was permitted because of its high price and size. F. 776, 1903, op. 22, d. 1, pp. 334-37. In 1898, the head of the Chief Board suggested prohibition of a popularization of Marxism. He thought followers of Marxism would be overwhelmed when they read the original. Polianskii, "Arkhivnyi...," *Literaturnoe Nasledstvo* vol. 22-24 (1935), pp. 615-16; F. 776, 1896, op. 21, d. 2, pp. 96-99b (here a censored Marxist text was forbidden). Despite prohibition by the censors, the newspaper *Don Speech* distributed 10,000 copies at 35 kopecks each, of a tale *For the Fatherland* that the police accused of spreading revolutionary ideas. N. S. Travushkin, "Izdatel'stvo 'Donskaia Rech'" *Kniga* Vol. 22 (1972), pp. 108-110; Dobrovol'skii, *Zapreshchennaia kniga...*, pp. 214-215.

110. F. 776, 1903, op. 22, d. 1, pp. 346-51b. Sombart's <u>Sketch of the History of Social Democracy</u> was forbidden because it justified the struggle of workers. Vorlander's <u>Capitalism and Marxism</u> was forbidden for arguing that moral imperatives required socialists to struggle. F. 776, 1896, op. 21, d. 2, pp. 198a and b. See Berezhnoi, <u>Tsarskaia...</u>, pp. 44-45 for restrictions on references to workers' disorders.

111. F. 776, 1896, op. 21, d. 2, pp. 77a and b, 340a and b; F. 776, 1905, d. 1, p. 153b. A work defending birth control was forbidden in 1902 because it popularized Malthusianism. F. 776, 1903, op. 22, d. 1, pp. 351b-52.

112. F. 776, 1901, d. 1, pp. 238b-39.

113. F. 776, 1903, op. 22, d. 1, p. 129b; F. 776, 1896, d. 2, pp. 78b, 198b.

114. F. 776, 1902, d. 1, p. 27b. See also F. 776, 1905, d. 1, p. 172 (the censors forbid a work because the author was an apologist for Nietzsche.)

115. F. 776, 1902, d. 1, p. 28. For the reading taste of the public, see N. V. Tulupov, "Narodnyia chteniia v gorodakh i selakh," <u>Russkaia Mysl'</u> No. 4 (1902), pp. 5-6.

116. F. 776, 1903, op. 22, d. 1, p. 356. In 1898 the Chief Board noted the "tendentious" character of books intended for the common people that the firm of Popov published. Liublinskii, "Knigoizdatel'stvo....," <u>Kniga</u> Vol. 13 (1966), p. 127.

117. F. 776, 1903, op. 22, d. 1, pp. 121a and b; Polianskii, "Arkhivnyi....," <u>Literaturnoe Nasledstvo</u> Vol. 22-24 (1935), p. 631. See also Travushkin, "Izdatel'stvo....," <u>Kniga</u> Vol. 22 (1972), p. 108.

118. Polianskii, "Arkhivnyi....," <u>Literaturnoe Nasledstvo</u> Vol. 22-24 (1935) p. 625; Rigberg, "Tsarist Censorship....," <u>Jahrbucher fur Geschichte osteuropas</u> (Mar., 1969), p. 71.

119. F. 776, 1905, d. 1, p. 171; F. 776, 1902, d. 1, p. 27b; F. 776, 1896, op. 21, d. 2, pp. 242a and b; Aizenshtok, "Frantsuzskie pisateli....," <u>Literaturnoe Nasledstvo</u> Vol. 33-34 (1939), pp. 823-33.

120. B. I. Esin, "Pravitel'stvennyi ofitsioz dlia naroda 'Selskyi Vestnik' 1881 g," <u>Vestnik Moskovskogo Universiteta. Seria XI Zhurnalistika</u> No. 5 (1972), p. 41. In almost one half of the volosts in Russia there were no subscribers to the newspaper.

121. F. 776, 1905, d. 1, p. 151; F. 776, 1903, op. 22, d. 1, pp. 130a and b; F. 776, 1905, d. 1, p. 156. Sytin published works of Pushkin and Gogol in inexpensive editions and in toto 47 books in the Library for Self-Education from 1899 to 1905. Sytin, Zhizn'...., pp. 11, 54, 58-60. See also Travushkin, "Izdatel'stvo....," Kniga Vol. 22 (1972), pp. 110-11; Aizenshtok, "Frantsuzskie pisateli....." Literaturnoe Nasledstvo Vol. 33-34 (1939), p. 837 for works for the common people. Tulupov notes that about 38% of the titles permitted in popular reading rooms were in belles-lettres, 25% were spiritual works, 11% in natural sciences, 9% in geography, and 9% in history. Tulupov, "Narodnyia..." Russkaia Mysl' No. 4 (1902), pp. 1-2.

122. F. 776, 1896, op. 21, d. 2, pp. 108, 110, 112.

123. F. 776, 1901, d. 1, pp. 18, 20, 22.

124. F. 776, 1896, op. 21, d. 2, p. 17b; F. 776, 1901, d. 1, pp. 2, 4, 5b, 63b, 164b, 165b.

125. F. 776, 1904, op. 22, d. 1, pp. 23b-25b; F. 776, 1895, d. 1444, p. 58, 84.

126. F. 776, 1902, d. 1, p. 55; F. 776, 1904, op. 22, d. 1, pp. 173-87, 188-93b.

127. F. 776, 1905, d. 1, p. 442. Russian orthography had to be used in periodicals. Polianskii, "Arkhivnyi....," Literaturnoe Nasledstvo Vol. 22-24 (1935), p. 632. See Polianskii also for prohibition of works of Franko and Shevchenko.

128. F. 776, 1902, d. 1, p. 27b.

129. F. 776, 1905, d. 1, pp. 171a and b (Gorkii's Vagabond's Den (Bosiak priton) and Night Circuit were forbidden); F. 776, 1905, d. 1, pp. 174b, 309b (Bal'mont's Mountain Summit (Gornyia vershiny) was expurgated); F. 776, 1905, d. 1, p. 178. (Sologub's Dear Page was excluded); F. 776, 1904, op. 22, d. 1, pp. 188-93b (Briusov's poem Meeting and Bal'mont's We Will be like the Sun. A Book of Symbols required correction before printing). See Polianskii, "Arkhivnyi...," Literaturnoe Nasledstvo Vol. 22-24 (1935), p. 627 for fate of two works by Sologub.

130. F. 776, 1903, op. 22, d. 1, pp. 124b, 128b.

131. F. 776, 1896, op. 21, d. 2, p. 196b; F. 776, 1903, op. 22, pp. 121b-22.

132. In 1900, a new edition of Tolstoy's *Kreutzer Sonata* was permitted. F. 776, 1901, d. 1, p. 241b.

133. F. 776, 1903, op. 22, d. 1, p. 133, 135-39b; F. 776, d. 1444, p. 85.

134. F. 776, 1901, d. 1, p. 241.

135. F. 776, 1901, d. 1, p. 153.

136. F. 776, 1905, d. 1, p. 169b. Iakushkin's *Memoirs* were temporarily arrested in 1904. F. 776, 1905, d. 1, p. 179b.

137. F. 776, 1896, op. 21, d. 2, pp. 219-23b; F. 776, 1901, d. 1, pp. 175-77b; F. 776, 1904, op. 22, d. 1, p. 404b. The figure for imports in 1904 was 29.5 million. F. 776, 1905, d. 1, pp. 391-96b; Rozenberg and Iakushkin, pp. 186-87.

138. F. 776, 1896, op. 21, d. 2, pp. 211-16b.

139. F. 776, 1898, op. 22, d. 1, p. 48; F. 776, 1901, d. 1, pp. 179-80.

140. F. 776, 1901, d. 1, pp. 179-80; F. 776, 1903, d. 1, pp. 311-12.

141. F. 776, 1896, op. 21, d. 2, pp. 219-23b (12,543 permitted, 384 expurgated, 609 forbidden); F. 776, 1901, d. 1, pp. 251b-52 (12,496 total, 274 expurgated, 606 forbidden); F. 776, 1903, d. 1, pp. 311-19b (10,882 total, 390 expurgated, 825 forbidden); F. 776, 1905, d. 1, pp. 391-96b (14,317 total, 761 expurgated, 943 forbidden).

142. F. 776, 1902, d. 1, pp. 29b-33b.

143. F. 776, 1896, op. 21, d. 2, pp. 219-23b.

144. F. 776, 1904, op. 22, d. 1, p. 404b. In 1902, French works were forbidden more often. F. 776, 1903, d. 1, pp. 311-19b.

145. F. 776, 1902, d. 1, pp. 29b-33b.

146. F. 776, 1902, kn. 1, pp. 95-98.

147. F. 776, 1902, kn. 1, pp. 100-12b.

148. F. 776, 1902, d. 1, p. 34. The year 1900 is incorrectly written as 1890.

149. F. 776, 1901, d. 1, pp. 244a and b. In 1899, 2,281 plays examined, 891 permitted, 81 rejected and 1309 returned for correction (skrepleno). In 1900, 2408 examined, 1086 permitted, 114 unsuitable and 1280 returned for correction (skrepleno).

150. F. 776, 1901, d. 1, pp. 249b-50.

151. F. 776, 1905, d. 1, p. 194.

152. F. 776, 1895, d. 1444, pp. 208b-11; F. 776, 1902, op. 22, d. 1a, p. 367b; F. 776, 1904, op. 22, d. 1, p. 431. The figure was 14% in 1904. F. 776, 1905, d. 1, p. 432.

153. F. 776, 1901, d. 1, pp. 277a and b. In 1896 the Kiev censors rejected 42% of the Ukrainian manuscripts they examined.

154. F. 776, 1905, d. 1, pp. 150-73.

155. F. 776, 1895, d. 1444, pp. 288-90.

156. F. 776, 1901, d. 1, p. 101b; F. 776, 1905, d. 1, pp. 148-49.

157. F. 776, 1903, d. 1, p. 323.

158. F. 776, 1905, d. 1, pp. 56b-57b, 70-72, 89-90, 107-109, 214, 317b, 333, 335.

159. Rozenberg and Iakushkin, p. 172. Special censors were appointed for periodicals in Nizhnyi Novgorod, Saratov, Vladivostok in 1902 and Rostov on the Don, Ekaterinoslav and Tomsk in 1903. Esin, "Russkaia legal'naia....," in Esin, Iz istorii... (Moscow: 1973), p. 13.

160. F. 776, 1898, op. 22, d. 1, pp. 61b-62; F. 776, 1902, op. 20, d. 1, pp. 3-6; F. 776, 1901, d. 1, pp. 237, 240a and b.

161. F. 776, 1902, op. 20, kn. 1, pp. 2a and b; F. 776, 1901, d. 1; p. 236.

162. F. 776, 1902, d. 1, p. 35. The archives mention daily surveys for the minister of interior in 1901.

163. F. 776, 1902, d. 1, pp. 13b, 28b.

164. F. 776, 1902, d. 1, p. 12b. In two other cases the Council supported the complaints of the publishers and in one other, it supported the censor. F. 776, 1902, d. 1, pp. 12b-13.

165. F. 776, 1901, d. 1, pp. 237, 240a and b.

166. Arsen'ev, Zakondatel'stvo..., pp. 154, 166-67, 170. In 1867 the Minister of Interior had ruled that a printed sheet must contain 11,000 letters if the work was to qualify for exemption from censorship. Ten sheets or 160 pages in octavo freed the work. Goremykin's order raised the requirement to 33,000 letters. See Materialy...1869, Part V, p. 13 note - for the 1867 rule that each printed page in octavo have a minimum of 5400 spaces. Therefore a sheet must have 86,400 spaces.

167. Rozenberg and Iakushkin, pp. 136-37.

Footnotes   Chapter IX

1. Berezhnoi, Tsarskaia...., p. 125; Materialy....1905, pp. 1-6 (Special journal of the Committee of Ministers, 28 and 31 Dec., 1905); also in Proekt ustava vysochaishe uchrezhdennogo osobogo soveshcheniia dlia sostavleniia novogo ustava o pechati (SPB: 1906).

2. Materialy... 1905, pp. 6-20 (Special journal of Committee of Ministers 28 and 31 Dec., 1904); also in Proekt... 1905; Berezhnoi, Tsarskaia...., pp. 137-38.

3. Ibid., pp. 138, 178-79; Materialy... 1905, pp. 1-2 (Explanatory memorandum to project).

4. Lemke (ed.), Stasiulevich... , II, pp. 246-47 (Letter of March 14, 1905); Protokoly vysochaishe uchrezhdennago osobago soveshcheniia dlia sostavleniia novogo ustava o pechati (SPB: 1906), Protocol No. 6, pp. 3-4 (Meeting of March 3, 1905); V. D. Nabokov, "K istorii nashego zakonodatel'stva o pechati (komissiia Kobeko)" Pravo No. 33 (1911), pp. 1828-29.

5. For an explanation of the project, see Materialy... 1905, pp. 2-13 (Explanatory memorandum to project). For deliberation see Protokoly... 1905.

6. Materialy... 1905, p. 13 (Explanatory memorandum to project) S. Witte,Vospominaniia 3 vols. (Moscow: 1960), III, pp. 318-21 II, 356-58; Berezhnoi, Tsarskaia..., pp. 178-79, 181-83. Berezhnoi says the Temporary Press Rules were issued independently of the Commission. He cites Suvorin's statement in the Commission on the day the Rules were published that he considered the time he spent in the Commission lost and unnecessary; Polnoe sobranie zakonov, 3rd Collection, No. 26962, pp. 837-40. Witte reports that the Emperor said of Kobeko "I will never forget his attitude in press affairs." Kobeko was dropped from the State Council after the Commission ended its work.

7. Materialy... 1905, pp. 13-20 (Explanatory memorandum to project).

8. Materialy...1905, pp. 20-37 (Explanatory memorandum to project); also separately paged "Proekt vyzyvaemykh izdaniem ....izmenenii....", pp. 2-24. Koni did not explain his refusal to sign the project. In his recollections, he printed his memoranda for the Kobeko Commission. While favoring abolition of prior censorship, he advised a seven day period between printing and distribution. Koni had

8. (continued) previously remarked that the list of press crimes in the Code might have to be supplemented. But he believed that the existing Code would cover most press crimes. Koni, II, pp. 769-70, 776.

9. See memorandum of d.s.s.V.M. Iuzofovich in Materialy....1905, and in protocol No. 14, pp. 1-6 in Protokoly...., 1905.

10. Even Prince Shakhovskoi, the head of the Chief Board, in the first meeting of the Kobeko Commission, admitted that the concept of a "harmful tendency" had been expanded in such a way as to irritate writers. See protocol No. 1 (Feb. 10, 1905), p. 11 in Protokoly....1905. Shakhovskoi particularly feared inexpensive publications for the common people. He noted that the publisher Sytin alone published 6 million calendars; also 36 firms published 85 million copies of printed works for the common people. S. I. Stykalin, "Russkoe samoderzhavie i legal'naia pechat' 1905 goda" in Esin, Iz istorii....,(Moscow: 1973), p. 82.

11. Rigberg, "Tsarist Press..." Jahrbucher fur Geschichte osteuropas (Sept., 1965), p. 341; Stykalin, "Russkoe sam....," in Esin, Iz istorii....(Moscow: 1973), pp. 70-71. Trepov was the St. Petersburg governor-general until April 1905 when he became Vice-Minister of Interior.

12. S. I. Stykalin, "Politicheskaia satira v 'Zritel' 1905 g." in A. V. Zapadov (ed.), Iz istorii russkoi zhurnalistiki (Moscow: 1959), pp. 170-75, 184-88; Vezirova and Eikhengol'ts (ed.), pp. 330-32.

13. Berezhnoi, Tsarskaia...., p. 145.

14. O. D. Golubeva, "Izdatel'skoe delo v Rossii v period pervoi russkoi revoliutsii (1905-1917 gg.), Kniga Vol. 22 (1972), pp. 119-20; Berezhnoi, Tsarskaia...., p. 189.

15. Golubeva, "Izdatelskoe delo...," Kniga Vol. 22 (1972), pp. 120-21; Berezhnoi, Tsarskaia...., p. 185. The Moscow Soviet banned Bolshevik newspapers and permitted only the Izvestiia of the Moscow Soviet to appear.

16. Berezhnoi, Tsarskaia...., pp. 175, 187-89, 198. In Chita, a printer refused to print "Black Hundred" newspapers. The Soviet of New Russia sealed the press of what Berezhnoi calls reactionary newspapers and the Samara Soviet demanded that press workers present all publications to it for preliminary examination. Early in December, 1905, the police obtained a court order banning publication of the Bolshevik New Life, (Novaia Zhizn') no. 27. The courts did not decide the case until 1913 when they ruled that the confiscated issue be

16. (continued) destroyed. The Union for the Defense of Freedom of the Press protested against such decisions to print only revolutionary publications.

17. V. D. Nabokov, "Ugolovnaia otvetstvennosti' knigoprodavtsa," Pravo No. 18 (1908), pp. 1128-36; Berezhnoi, Tsarskaia...., pp. 199-203; Vitte, III, p. 319; M. Florinsky, Russia, A History and An Interpretation 2 vols. (New York: 1953), II, p. 1186; J. Walkin, "Government Controls over the Press in Russia, 1905-1914," Russian Review Vol. 13 (July, 1954)p. 204. A minority (16) of the Council wanted to have the press rules considered in the Duma. The duty of presenting printed material was imposed on the owner of the press. Publishers of suspended periodicals could not replace the banned periodical with a new one until judgment by the courts. Often this took a long time. Penalties were increased from a maximum of 300 rubles, in the November, 1905 rules, to 3000. At the end of 1906, the praise of criminal actions was made punishable by imprisonment from 2 to 8 months or a fine of up to 500 rubles. Polnoe sobranie zakonov 3rd Collection, No. 27574, pp. 281-83, No. 27815, pp. 482-83.

18. Walkin, "Government....," Russian Review (July, 1954), p. 205.

19. Ibid., pp. 208-209; Berezhnoi, Tsarskaia..., p. 208.

20. Vitte, III, pp. 320-21. Witte recognized the importance of public opinion. On October 18, 1905, he summoned editors and a few writers from capital periodicals and appealed for their support in the effort to pacify public opinion. This support, he said, would allow the government to play the role that governments did in "cultured countries." Stykalin, "Russkoe sam....," in Esin, Iz istorii... (Moscow: 1973), pp. 95-96.

21. V. Obninskii, Polgoda russkoi revoliutsii (Moscow: 1906), I, pp. 131, 135, 137. Closed periodicals often reappeared under a new name. Berezhnoi, Tsarskaia...., pp. 208-209.

22. S. R. Mintslov, "14 mesiatsev' svobody pechati'. Zametka bibliografa," Byloe No. 3 (1907), p. 134.

23. Berezhnoi, Tsarskaia...., pp. 194, 204-205. In St. Petersburg in 1906, officials warned booksellers not to sell the journal Zhalo on pain of losing their right to sell printed works. In sum, for the 11 months of 1913, the "workers' press" paid 322 fines, had 371 issues confiscated, 35 newspapers closed and 34 periodicals brought to court for prosecution. Berezhnoi, Tsarskaia..., p. 225.

24. B. Pinchuk, The Octobrists in the Third Duma (Seattle: 1974) p. 84.

25. Rozenberg (ed.), Russkiia Ved...., pp. 42-43, 305-307. The editor of the Kadet newspaper Speech (Rech) was imprisoned for 8 months. Walkin, "Government.....," Russian Review (July, 1954), p. 206.

26. Berezhnoi, Tsarskaia...., p. 226.

27. Walkin, "Government....," Russian Review (July, 1954), p. 207. In that period Pravda published 416 issues, Luch 294 issues, and Trudovoi Golos 96 issues.

28. Berezhnoi, Tsarskaia...., pp. 208-209.

29. Walkin, "Government....," Russian Review (July, 1954), p. 207.

30. From October, 1905 to April, 1906, about 1,699 brochures were issued, half by the Social Democrats. Golubeva, "Izdatel'skoe delo....," Kniga No. 22 (1972), p. 140. Publishers of Social Democratic pamphlets stated that their pamphlets were being issued in 5-6,000 copies when in fact the number was 10 times greater. Berezhnoi, Tsarskaia...., p. 209.

31. Obninskii, I, p. 5. Stykalin names a series of subsidized periodicals: I. V. Skvortsov's Slovo, F. N. Berg's Den', A. P. Piatkovskii's Nabliudatel' and Glasnost'. Stykalin also cites a memorandum read by the Emperor on March 16, 1905 which proposed to buy the S- Peterburgskie Vedomosti from E. Ukhtomskii for 100,000 rubles. Nicholas apparently vetoed the proposal. But in 1906, the Village Messenger, previously a weekly supplement to the Pravitel'stvennyi Vestnik, became a separate daily spokesman of the government. Stykalin, "Russkoe sam....," in Esin, Iz istorii..., (Moscow: 1973), pp. 74-76, 84-86, 88.

32. Rozenberg (ed.), Russkiia Ved...., pp. 42-43, 305-307. The establishment of the newspaper cost the government 100,000 rubles. It began to issue in November, 1905. Stykalin, "Russkoe sam....," in Esin, Iz istorii...., (Moscow: 1973), pp. 87-88. In 1912 and 1913, the government gave out 600,000 and 800,000 rubles in subsidies. In 1914, 1915, and 1916 the subsidies rose to 900,000, 1,000,000 and 1,600,000 respectively. A. F. Berezhnoi, Russkaia legal'naia pechat' gody pervoi mirovoi voiny (Leningrad: 1975), p. 26.

33. B. Rigberg, "The Efficacy of Tsarist Censorship Operations 1894-1917," Jahrbucher fur Geschichte osteuropas Vol. 14 (Sept., 1966), pp. 333-35; Esin, Russkaia dorevoliutsionnaia gazeta...., p. 74; J. Walkin, The Rise of Democracy in Pre-Revolutionary Russia (New York: 1962), p. 272.

34. G. Hosking, The Russian Constitutional Experiment (Cambridge: 1973), p. 200. Berezhnoi, Tsarskaia....., pp. 237-38.

35. Berezhnoi, Tsarskaia...., pp. 232-38.

36. Berezhnoi, Tsarskaia...., pp. 239, 253, 274; in 1915, Maklakov's law was again introduced into the State Council but died there. Berezhnoi, Russkaia...., pp. 54-55.

37. Berezhnoi, Tsarskaia...., pp. 280-82. Berezhnoi, Russkaia.. pp. 21-22, 56-57, 58-59, 71-72. In 1917, the government was preparing a law that would increase penalties for press violations.

Footnotes Conclusion

1. F. S. Siebert, T. Peterson, W. Schramm, <u>Four Theories of the Press</u> (Urbana: 1969 (1956)), pp. 2-3, 18. Siebert notes that the authoritarian theory of the press was strong in western Europe until the rise of libertarian theories in the 18th century.

2. Koz'ma Prutkov was a pseudonym for the writers Aleksei, Vladimir, and Aleksandr Zhemchuzhnikov and the poet, A. K. Tolstoy. See A. V. Zapadov (ed.), <u>Khrestomatiia po istorii russkoi zhurnalistiki XIX veka</u> (Moscow: 1965), pp. 290-93.

3. K. P. Pobedonostsev, <u>Reflections of a Russian Statesman</u> (Ann Arbor: 1965), p. 63.

4. Arsen'ev, <u>Za chetvert' veka, 1871-1894. Sbornik stat'ei</u> (Petrograd: 1915), pp. 552-60.

5. <u>Materialy....1869</u>, Part II, pp. 284-93.

Bibliography of Sources cited

The following /except for bibliographies/ is a list of sources that are cited in the body of the work. Many additional titles were used in the preparation of this work but are not listed here. For a full listing of sources on the censorship, see references in Part III of the bibliography.

I. Unpublished Sources

   Central State Historical Archives of the USSR (Leningrad)
   Fund 772 Chief Board of Censorship
   Fund 776 Chief Board of Press Affairs
   Fund 777 St. Petersburg Censorship Committee
   Fund 851 A. V. Golovnin
   Fund 908 Count P. A. Valuev

   Central State Archives of the October Revolution (Moscow) now

   Central State Historical Archives (Moscow)
   Fund 109 Third Section Archives
   Fund 728 Baron Modest Korf

   Manuscript Room of the Saltykov-Shchedrin Library (Leningrad)
   Fund 208 A. V. Golovnin
   Fund 833 V. Tsee (Tsey)

   Manuscript Section, Institute of Russian Literature
      (Pushkinskii Dom)
   Fund 559 P. A. Valuev

II. Published Official Documents
   (S. A. Adrianov) Ministerstvo vnutrennikh del. Istoricheskii ocherk 2 v. SPB: 1901.
   Alfavitnyi katalog izdanniiam na russkom iazyke zapreshchennym k obrashcheniiu i perepechataniiu v Rossii SPB: 1894
   Printed on order of the Chief Board of Press Affairs.

   Alfavitnyi katalog izdanniiam na russkom iazyke zapreschennym k obrashcheniiu i perepechataniiu v Rossii SPB: 1899
   Printed on order of Chief Board of Press Affairs.

   Alfavitnyi katalog knigam po russkom iazyke zapreshchennym k obrashcheniiu i perepechataniiu v Rossii SPB: 1870-1876.
   Printed on order of Chief Board of Press Affairs.

   Alfavitnyi spisok proizvedenii pechati zapreshchennykh k obrashcheniiu v publichnikh bibliotekakh i obshchestvennykh chital'niakh SPB: 1903. Printed on order of Chief Board of Press Affairs.

Dopolnenie k alfavitnomu katalogu izdanii na russkom iazyke zapreshchennykh k obrashcheniiu i perepechataniiu v Rossii SPB: 1899. Printed on order of Chief Board of Press Affairs.

Gosudarstvennyi Sovet, 1801-1901 SPB: 1901

Istoricheskiia svedeniia o tsenzure v Rossii SPB: 1862. Printed at press of Naval Ministry. Composed by P. Shchebalskii on the order of Golovnin, this volume was published in three editions. The above, without omissions and with supplements, a second at the Naval Ministry with no supplements, and a third, at the press of F. Person, with great omissions and no supplements.

Izvlechenie iz otcheta ministerstva vnutrennikh del za 1861, 1862 i 1863 gg. SPB: 1865. Official account of the ministry.

Katalog razsmotrennykh inostrannoiu tsenzuroiu sochinenii zapreshchennykh i dozvolennykh s iskliucheniiami s i-go Iulia 1871 po Ianv. 1897 g. SPB: 1897.

Kratkoe obozrenie napravleniia periodicheskikh izdanii i otzyvov ikh po vazhneishim pravitel'stvennym i drugim voprosam za 1862 g. SPB: 1862. At the press of F. Person. Composed on order of Golovnin by P. I. Kapnist, this work can also be found in Kapnist's works.

Materialy sobrannye osoboiu kommissieiu vysoch. uchrezhd. 2 noiabria 1869g. dlia peresmotra deistvuiushchikh postanovlenii o tsenzure i pechati 5 Parts, SPB: 1870. Material gathered by the Urusov Commission.

Materialy vysochaishe uchrezhd. osobago soveshchaniia dlia sostavleniia novogo ustava o pechati SPB?: 1906? No date, no place, no consecutive paging, no table of contents.
Some of this material, which is from the Kobeko convocation on the press laws in 1905 is contained in the Protokoly of the convocation.

Polnoe sobranie zakonov 3rd Collection.

Proket ustava o knogopechatanii SPB: 1862 Printed on order of the ministry of education. This is the first project of the Obolenskii Commission.

Proekt ustava o knigopechatanii SPB: 1863. Printed on order of the ministry of interior. This is the second project of the Obolenskii Commission.

Proekt ustava o pechati i tsenzure. SPB: 1870. This is
the project of the Urusov Commission of 1869.

Proekt ustava vysochaishe uchrezhd. osobago soveshcheniia
dlia sostavleniia novogo ustava o pechati SPB: 1906. This
is the project of the 1905 Kobeko Commission. Contains
separately paged Proekt, Ob'iasnitelnaia zapiska k proektu,
and Proekt vyzyvaemykh izdaniem...izmenenii...

Proekty i zapiski o tsenzure (n.p: n.d) Copy from library
of A. V. Golovnin in Library of Congress contains many
separately published works: Uvarov's 1849 project,
Kovalevskii project of 1859, Opinions of various peoples
on the transformations of the censorship (Feb., 1862),
Memorandum of Bert and Iankevich (1862), Memorandum of
Fridberg (1862), Memorandum of Fuks (1862), Collection of
Censorship Decrees from 1828 to 1862, Extracts from French,
Prussian and Austrian Press Laws.

Protokoly vysochaishe uchrezhdennago osobago soveshcheniia
dlia sostavleniia novogo ustava o pechati SPB: 1906.
Separate proceedings for each meeting of the 1905 Kobeko
Commission. Each meeting is paged separately.

Sbornik postanovlenii i rasporiazhenii po delam pechati
1865 goda SPB: 1866 Printed at the press of the ministry
of interior.

Sbornik postanovlenii i rasporiazhenii po delam pechati s 5
Aprelia 1865g po 1 Avgusta 1868 g. SPB: 1868. Printed on
order of the Head of the Chief Board.

Sbornik rasporiazhenii po delam pechati s 1863 po 1-e
sentiabria 1865 goda SPB: 1865 Printed on order of
Minister of Interior.

Sbornik stat'ei nedozvolennikh tsenzuroiu v 1862 g. 2 vols.
SPB: 1862 Printed on order of Golovnin.

(S. M. Seredonin) Istoricheskii obzor deiatel'nosti
komiteta ministrov 5 vols. SPB: 1902.

Vsepoddanneishii doklad stat' sekretaria Golovnina o knigopechatanii 10 Dek. 1862 g. SPB: 1862.

Vsepoddaneishii doklad ministra narodnago prosveshcheniia
po proektu ustava o knigopechatanii chitannyi v sovet
ministrov 10 Ianvaria 1863... (n.d., n. p.) Printed at
press of Naval Ministry.

Zakony o pechati. Sobranie deistvuiushchikh zakonodatel'nykh postanovlenii o pechati SPB: 1873.

Zhurnaly osoboi kommissii vysochaishe uchrezhdennoi 2-go noiabria 1869 g. dlia peresmotra deistvuiushchikh postanovlenii o tsenzure i pechati 2 vols. SPB: 1870. Proceedings of the Urusov Commission.

Zhurnaly vysochaishe uchrezhdennoi kommissii dlia razsmotreniia proekta ustava o knogopechatanii SPB: 1863 Proceedings of the second Obolenskii Commission, printed on order of the ministry of interior.

III. Bibliographies

Alfavitnyi sluzhebnyi katalog russkikh dorevoliutsionnykh gazet (1703-1916) Leningrad: 1958. Publication of the Saltykov=Shchedrin Library.

Cherepakhov, M. S. and Fingerit, E. M. Russkaia periodicheskaia pechat' 1895 - Okt. 1917, Spravochnik. Moscow: 1957.

Dement'ev, A. G., Zapadov, A. V., Cherepakhov, M. S. Russkaia periodicheskaia pechat' 1702-1894, Spravochnik Moscow: 1959.

Dobrovolskii, L. M. "Bibliograficheskii obzor dorevoliutsionnoi i sovetskoi literatury po istorii russkoi tsenzury" Trudy biblioteki Akad. Nauk SSSR Vol. 5 (Moscow: 1961), pp. 245-52.

Mashkova, M. V. and Sokurova, M. V. Obshchie bibliografii russkikh periodicheskikh izdanii 1703-1954 gg i materialy po statistiki russkoi periodicheskoi pechati. Annotirovannyi ukazatel' Leningrad: 1956.

Mez'er, A. V. Slovarnyi ukazatel' po knigovedeniiu Leningrad: 1924.

Mez'er, A. V. Slovarnyi ukazatel' po knogovedeniiu 3 vols. Moscow-Leningrad: 1931-34.

Muratova, K. D. Istoriia russkoi literatury XIX veka. Bibliograficheskii ukazatel' Moscow-Leningrad: 1962.

Muratova, K. D. Istoriia russkoi literatury kontsa XIX-- nachala XX veka. Bibliograficheskii ukazatel' Moscow- Leningrad: 1963.

Prokhorov, E.P. "Russkaia zhurnalistiki, publitsistika kritika vtoroi poloviny XIX veka. Materialy dlia bibliografii. Literatura 1961-65 gg." In B. I. Esin (ed.), *Iz istorii russkoi zhurnalistiki kontsa XIX-nachala XX v.* Moscow: 1973 pp. 246-66.

Rubakin, N. A. *Sredi knig: opyt obzora russkikh knizhnykh bogatstv.* 2nd ed. 3 vols. Moscow: 1911-15.

Simkina, S. K. "Zhanry russkoi periodiki i masterstvo kritikov, publitsistov i ocherkistov XIX veka sovetskoi kriticheskoi literature. (Materialy k bibliografii)" in N. P. Emel'ianov, *Russkaia zhurnalistika XVIII-XIX vekov. Iz istorii zhanrov* Leningrad: 1969 pp. 132-67.

Ul'ianinskii, D. V. *Biblioteka D. V. Ul'ianinskago: bibliograficheskoe opisanie* 3 vols. Moscow: 1912-15.

Val'denberg, D. V. *Spravochaia kniga o pechati vsei Rossii* SPB: 1911.

IV. Books and Articles Cited

Aizenshtok, I., "Frantsuzskie pisateli v otsenkakh tsarskoi tsenzury," *Literaturnoe Nasledstvo* Vol. 33-34 (1939), pp. 769-858.

Aizenshtok, I. (ed.), "Pis'ma K. P. Pobedonostseva k E. M. Feoktistovu 1883-1896" *Literaturnoe Nasledstvo* Vol. 22-24 (1935), pp. 497-560.

Alekseev, A. D. *Letopis' zhizni i tvorchestva I. A. Goncharova* Moscow-Leningrad: 1960.

Ambler, E. *Russian Journalism and Politics 1861-1881. The Career of Aleksei S. Suvornin* Detroit: 1972.

Anninskii, A. "Tsenzura i L. N. Tolstoi," *Krasnyi Arkhiv* Vol. 1 (1922), pp. 412-16.

Arsen'ev, K. K. "Iz vospominanii K. K. Arsen'eva," *Golos Minuvshago* No. 2 (1915), pp. 117-29.

Arsen'ev, K. K. *Za chetvert' veka, 1871-94. Sbornik stat'ei* Petrograd: 1915.

Arsen'ev, K. K. *Zakondatel'stvo o pechati* SPB: 1903.

Balmuth, D. "Origins of the Russian Press Reform of 1865," *Slavonic and East European Review* No. 109 (Jan., 1969), pp. 369-88.

Balmuth, D. Review of B. P. Baluev, Politicheskaia reaktsii 80-kh godov XIX veka i russkaia zhurnalistika in Kritika No. 3 (Spring, 1973).

Baluev, B. P. Politicheskaia reaktsiia 80-kh godov XIX veka i russkaia zhurnalistika Moscow: 1971.

Bank, B. V. Izuchenie chitatelei v Rossii (XIX v.) Moscow: 1969.

Barenboim, I. E. "Tipograf M. A. Kukol'-Iasnopol'skii i demokraticheskoe knizhnoe delo 60-kh godov" in Problemy rukopisnoi i pechatnoi knigi (Moscow: 1976).

Bel'chikov, N. and Pereselenkov, O., "N. A. Nekrasov i tsenzura," Krasnyi Arkhiv Vol. I (1922), pp. 355-61.

Belonskii, I. P. Essay in V zashchitu slov (see below) pp. 224-34.

Berezhnoi, A. F. Russkaia legal'naia pechat' gody pervoi mirovoi voiny Leningrad: 1975.

Berezhnoi, A. F. Tsarskaia tsenzura i bor'ba bol'shevikov za svobodu pechati (1895-1914) Leningrad: 1967.

Berezina, V. G., Emel'ianov N. P. et al (ed.), Ocherki po istorii russkoi zhurnalistiki i kritiki Leningrad: 1965 Vol. II.

Binshtok, V., "Materialy po istorii russkoi tsenzury (60-kh godov)" Russkaia Starina Vol. LXXXIX (Mar., 1897).

Bogucharskii, V. "Tsenzurnye vzykaniia," Entsiklopedich-eskii slovar' Brokgaus -Efron

Bogucharskii, V. Iz proshlogo russkogo obshchestva SPB: 1904.

Brooks, J., "Readers and Reading at the End of the Tsarist Era," pp. 97-150 in W. M. Todd (ed.), Literature and Society in Imperial Russia 1800-1914 Stanford: 1978.

Chirikov, E. Essay in V zashchitu slov (see below), pp. 142-144.

Chukovskii, K., "F. M. Tolstoi i ego pis'ma k Nekrasovu," Literaturnoe Nasledstvo Vol. 51-52 (1949), pp. 569-622.

Collins, I., The Government and the Newspaper Press in France 1814-1881 London: 1959.

"Delo III otd. S.E.I.V. Kantseliarii 1862 g." Vsemirnyi Vestnik No. 6 (June, 1906), Supplement, pp. 1-32, No. 7 (July, 1906), Supplement, pp. 33-74.

D'iakov, V. A., Linkov, Ia.I et al (ed.), Revoliutsionnaia situatsiia v Rossii v 1859-1861 gg. Moscow: 1962.

Diuneo, Essay in V zashchitu slov (see below), pp. 49-56

Dmitriev, S. S. (ed.), Khrestomatiia po istorii SSSR 2nd ed. Moscow: 1952, Vol. III, 1857-1894.

Dobrovol'skii, L. M. "K istorii tsenzurnoi politiki russkoi pravitel'stva vo vtoroi polovine XIX v." Uchenye Zap. Leningrad. Pedagogicheskogo Inst.-ta imeni A. I. Gertsena Vol. 67 (1948), pp. 260-69.

Dobrovol'skii, L. M. "Parizhskaia kommuna v russkikh zapreshchennykh izdaniiakh 70-kh godov," Kniga o knige Vyp 3 (1932) (Leningrad), pp. 289-92.

Dobrovol'skii, L. M. "Zapreshchennye i unichtozhennye knigi V. V. Bervi-Flerovskogo," Literaturnoe Nasledstvo Vol. 7-8 (1933), pp. 163-80.

Dobrovol'skii, L. M. Zapreshchennaia kniga v Rossii 1825-1904 Moscow: 1962.

Doroshevich, V. M. Polveka dlia knigi Moscow: 1916.

Doroshevich, V. M. Rasskazy i ocherki Moscow: 1962.

Elenev, F. O zloupotrebleniiakh literatury i o deistviiakh tsenzurnago vedomstva s kontsa piatidesiatikh godov po nastoiashchee vremia Geneva: 1898 Vol. II of Materialy dlia kharakteristiki polozheniia russkoi pechati published by Union of Russian Social Democrats.

Emel'ianov, N. "Iz istorii russkikh ofitsiozov 1879-1880 g." Voprosy zhurnalistiki.mezhvuzovskii sbornik statei, V. 2, Bk. 2 (Leningrad: 1960), pp. 72-80.

Esin, B. I., "K kharakteristike zhurnala 'Russkaia Mysl' v 1880-1885 gg." Iz istorii russkoi zhurnalistiki ed. by A. V. Zapadov, Moscow: 1959, pp. 237-48.

Esin, B. I., and Myl'tsyn, I. V. "K kharakteristike zhurnala'Delo'. Pis'mo N. F. Bazhina D. N. Maminu-Sibiriaku" B.I.Esin (ed.) Iz istorii russkoi zhurnalistiki (Moscow: 1973).

Esin, B. I. Kratkii ocherk razvitiia gazetnogo dela v Rossii XVIII-XIX vekov Moscow: 1967.

Esin, B. I. "Pravitel'stvennyi ofitsioz dlia naroda 'Sel'skyi Vestnik' 1881 g," Vestnik Moskovskogo Univ. No. 5 (1972) Seriia XI Zhurnalistika pp. 38-48.

Esin, B. I., Russkaia dorevoliutsionnaia gazeta 1702-1917 gg. Moscow: 1971.

Esin, B. I., "Russkaia legal'naia pressa kontsa XIX-nachala XX veka" in B. I. Esin, ed., Iz istorii russkoi zhurnalistiki (Moscow: 1973).

Esin, B. I. Russkaia zhurnalistikia 70-80-kh godov XIX veka Moscow 1963.

Esin, B. I. "Skvoz'prepony tsenzury," Kniga Vol. 14 (1967) pp. 236-40.

Esin, B. I., "Zakrytie 'Otechestvennye Zapiski' i sud'ba ego sotrudnikov posle 1884 goda," Iz istorii russkoi Zhurnalistiki vtoroi poloviny XIX v. ed. by A. V. Zapadov, Moscow: 1964.

Evgen'ev, V. "D. I. Pisarev i okhraniteli," Golos Minuvshago No. 1-4 (1919), pp. 131-61.

Evgen'ev, V. "I. A. Goncharov kak chlen soveta glavnogo upravleniia po delam pechati," Golos Minuvshago No. 11 (1916), pp. 117-56, No. 12 (1916), pp. 141-74.

Evgen'ev-Maksimov, V.   I. A. Goncharov Moscow-Leningrad: 1925

Evgen'ev-Maksimov, V. "Iz tsenzurnoi istorii 'Otechestvennye Zapiski' (1868-1884), Russkoe Bogatstvo No. 1-3 (1918), pp. 109-45, No. 4-6 (1918), pp. 40-72.

Evgen'ev-Maksimov, V.   Ocherki po istorii sotsialisticheskoi zhurnalistiki v Rossii XIX veka Moscow-Leningrad: 1927.

Evgen'ev-Maksimov, V. "Pis'ma k Nekrasovu," Literaturnoe Nasledstvo Vol., 51-52 (1949), pp. 85-569.

Fedorov, A. "Genrikh Geine v tsarskoi tsenzure," Literaturnoe Nasledstvo Vol. 22-24 (1935), pp. 635-78.

Feoktistov, E. M. Vospominaniia E. M. Feoktistova. Za kulisami politiki i literatury 1848-1896 Leningrad: 1929.

Field, D., The End of Serfdom (Cambridge, Mass., 1976).

Florinsky, M. Russia, A History and An Interpretation 2 vols. New York: 1953.

Garkavi, A. M., N. A. Nekrasov v bor'be s tsarskoi tsenzuroi (Kaliningrad: 1966).

Garmiza, V. V. "Predlozheniia i proekty P. A. Valueva po voprosam vnutrennei politiki 1862-1866 gg." Istoricheskii Arkhiv No. 1 (1958).

Gerasimova, Iu. I., Iz istorii russkoi pechati v period revoliutsionnoi situatsii kontsa 1850-kh-nachala 1860-kh gg. (Moscow: 1974).

Gerasimova, Iu. "Krizis pravitel'stvennoi politiki v gody revoliutsionnoi situatsii i Aleksandr II," in D'iakov, Linkov et al (ed.), Revoliutsionnaia situatsiia v Rossii v 1859-1861 gg. (see above).

Giliarovskii, V. L. Sochineniia v chetyrekh tomakh Moscow: 1967, Vol. III.

Golitsyn, Prince N. V. "Konstitutsiia grafa Loris-Melikova; materialy dlia eia istorii," Byloe No. 4-5 (1918), pp. 125-86.

Golubeva, O. D. "Izdatel'skoe delo v Rossii v period pervoi russkoi revoliutsii 1905-1907 gg)," Kniga Vol. 22 (1972), pp. 115-41.

Gradovskii, G. K. Itogi 1862-1907 Kiev: 1908.

Gurevich, P. "K kharakteristike reaktsii shestidesiatykh godov," O Minuvshem (SPB: 1909), pp. 100-109.

Gurenkov, M. N. " A. N. Tolstoi-voennyi korrespondent 'Russkikh Vedomostei' (1914-1917 gg)" Voprosy istorii russkoi zhurnalistiki Leningrad: 1957, Uchenye zapiski Lenin. Universiteta, No. 218, Seriia filologicheskoi nauk, Vyp. 33.

Hosking, G. The Russian Constitutional Experiment Cambridge: 1973.

Iampolskii, I., Satiricheskaia zhurnalistika 1860-kh godov Moscow: 1964.

Kapnist, Graf P. I. Sochineniia 2 vols. in one Moscow: 1901.

Koni, A. F. Na zhiznennom puti 2 vols. SPB: 1912.

Korolenko, V., "Chertochka iz avtobiografii," in V. Rozenberg, (ed.) Russkiia Vedemosti... (see below)

Kuznetsov, F. F. "Zhurnal 'Russkoe Slovo' i narodnichestvo," Iz istorii russkoi zhurnalistiki, ed. by A. V. Zapadov Moscow: 1959, pp. 84-119.

Lapshina, G. S. "Gazeta'Nedelia' v 1868-69 gg. i tsenzura," Vestnik Moskovskogo Universiteta. Zhurnalistika, No. 1 (1968), pp. 46-56.

Laverichev, V. Ia., "Russkie kapitalisty i periodicheskaia pechat' vtoroi poloviny XIX v." Istoriia SSSR, No. 1 (1972), pp. 26-47.

Lemke, M. K. Epokha tsenzurnikh reform SPB: 1904.

Lemke, M. K. "Istoriia 'belogo' nomera," Obrazovanie No. 9 (1906), pp. 123-35.

Lemke, M. K. "K sorokaletiiu 'velikoi reformy'", Mir Bozhii (Apr., 1905), pp. 1-26.

Lemke, M. K. (ed.), M. M. Stasiulevich i ego sovremenniki v ikh perepiske 5 vols. SPB: 1911-15.

Lemke, M. K. "Neobkhodimyia dopolneniia," Vestnik Prava (Oct., 1905), pp. 229-31.

Lemke, M. K. Ocherki po istorii russkoi tsenzury i zhurnalistiki XIX stoletiia SPB: 1904.

Lemke, M. K. "Rasporiazheniia komiteta ministrov ob unichtozhenii proizvedenii pechati za 1872-1904 gody," Vestnik Prava (Apr., 1905), pp. 119-34.

Lemke, M. K. "V mire usmotreniia (st. 140 i 156 ust. o tsen. i pech.)," Vestnik Prava (Sept., 1905), pp. 97-156.

Librovich, S. F. Na knizhnom postu. Vospominaniia, zapiski, dokumenty Petrograd: 1916.

Liublinskii, S. B. "Knigoizdatel'stvo O. N. Popovoi," Kniga Vol. 13 (1966), pp. 120-32.

(Lisovskii, N. M.) "Materialy dlia kharakteristiki polozheniia russkoi pressy," Vsemirnyi Vestnik No. 7 (1908) pp. 33-60, No. 8 (1908), pp. 27-54.

L'vova, M. I. "Kak podgotovlialos' zakritie 'Sovremennika' v 1862 g," Istoricheskie Zapiski, XLVI (1954).

Malykhin, N. G. "Izdatel'skaia deiatel'nost' P. P. Soikina," Kniga, Vol. 14 (1967), pp. 160-74.

Mamulova, L. G., "Zemskii vopros v russkoi periodicheskoi pechat' epokhi kontrreform," Vestnik Moskov. Universiteta Seriia IX, Istoriia, No. 2 (1966), pp. 57-68.

Mardar'ev, N. G. "Nechto iz proshlogo. Iz vospominanii byvshego tsenzora, 1886-1904," Golos Minuvshago No. 5-6 (1916), pp. 372-91.

Materialy dliz kharakteristiki polozheniia russkoi pechati Geneva: 1898. Vol. I of this publication by the Union of Russian Social-Democrats was prepared by V. V. Vodovozov.

Meshcherskii, Prince V. P. Moi vospominaniia SPB: 1912 Part III.

(Mikhnevich, V. O.) Piatnadtsatiletie gazety 'Golos' 1863-1877 SPB: 1878.

Miliutin, D. A. Dnevnik D. A. Miliutina 1873-1882. Ed. by P. A. Zaionchkovskii 4 vols. Moscow: 1947-50.

Mintslov, S. R. "14 mesiatsev svobody pechati. Zametka bibliografa," Byloe No. 3 (1907), pp. 123-48.

Mseriants, Z. Zakony o pechati; Nastoial'naia spravochnaia kniga 8th ed. Moscow: 1899.

Muratov, A. V. and Ulman, M. I. "Tipologicheskaia kharakteristika zhurnal'noi periodiki 1870-1890-kh godov," in Berezina and Emel'ianov, Ocherki po istorii russkoi zhurnalistiki..., (see above), II, pp. 253-67.

Nabokov, V. "K istorii nashego zakonodatel'stva o pechati

(komissiia Kobeko)," Pravo No. 33 (1911), pp. 1821-36, No. 34 (1911), pp. 1877-87, No. 35 (1911), pp. 1925-1937.

Nabokov, V. "Ugolovnaia otvetstvennost' knigoprodavtsa," Pravo No. 18 (1908), pp. 1128-36.

Nikitenko, A. V. Dnevnik Ed. by N. L. Brodskii, F. V. Gladkov F. M. Golovenchenko, N. K. Gudzii 3 vols. Moscow: 1955-56.

Nikitenko, A. Moia povest' o samom sebe i o tom 'chemu sviditel' v zhizni byl'. Zapiski i dnevnik 1804-1877 gg. Ed. by M. K. Lemke 2nd ed. SPB: 1904.

N. L. "Aleksandr III o L've Tolstom," Krasnyi Arkhiv Vol. 1 (1922), p. 417.

Oblinskii, V. Polgoda russkoi revoliutsii Moscow: 1906 Vol. I, pp. 130-52.

Orzhekhovskii, I. V. Administratsiia i pechat' mezhdu dvumia revoliutsionnymi situatsiiami (1866-1878 gg.) Gorkii: 1973.

Papkovskii, B. and Makashin, S. "Nekrasov i literaturnaia politika samoderzhaviia," Literaturnoe Nasledstvo Vol. 49-50 (1946), pp. 429-532.

Pinchuk, B. The Octobrists in the Third Duma Seattle: 1974.

Pintner, W. "Social Characteristics of Early 19th Century Russian Bureaucracy," Slavic Review (Sept., 1970).

Plotkin, A. A. Pisarev i literaturno-obshchestvennoi dvizhenie shestidesiatikh godov Leningrad-Moscow: 1945.

Polianskii, L., "Arkhivnyi fond glavnogo upravleniia po delam pechati," Literaturnoe Nasledstvo No. 22-24 (1935), pp. 603-34.

Privalova, M. I. and Ganshin, V. I. "Satiricheskaia zhurnalistika," in Berezina and Emel'ianov, Ocherki po istorii russkoi zhurnalistiki (see above), Vol. II, pp. 431-48.

Rigberg, B. "The Efficacy of Tsarist Censorship Operations 1894-1917," Jahrbucher fur Geschichte osteuropas Vol. 14, Bk. 3 (Sept., 1966), pp. 327-46.

Rigberg, B. "The Tsarist Press Law 1894-1905," Jahrbucher

fur Geschichte osteuropas Vol. 13 (Sept., 1965), pp. 331-43.

Rigberg, B. "Tsarist Censorship Performance 1894-1905," Jahrbucher fur Geschichte osteuropas, Vol. 17, Bk. 1 (Mar., 1969), pp. 59-76.

Rozenberg, V. (ed.), Russkiia Vedemosti 1863-1913. Sbornik stat'ei Moscow: 1913.

Rozenberg, V. and Iakushkin, V. Russkaia pechat' i tsenzura v proshlom i nastoiashchem Moscow: 1905.

Ruud, C., "A. V. Golovnin and Liberal Russian Censorship, Jan.-June, 1862," Slavonic and East European Review (Apr., 1972), pp. 198-219.

Ruud, C., "The Russian Empire's New Censorship Law of 1865," Canadian Slavic Studies, No. 2 (Summer, 1969), pp. 235-45.

Samoderzhavie i pechat' v Rossii Berlin: 1898.

Samoderzhavie i pechat' v Rossii SPB: 1906. With introduction by S. Vengerov.

Savenkov, A. V. "Vestnik Evropy" in Berezina, Emel'ianov, Ocherki po istorii russkoi zhurnalistiki...(see above), II, pp. 367-75.

Sidorov, A. "Iz vospominanii tsenzora," Golos Minuvshago No. 3 (1923), pp. 129-32.

Sinel, A. The Classroom and the Chancellery Cambridge, Mass. 1973.

Sladkevich, N. G. "Oppozitsionnoe dvizhenie dvorianstva v gody revoliutsionnoi situatsii' in D'iakov, Linkov et al (ed.), Revoliutsionnaia situatsiia...(see above).

Sokolov, N. I., "Delo" in Berezina, Emel'ianov (ed.), Ocherki po istorii russkoi zhurnalistiki...(see above), II, pp. 310-36.

Sokolov, N. I. Russkaia literatura i narodnichestvo Leningrad: 1968.

Sytin, M. D. Zhizn' dlia knig Moscow: 1960.

Stykalin, S. I. "Politicheskaia satira v 'Zritele' 1905g,"

Iz istorii russkoi zhurnalistiki Ed. by A. V. Zapadov, Moscow: 1959, pp. 137-202.

Stykalin, S. I., "Russkoe samoderzhavie i legal'naia pechat' 1905 goda" B. I. Esin (ed.), *Iz istorii russkoi zhurnalistiki* (Moscow: 1973).

Teplinskii, M. V. *"Otechestvennye Zapiski" 1868-1884* Iuzhno-Sakhalinsk: 1966.

Travushkin, N. S. "Izdatel'stvo 'Donskaia Rech'", *Kniga* Vol. 22 (1972), pp. 106-23.

Tulupov, N. V. "Narodnyia chteniia v gorodakh i selakh," *Russkaia Mysl'* No. 3 (1902), pp. 154-69, No. 4 (1902), pp. 1-18.

Valuev, P. A. "Graf P. A. Valuev v 1881-1883 godakh," *O Minuvshem* (SPB: 1909), pp. 417-80.

Valuev, P. A. *Dnevnik P. A. Valueva* Ed. by P. A. Zaionchkovskii, 2 vols. Moscow: 1961.

Veselovskii, K. S., "Vospominaniia K. S. Veselovskago. Vremia prezidentstva gr. D. N. Bludova v Akad. Nauk. 1855-1864," *Russkaia Starina* CVII (Dec., 1901), pp. 495-528.

Vezirova, L. A. and Eikhengol'ts, A. D. (ed.) *Khrestomatiia po istorii russkoi knigi 1564-1917* Moscow: 1965.

Vitte, S. Iu. *Vospominaniia* 3 vols. Moscow: 1960.

Voenskii, K., "Goncharov -tsenzor. Neizdannye materialy dlia ego biografii," *Russkii Vestnik*, Vol. 305, No. 10 (1906), pp. 571-619.

V zashchitu slova. Sbornik 4th ed., SPB: 1906.

Walkin, J., "Government Controls over the Press, 1905-1914," *Russian Review* Vol. 13 (July, 1954).

Walkin, J. *The Rise of Democracy in Pre-Revolutionary Russia* New York: 1962.

Wortman, R. *The Development of a Russian Legal Consciousness*, Chicago: 1976.

Zaionchkovskii, P. A. *Krizis samoderzhaviia na rubezhe 1870-1880 godov* Moscow: 1964.

Zaionchkovskii, P. A. Rossiiskoe samoderzhavie v kontse XIX stoletiia Moscow: 1970.

Zapadov, A. V. (ed.), Iz istorii russkoi zhurnalistiki vtoroi poloviny XIX v. Moscow: 1964.

Zapadov, A. V. (ed.), Iz istorii russkoi zhurnalistiki Moscow: 1959.

Zapadov, A. V. (ed.), Khrestomatiia po istorii russkoi zhurnalistiki XIX veka Moscow: 1965.

Zhuravlev, K. N. "K voprosu ob avtore zapiski redaktsii zhurnala 'Sovremennika' i preobrazovanii tsenzury," Istoricheskie Zapiski XXVII (1951).

Index

Abaza, A. 87, 91, 92

Abaza, N. S. 85, 86, 87, 92

Academy of Sciences 109, 112, 113, 129, 130, 131

Aksakov, I. 14, 35, 36, 37, 68, 84, 165

<u>Alarm Clock</u> (Budil'nik) 30, 70

Alexander II 1, 2, 4, 5, 6, 7, 10, 11, 20, 22, 24, 25, 29, 30, 31, 36, 37, 39, 45, 48, 50, 51, 59, 60, 72, 74, 75, 79, 81, 82, 83, 84, 88, 89, 90, 91, 92, 101, 107, 109, 112, 139, 140, 149

Alexander III 45, 72, 75, 81, 83, 88, 89, 90, 91, 92, 93, 94, 96, 97, 98, 102, 103, 107, 109, 193, 200

Alexandra Fedorovna, Empress 109

Antonovich, M. 33, 47

Arsen'ev, K. K. 34, 53, 57, 58, 69, 117, 131, 140

Aulard, A. 126

Bal'mont, K. 125, 213

Baluev, B. 103, 198, 199

Batalin, I. 83

Beaumarchais 169

<u>The Beginning</u> (<u>Nachalo</u>) 121, 123, 142

Bernstein, E. 123, 211

<u>The Bessarabian</u> (Bessarabets) 127

Bezobrazov, V. 74

Bibikov, P. 55, 75

Bilbasov, V. 104

Blagosvetlov, G. 54, 65

Blanc, Louis 56, 61, 177

Boborykin, 18

Bogdanov, Censor 69

Bourget, P. 106

Brandes, George 61, 102

Briusov, V. 213

Bulygin, A. 137

Carlyle, T. 40, 41

Catherine II 76, 104

Cherniaev, M. 68

241

Chernyshevsky, N. 65

Chicherin, B. 89, 94, 121, 124

Chief Board of Press Affairs 17, 22, 27, 30, 33, 34, 35, 36, 37, 39, 40, 41, 42, 43, 44, 46, 47, 48, 49, 51, 52, 53, 54, 55, 60, 62, 63, 64, 65, 66, 67, 71, 72, 77, 78, 85, 90, 92, 94, 95, 99, 106, 107, 109, 110, 111, 115, 116, 117, 119, 121, 122, 123, 125, 127, 129, 131, 134, 135, 142, 177, 189, 212, 215

The Citizen (Grazhdanin) 98, 118, 131

Committees on Press Affairs (after 1905) 135

Comte, A. 77

Constantine Nikolaevich, Grand Duke 1, 24

Constantine, Constantinovich, Grand Duke 129

The Contemporary (Sovremennik) 5, 9, 10, 20, 30, 31, 32, 33, 46, 47, 49, 55, 65, 68, 91, 97, 139

Conversation (Beseda) 73

The Country (Strana) 90, 99

The Courier (Kur'er) 118

Darwin, C. 76

The Day (Den') 14, 17, 35

The Deed (Delo) 42, 47, 64, 65, 67, 142, 180, 181

De Maistre, J. 76

DeMaupassant, G. 119

Diderot, D. 61

Diversion (Razvlechenie) 30, 70

Dolgorukov, Prince V. A. 4, 29, 45

Don Speech (Donskaia Rech') 116, 211

Doroshevich, V. 120

The Dragonfly (Strekoza) 184

Drentel'n, General A. R. 82

Durnovo, I. N. 89, 109

Dzhanshiev, G. 121

Echoes (Otgoloski) 82, 83

Efros 118

Elenev, F. (Skaldin, pseudonym) 49, 50, 109, 110, 111, 117, 118, 140

Eliseev, G. 121

Esin, B. 105

Evgen'ev-Maksimov, V. 66

"Expose" literature 7, 8, 16, 17, 28, 65, 70, 71, 72, 74, 103

Faure, President of France 118

Feoktistov, E. 3, 4, 9, 92, 94, 95, 109, 111, 114, 143, 200

The Field (Niva) 63, 95, 113

Finland 114

Finley, G. 74

Fourierism 122

Fyfe 104

Gagarin, Prince P. P. 30, 46, 171

Gibbon, E. 104

Giliarov-Platonov 63

God's World (Mir Bozhii) 113

Golovnin, A. V. 4, 5, 6, 7, 8, 9, 10, 11, 12, 13, 15, 20, 21, 22, 23, 29, 32, 51, 139, 150, 151, 153, 158

Gol'tsev, V. 100

Goncharov, I. 33, 35, 38, 39, 40, 167

Goremykin, I. 109, 123, 128

Gorkii, M. 124, 125, 213

Government Messenger (Pravitel'stvennyi Vestnik) 59, 220

Grigor'ev, V. 67, 83, 85, 182

Haeckel, E. 61

Hauptmann, G. 61

Heine, H. 153

Hobbes, T. 61, 75, 112

Hugo, V. 10, 56, 152, 182

Iakushkin, V. 117, 121

Ignat'ev, N. 89, 93, 98, 200

Iollos 119

Iuferov, Censor 70

Iuzefovich, V. 133

Ivan the Terrible 19, 76

Jews 8, 63, 72, 75, 78, 101, 102, 110, 116, 118, 119, 124, 126, 127, 200, 209

Journal de Ste- Peterbourg 15, 16

Journal for All (Zhurnal dlia vsekh) 113

Juridical Messenger (Iuridicheskii Vestnik) 85

Kakhanov 85, 87

Karakozov Affair 27, 29, 34, 38, 40, 41, 45

Karamzin, N. 76

Katkov, M. 15, 37, 38, 63, 64, 92, 93, 101, 104, 141, 166, 171, 172, 179, 198

243

Kavelin, K. 84, 107

Kardo-Sysoev, V. 83

<u>Kharkov Leaves</u> (<u>Khar'kovskii Listok</u>) 116

Khomiakov, D. 121

Khrushevan, P. 127

Khudiakov, I. 40, 169

<u>The Kievan</u> (<u>Kievlianin</u>) 131

Kliuchevskii, V. 131

Kobeko, D. 131, 132, 217, 218

Kolonn, E. 54

Koni, A. F. 131, 133, 150, 217

Korf, Baron Modest 2, 23, 24, 125

Korolenko, V. 124

Koshelev, A. 73

Kovalevskii, Evgraf 24

Kraevskii, A. 32, 34, 64, 98, 171, 179, 181, 193

Krasinskii, S. 121

Krestovskii, V. 18

Krivenko, S. 99

La Croix 76

Lassalle, F. 61, 177

Lazarevskii, V. 65, 66, 67, 68, 77

Lebedev, Censor 65, 66

Lecky, W. 61, 77, 120

Lemke, M. 115, 116

Lenin, V. 138

Leskov, N. 103

<u>Library for Reading</u> (<u>Biblioteka dlia Chteniia</u>) 10

<u>Light</u> (<u>Luch</u>) (Periodical in 1880s) 95

<u>Light</u> (<u>Luch</u>) (Anthology) 54, 162

<u>Light</u> (<u>Luch</u>) (Menshevik newspaper) 136

Liutostankii, 72

Longinov, M. 51

Loris-Melikov, M. 59, 63, 83, 84, 85, 87, 88, 89, 90, 91, 92, 93, 96, 101, 103, 139, 193

Maklakov, N. 137, 221

Makov, L. S. 59, 79, 82, 84, 85, 87

Maria Fedorovna, Empress 109

<u>Market Reports</u> (<u>Birzhevye Vedomosti</u>) 16, 32, 68, 113

Marx, Karl 102, 122, 123, 124, 202, 211

Maude, A. 126

Meshcherskii, Prince 98, 118, 131, 141, 195

Messenger of Europe (Vestnik Evropy) 57, 63, 69, 70, 73, 84, 85, 95, 100, 113, 131, 183, 184, 186, 209

Mezentsov, General N. V. 82

Michelet, J. 104

Mikhailovskii, N. K. 66, 116

Miliukov, P. 138

Miliutin, D. 4, 24, 25, 45, 46, 81, 82, 84, 91, 92, 101, 151

Miliutin, N. 4

Mill, John Stuart 56, 77, 102

Mirabeau, Octave 122

Morley, J. 77, 104, 123

Moscow (Moskva) 35, 36, 68, 165, 175

Moscow Leaves (Moskovskii Listok) 95, 113, 114

Moscow Reports (Moskovskie Vedemosti) 14, 18, 32, 37, 38, 39, 92, 118, 140, 156, 165, 166, 171, 172

Moscow Telegraph (Moskovskii Telegraf) 99, 100

Motherland (Rodina) 113

Munt, N. P. 69

Murav'ev, M. N. 30, 37, 40, 70, 162

Muromtsev, S. 85

The Muscovite (Moskvich) 31, 36

Nechaev Affair 64, 69

Nekrasov, N. 32, 33, 65, 67, 73, 181, 185

The News (Novosti) 118

The News (Vest') 42, 56, 174

News of the Day (Novosti Dnia) 118

Newspaper of A. Gatsuk (Gazeta Gatsuka) 98

New Russian Telegraph (Novorossiiskii Telegraf) 102

New Times (Novoe Vremia) 57, 85, 95, 113, 131, 138

The New Word (Novoe Slovo) 123

Nicholas I 76, 94, 139

Nicholas II 109, 111, 112, 114, 118, 119, 129, 138

Nietzsche, F. 123, 126

Nikolai, Baron A. P. 22

Northern Bee (Severnaia Pchela) 15

Northern Post (Severnaia Pochta) 13, 16, 28, 37, 43, 59, 68

Notes of the Fatherland (Otechestvennye Zapiski) 32, 64, 65ff., 68, 97, 98, 99, 100, 109, 142, 173, 181, 183, 198

Notovich, O. K. 118

Obolenskii Commission 10, 11, 13, 19, 20, 21, 22, 23, 28, 155

October Manifesto 129, 132, 136, 137

Order (Poriadok) 84, 90, 193

Pahlen, Count C. 46, 48, 173

Panin, Count V. N. 24, 46

Pastukhov, N. I. 95

Paul I 76, 125

Pavlenkov, F. 39, 52, 53, 174

Pazukhin, A. D. 101, 198

Perets, E. A. 85, 89

Peter the Great 76

Peter III 61

Petersburg Gazette (Peterburgskaia Gazeta) 95

Petersburg Leaves (Peterburgskii Listok) 56

St. Petersburg Reports (S-Peterburgskie Vedomosti) 32, 42, 57, 74, 90, 137, 195, 220

Pikhno, D. I. 131

Pisarev, D. 33, 39, 40, 52, 53

Pleve, V. K. 99, 109, 112, 115, 117, 119, 129

Pobedonostsev, K. P. 85, 87, 88, 89, 91, 92, 93, 94, 98, 99, 103, 109, 111, 119, 130, 140

Poletika, V. 68

Popular Sheet (Narodnyi Listok) 83

Pravda 136

Press Law 1865 24, 25, 27, 29, 45, 84, 85, 87, 94, 112, 130, 139

Prokopovich, S. 122

Prugavin, A. S. 103

Prutkov, Koz'ma 110, 139, 223

Purishkevich, V. M. 137

Putiatin, Admiral E. V. 20

Pypin, A. 34

Razin Stenka 121, 125

Renan, E. 61, 77, 123

Rodbertus, K. 122

Rodzianko, M. 136

Rola (Warsaw newspaper) 102

Rozenberg, V. 97, 117, 121, 200

Rumor (Molva) 90

Rus (Rus') (Aksakov's newspaper) 84

Russia (Rossiia) 137

Russian Antiquity (Russkaia Starina) 76, 82, 104, 125

Russian Archive (Russkii Arkhiv) 76, 104

Russian Courier (Russkii Kur'er) 90, 100

Russian Invalid (Russkii Invalid 5, 15, 16

Russian Leaves (Russkii Listok) 113, 119

Russian Messenger (Russkii Vestnik) 101, 171

Russian Reports (Russkie Vedomosti) 70, 95, 107, 113, 114, 119, 120, 121, 136, 182, 184

The Russian State (Russkoe Gosudarstvo) 137

Russian Survey (Russkoe Obozrenie) 74

Russian Thought (Russkaia Mysl') 95, 97, 100, 106, 120, 198

Russian Wealth (Russkoe Bogatstvo) 113, 117, 121

Russian Word (Russkoe Slovo) (Journal of the 1860s) 20, 30, 31, 32, 33, 42, 46, 49, 54, 65, 91, 97

Russian Word (Russkoe Slovo) (Newspaper of the 1900s) 113, 114, 120

Russian Worker (Russkii Rabochii) 59, 75

Russian World (Russkii Mir) 6

Russo-Turkish War (1877-78) 59, 73

Saltykov-Shchedrin, M.E. 65, 66, 67, 99

Samara Messenger (Samarskii Vestnik) 122

Schiller, F. 169

Schopenhauer, F. 102

Sechenov, I. 55

Semevskii, M. I. 82, 83

Shakhovskoi, Prince N. V. 109, 114, 116, 127, 218

Shchegolev, P. 102

Shcheglov, D. 10

Shcherbinin, M. 30, 31, 33, 38

Shelgunov, N. V. 33, 65, 106, 121, 163, 177

Shil'der, N. 125

The Shore (Bereg) 83

Shuvalov, Count P. 30, 45, 46, 64, 171, 173

Siberian Messenger (Sibirskii Vestnik) 116

Sipiagin, D. S. 109, 116

Skabichevskii, A. 106

Smolensk Messenger (Smolenskii Vestnik) 90

Sokolov, N. 56

Sologub, F. 125, 213

Solov'ev, M. P. 109

Solov'ev, V. 200

Sombart, W. 212

Son of the Fatherland (Syn' Otechestva) 32, 63

The Spark (Iskra) 30, 70, 184

The Spectator (Zritel') 134

Spencer, H. 56

Spinoza 112

Stasiulevich, M. 86, 107, 131, 183

Stein, Lorenz 74

Stolypin, Peter 135, 136, 137

The Sunrise (Voskhod) 102, 124

Suvorin, A. 40, 57, 95, 131, 217

Sviatopolk-Mirskii, Prince D. 129

Sytin, I. 120, 213, 218

Tarde, G. 106

Temporary Censorship Rules (May, 1862) 5, 10, 97, 130

Temporary Press Laws 1905 132, 133, 134, 217, 219

Temporary Press Rules of 1882 93, 94, 97, 98, 99, 100, 112

Teplinskii, M. 65, 66, 67, 73, 74

Theatrical Censorship 42, 78, 126

Third Section 3, 4, 16, 17, 29, 30, 45, 46, 64, 65, 71, 75, 82, 83, 179

Tikhomirov, L. 140

Timashev, A. E. 36, 45, 46, 47, 48, 49, 51, 52, 54, 57, 59, 60, 61, 62, 64, 67, 69, 72, 73, 78, 79, 81, 82, 84, 85, 103, 139, 140, 172, 173

Tkachev, P. 33

Tolstoy, D. 37, 40, 64, 89, 93, 94, 98, 99, 101, 143, 173, 183

Tolstoy, F. 64, 65, 66, 67, 68, 142

Tolstoy, Leo 8, 9, 103, 118, 122, 124, 126, 152, 201, 214

Trepov, General D. F. 134

Trepov, General F. 79, 81

Tsey (Tsee), V. A. 4, 5, 153

Tugan-Baranovskii, M. 122

Turunov, Senator M. 49

Ukrainian 15, 71, 72, 101, 102, 105, 125, 126, 130

Unkovskii, A. M. 121

Urusov, Prince S. 48, 49, 50, 55, 85, 87, 91, 109, 173

Uspenskii, G. 73, 102, 199

Valuev, P. 5, 6, 7, 8, 9, 10, 11, 12, 13, 14, 15, 16, 17, 18, 19, 23, 24, 25, 26, 27, 28, 29, 30, 31, 34, 35, 36, 37, 39, 40, 41, 43, 44, 45, 46, 48, 49, 51, 53, 55, 56, 59, 64, 65, 66, 67, 69, 71, 78, 82, 83, 84, 85, 86, 88, 104, 139, 140, 143, 151, 153, 155, 156, 157, 161, 166, 171, 173, 174, 177, 191, 192

Viazemskii, Prince P. 92

Village Conversation (Sek'skaia Beseda) 83

Village Messenger (Sel'skii Vestnik) 113, 124, 137, 220

Village Reading (Sel'skoe Chtenie) 71

Voice of Labor (Trudovoi Golos) 136

The Voice (Golos) 32, 34, 42, 60, 63, 64, 68, 69, 90, 95, 98, 171, 183

Volga Leaves (Volzhskii Listok) 114, 115

Vorlander, E. 212

Wallace, Mackenzie 74

Ward, Lester 102

The Week (Nedelia) 32, 69

Witte, S. 122, 130, 132, 135, 136, 137, 205, 217, 219

The Word (Slovo) 67

Wundt, W. 56

Zaionchkovskii, P. A. 85, 87, 89, 90, 91, 92, 100, 203

Zamiatnin, D. N. 24

Zasulich, V. 79, 81

Zelenoi, A. (Zelenyi) 37

Zola, E. 61, 75, 102, 122

Zverev, N. A. 109, 131

UNIVERSITY OF PITTSBURGH AT GREENSBURG LIBRARY

Z658
.S65B2   Balmuth
1979   Censorship in Russia, 1865-1905

DATE DUE

AP 11 86			
APR 14 1997			
DISCARDED MILLSTEIN LIBRARY			

LIBRARY
UNIVERSITY OF PITTSBURGH
AT GREENSBURG

DEMCO